William and Mary

William and Mary

A History of Their Most Important Places and Events

Deborah Fisher

First published in Great Britain in 2024 by
Pen & Sword History
An imprint of Pen & Sword Books Limited
Yorkshire – Philadelphia

Copyright © Deborah Fisher 2024

ISBN 978 1 39907 561 9

The right of Deborah Fisher to be identified as
Author of this Work has been asserted by her in accordance
with the Copyright, Designs and Patents Act 1988.

A CIP catalogue record for this book is
available from the British Library

All rights reserved. No part of this book may be reproduced or
transmitted in any form or by any means, electronic or mechanical
including photocopying, recording or by any information storage and
retrieval system, without permission from the Publisher in writing.

Typeset by Mac Style
Printed in the UK by CPI Group (UK) Ltd, Croydon, CR0 4YY.

Pen & Sword Books Limited incorporates the imprints of After
the Battle, Atlas, Archaeology, Aviation, Discovery, Family History,
Fiction, History, Maritime, Military, Military Classics, Politics,
Select, Transport, True Crime, Air World, Frontline Publishing, Leo
Cooper, Remember When, Seaforth Publishing, The Praetorian Press,
Wharncliffe Local History, Wharncliffe Transport, Wharncliffe True
Crime and White Owl.

For a complete list of Pen & Sword titles please contact

PEN & SWORD BOOKS LIMITED
47 Church Street, Barnsley, South Yorkshire, S70 2AS, England
E-mail: enquiries@pen-and-sword.co.uk
Website: www.pen-and-sword.co.uk
or
PEN AND SWORD BOOKS
1950 Lawrence Rd, Havertown, PA 19083, USA
E-mail: uspen-and-sword@casematepublishers.com
Website: www.penandswordbooks.com

Contents

Introduction		vi
Chapter 1	The Posthumous Prince	1
Chapter 2	The Stuart Princesses	30
Chapter 3	Marriage	45
Chapter 4	A Joint Monarchy	78
Chapter 5	King William the Widower	128

Acknowledgements   171
Appendix: Artists and Architects Associated with William and Mary   173
Bibliography   179
Index   189

Introduction

William and Mary are in some ways Britain's most mysterious monarchs. Everyone has heard of them, but few British people know much about them. Their joint reign lasted less than six years, and William's solo reign barely seven years after Mary's death, but those thirteen years were critical ones in the history of the British Isles.

By the standards of their time, they were a well-travelled couple. In William's case, he was born a ruler and became a soldier, and his travels were due to his responsibilities as a military leader as well as a prince. For Mary, moving to the Netherlands was all part of what a woman of royal birth might expect; her duty was to form a union with a suitable husband of appropriate status, wherever in Europe he might be found. The palace of Het Loo at Apeldoorn was built for the couple. What neither of them expected was that the latter part of their married life would take them back across the North Sea to the land of Mary's birth.

To call them 'British' monarchs is not entirely accurate; to call them 'English' would be almost equally inaccurate. England, Scotland, and Ireland, although ruled by the same monarchy, were still separate countries, with their own parliaments, laws and economic governance. The final union did not occur until 1707, and the 'United Kingdom of Great Britain and Ireland' did not come into existence for another century. Yet the years of their reign were critical ones for those countries, since they came to power after more than a century of religious conflict and political controversy.

The 'Glorious Revolution' (sometimes misleadingly called the 'Bloodless Revolution') that placed William and Mary on the throne was intended to sign the way for the future of England, Wales, Scotland

and Ireland, a future that would be peaceful and bring an end to the squabbling, allowing the economy to settle down and the country to become prosperous in the run-up to the Agricultural and Industrial Revolutions. As a result, in the eyes of the rest of Europe, Britain developed a growing reputation for enlightened government.

The world of William and Mary was one that in many ways would be recognisable to us today. The British had almost passed the stage of executing Roman Catholic priests, the last of the 'Forty Martyrs of England and Wales' having gone to the gallows in 1679. At the same time, Protestants – who had felt threatened under Mary's Catholic father, King James II – could relax again under a more sympathetic government. Ireland was not as fortunate as the British mainland, and the Battle of the Boyne in 1690 would spawn a new variety of religious dissent that led to centuries of unrest.

The monarchy was now fully answerable to Parliament. The satire boom had begun, with even the most outspoken writers gradually ceasing to live in fear of a treason charge. Commerce and culture were thriving throughout the British Isles. London, rebuilt after the Great Fire of 1666, was a bustling city with some fine new buildings. Hackney carriages, though still a long way from motorised taxis, had been introduced to the capital sixty years earlier. Department stores and banks were beginning to come into existence, along with coffee houses and newspapers. None of these developments can be directly attributed to William or Mary, but their reign provided a period of stability during which these institutions could thrive. North of the border, the way was being paved for the Scottish Enlightenment, despite Edinburgh being one of Europe's most crowded cities. Dublin, too, was growing dramatically. Oxford and Cambridge were full of scientists and physicians, while Scottish, English, Welsh and Irish philosophers were arguing for liberty, equality and toleration.

By the time they arrived in Britain, Prince William of Orange and his wife, Princess Mary, had acquired and improved several palaces in William's homeland, then known as the United Provinces of the Netherlands. Their palace at Het Loo, near The Hague, was much admired for its design, and William's art collection was second to none, but the couple were becoming particularly known for their contributions to horticulture. Gardens were a speciality of the Dutch, who, like the British, were exploring the far corners of the known world and bringing home many exotic plants and fruits.

Dissatisfied with the palace of Whitehall (eventually destroyed by fire in 1698), the couple had Kensington Palace built, to a design by Sir Christopher Wren. Their renovations at Hampton Court Palace, also by Wren, gave the palace much of its present character. It is worth noting here that the construction costs involved in building or rebuilding royal residences typically accounted for less than half of the total expenditure, with interior and exterior decoration, furniture and home comforts making up the rest. In addition to her interest in gardening, Mary was an enthusiastic collector of ceramics, founded Greenwich Hospital for retired sailors, and influenced contemporary culture. After her premature death, William's popularity naturally fell off, and his reputation was tarnished by accusations of favouritism and greed, but his rule was never seriously threatened, ensuring a peaceful transition of power to his sister-in-law Anne.

Things were not perfect. William was regarded as a foreigner, and foreigners had never been popular with the English. He was accepted because of his Stuart queen, and it would take several gaffes before his good qualities were recognised; by many of the population, they never were. He did, however, acknowledge that he owed his position to the wishes of the English and Scottish parliaments. With the death of Mary's younger sister Anne, in 1714, the stability of the realm would again be threatened, and many subjects of the new Hanoverian dynasty may have thought back fondly on the events of 1688 that had brought them nearly three decades of peace and prosperity.

Family tree

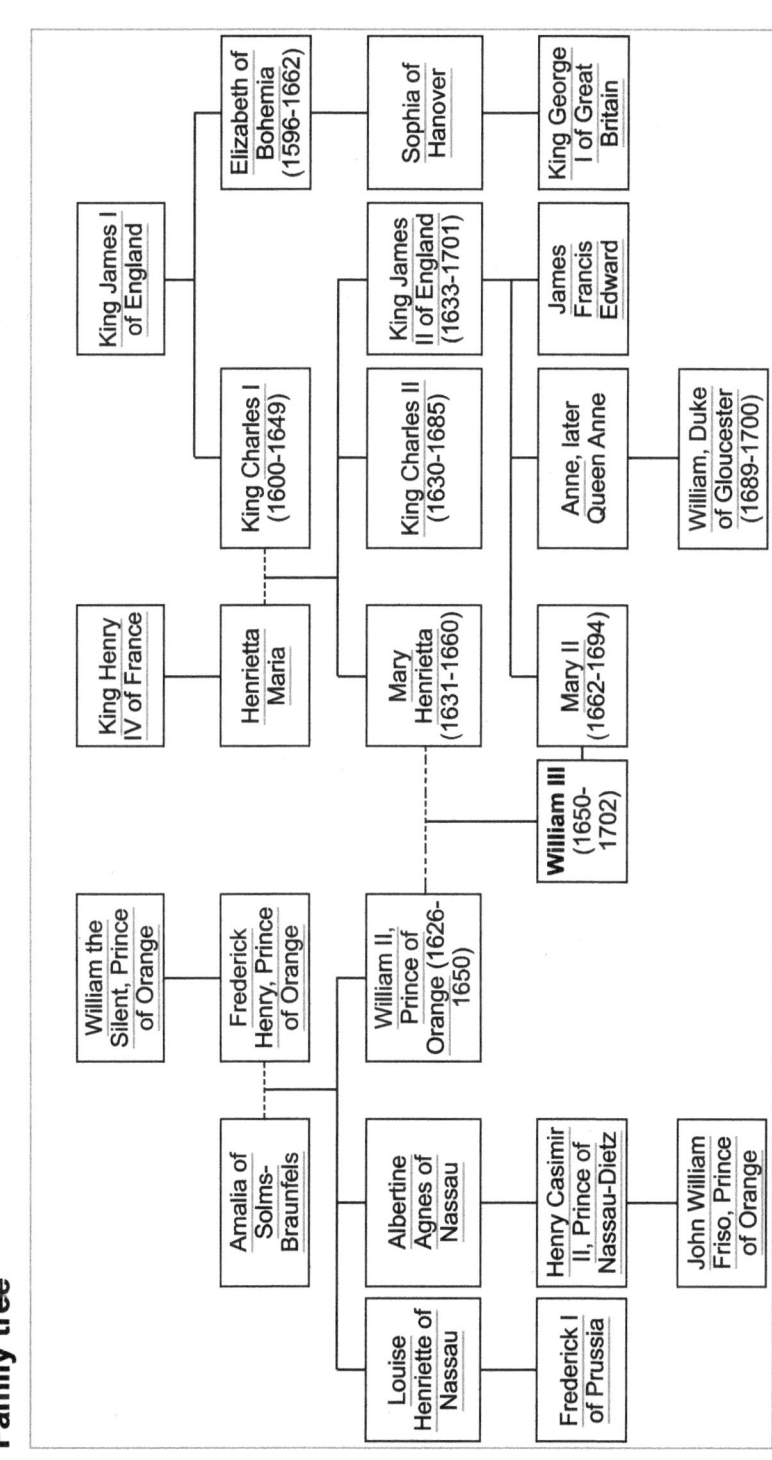

Chapter 1

The Posthumous Prince

The man known as King William III of England was born Willem Hendrik, Prince of Orange, a 'stadtholder' born to rule one of the seven provinces of the Dutch Republic, which lasted from 1588 to 1795. The territories of Holland, Zeeland, Utrecht, Guelders, and Overijssel, which he had inherited from his father, made up most of the United Provinces – more or less the same country as the present-day Netherlands. The other two provinces, Groningen and Friesland, mostly went along with this arrangement. Although the stadtholder's position was passed down in the same family, the ruler was subject to formal election. It should be noted that a stadtholder was not the same as a king, and that William III of the Netherlands (1817–1890) was a completely different person from William III of England, even though both were Princes of Orange.

William's father, the previous stadtholder, had married Princess Mary Henrietta, eldest daughter of King Charles I of England and Scotland, a man who had failed to live up to what was expected of a constitutional monarch and had been executed by his own people less than two years before William's birth. Thus William was half-English, but by the time of his birth in 1650, not only was his father already dead of smallpox, but hostilities were about to break out between his own country and that of his mother. Mary Henrietta, who had been living in exile in the Netherlands since the outbreak of the English Civil War, was perceived by her subjects as anti-Dutch, partly because her adopted country now shared the religious beliefs of Oliver Cromwell's government which had removed her family from the throne in order to come to power across the North Sea.

2 William and Mary

It was not an auspicious start for Mary Henrietta's son, who was born on 4 November 1650, in The Hague, at the Binnenhof ('inner court'), a castle that had become the centre of the country's government towards the end of the previous century. His cradle was swathed in black in mourning for his father. On the other hand, a story went about that, at the moment of his birth, a gust of wind blew out the candles in the room, and the attending midwife claimed that she clearly saw three circles of light above his head, indicating his likely succession to three crowns. The claim appears outlandish to us, even if made in retrospect, but the fact remained that William was, at the time, fourth in line for the thrones of England and Scotland – after the dispossessed Charles II and his younger brothers, James and Henry, and perhaps also behind his own mother, their sister. He grew up with an awareness of this distant possibility, and he was brought up as a Calvinist, so he believed in predestination.

The Dutch Republic, whose leader William was destined to become, was at the zenith of its 'Golden Age', during which the Netherlands had excelled in both science and the visual arts and become one of the world's most powerful military and trading nations. From 1568, the country had been embroiled in the Eighty Years' War, eventually throwing off Spanish rule and permanently establishing a republic around forty years before William's birth. Fighting had, however, continued until 1648. Under the terms of the peace, Spain retained some of its territories, and the Roman Catholic faith was tolerated. The Low Countries had undergone their own Reformation: 'Beeldenstorm' is the Dutch term for the widespread destruction of religious icons that took place during the sixteenth century.

The leaders of the United Provinces called a meeting the very night William's father died. The late Prince of Orange had made progress towards devising a new constitution when smallpox suddenly claimed his life, but he had no time to secure the position of stadtholder for his unborn son. Even during his reign, the authority of the stadtholder had been undermined.

In the absence of an adult ruler, it was Frederick William, Elector of Brandenburg and brother-in-law of the late stadtholder, who eventually took charge. Mary Henrietta was obliged to give up some of her property in order to persuade the Dutch government to show favour towards her brother, the future King Charles II of England and Scotland, who would spend part of his exile among them. The political climate shifted back and forth along with the rivalry between England and the Netherlands as colonial powers. Mary Henrietta's death in 1660, from smallpox, would break the living link between the two countries, but Mary Henrietta's will entrusted her brother Charles with looking after her young son's interests.

For a short time after his mother's death, William's day-to-day care was handled by an English governess, Katherine Stanhope, the former Countess of Chesterfield, who had married a Dutchman following the death of the Earl of Chesterfield; she had been Mary Henrietta's own governess and had accompanied her to Holland. Shortly after the deaths of both her husband and the princess, she returned to England to take up a position in the household of the Duchess of York, mother of the woman William would one day marry. Another of his early governesses was Lady Anna Mackenzie (1621–1707), a Scotswoman and the wife of Lord Balcarres, a member of Charles II's court in exile.

One of the prince's childhood companions was his cousin, Charlotte Elizabeth, known as 'Liselotte', who would later marry the brother of King Louis XIV of France. Liselotte was by all accounts a lively child whose general conduct was in complete contrast with William's, but he seems to have participated actively in the children's games. Later in life, Lieselotte apparently confessed that she would not have objected to marrying William.

A painting of William at the age of seven, copied from an original by Cornelius Johnson, is one of over 140 portraits of the king held by the UK's National Portrait Gallery. He had already been painted by a mediocre French artist, Abraham Ragueneau, who was employed as a tutor in the royal household, and by Adriaen Hanneman. Various versions of Cornelius Johnson's picture exist, including one at Knole in Kent, signed and dated by Johnson. The young prince, appropriately dressed in an orange doublet, looks wide-eyed but not quite innocent, with pursed lips suggesting a somewhat puritanical nature. Perhaps, even at such an early age, he was already becoming cynical. Observing him at a banquet at the age of two, his great-aunt, Elizabeth of Bohemia, had commented on his stillness and good behaviour.

A council, the *Raad van de prinsen*, had been set up to advise William, his mother and his grandmother. The members included Frederic Rivet (1617–1666), a French Huguenot theologian highly regarded by his grandmother and the author of a publication called *De la premiere education d'un Prince, Depuis sa naissance jusqu'à l'age de sept ans* (*About the early education of a prince, from his birth to the age of seven years*). Rivet even advised on the prince's diet. Another advisor, Cornelis Trigland (1609–1672), a Calvinist preacher, would be given a more direct role in tutoring the child from the age of six onwards. With such an upbringing, it was no wonder he grew up with an awareness of his duty and a serious mind that seems to have rejected frivolity.

The Hague

The Hague, where William was born, is nowadays the administrative capital of the Netherlands, the seat of both the Dutch Parliament and the International Court of Justice, an arm of the United Nations. Generally overshadowed by Amsterdam when it comes to tourism, it is nevertheless a city rich in culture. Its official name, "s-Gravenhage', literally meaning 'the Count's wood', gives an idea of its origins. Yet in the late seventeenth century, The Hague did not have city status; nor did it ever have city walls.

The Hague was, however, a notable centre of the fine arts. Although it had its own branch of the 'Guild of St Luke', an organisation originally formed in Antwerp by painters, sculptors, engravers and other artists, The Hague also boasted enough home-grown visual artists to be able to establish its own society, the 'Confrerie Pictura', to protect the rights of an elite group that included several men who would work for William and Mary: Adriaen Hanneman, Robbert Duval, Jacob Roman, Daniel Marot and Gérard de Lairesse were among the most notable.

The *Panorama of Scheveningen*, a 360-degree panoramic painting by the Dutch master Hendrik Willem Mesdag (1831–1915), shows what parts of the city looked like in the nineteenth century. Completed and opened in 1881, it used contemporary photographs as well as Mesdag's own sketches to create an accurate picture of Scheveningen, a seaside district of The Hague. The Mesdag Collection, close by the building that houses the panorama, is an art museum that focuses on painters of the nineteenth-century 'Hague School'. However, we would need to go back another 200 years to get a convincing picture of what the city was like during William's lifetime, when he was in the habit of riding on the Scheveningen sands.

The Golden Age painters can perhaps help us get some idea of what The Hague was like in the prince's youth, by comparison with the present-day city of the same name. Jan van Goyen produced a 'View of the Hague' (sadly, not held in the Netherlands) in 1647, which shows a city skyline dominated by churches and windmills. Most of the churches can still be seen, but the traditional windmill has all but disappeared; only a handful from this period still stand in the outskirts of The Hague. The best-known are the 'Molendriegang', a row of three windmills in the flat countryside outside the city. Their original function was to drain the polders, flood plains and areas of reclaimed land. They have not been in use since 1951, and are not open to the public.

Binnenhof

The Binnenhof, originally a medieval residence for the Counts of Holland, had fallen out of use with the demise of the title in the fifteenth century, and the Ridderzaal or 'Hall of the Knights', a public area, was the only part of the building that remained in use as a government building, comparable in many ways to London's Westminster Hall. Constructed and finished in Gothic style, the Ridderzaal contains a tasteful gilded throne that was installed when the building was refurbished in 1898–

1904 (after being under threat of demolition for a time) and has been used in modern times by monarchs of the Netherlands to make their traditional annual speech.

Prince Maurice of Orange (1567–1625), William's great-uncle, was the first ruler to take up residence at the Binnenhof after the country's Spanish overlords fell from power in 1581. Maurice effectively rebuilt and extended the residence. At the time of William's birth in 1650, an artificial lake called the Hofvijver, created in the fourteenth century, surrounded the palace, presumably for defensive reasons, but other buildings gradually encroached. Besides the Ridderzaal, the complex includes the Torentje or 'Little Tower', now the office of the Prime Minister of the Netherlands. This was used as a kind of summer-house or gazebo for the Counts of Holland, adjacent to their gardens. In modern times, renewed security concerns led to the construction of an underwater gate in 2004, to prevent unauthorised access to government offices by that route.

Next to the Torentje, overlooking the water, is the Trêveszaal, where the Council of Ministers of the Netherlands now meets. This was virtually rebuilt in the late 1690s, when William's triumph in negotiating peace with France had placed the king in a position of enormous prestige throughout Europe. The States-General commissioned Daniel Marot to create a magnificent reception hall, which was completed in October 1697 and decorated in French style. Naturally, the paintings of key figures in the country's history include a portrait of William, this one by Jan Hendrik Brandon. It shows the king in armour, wearing his royal robes. Copies, with some variation, can be seen at the National Portrait Gallery in London and at Het Loo, William's country retreat.

Surrounding the palace complex was a commercial area that had developed during the Middle Ages. Some of the streets in this area, especially the narrow Venestraat, contain architectural survivals from that period. Venestraat was built on peat, with additional marshland being drained in order to expand it. The Rijksmuseum de Gevangenpoort (Rijksmuseum being a general term for a national museum in Holland, not only the famous one of the same name in Amsterdam) has been a museum since 1882. The square outside, the Buitenhof ('outer court') was the setting for one of the most horrific events in Dutch history, the murder of the De Witt brothers, which took place when William was in his early twenties. When first built, the courtyard contained stables and houses and even a zoo. The Gevangenpoort or 'Prisoner's Gate', also originally a medieval building, was the only access to the Buitenhof until the early nineteenth century. Several of the houses around the square, now disguised as hotels and restaurants, were already present at that time.

As the Binnenhof developed into a centre of government, some of the major players decided to build residences close by, as a way of ensuring they could see and be seen by those in power. The Mauritshuis, now one of Europe's great art museums, was built in the 1630s, close to the palace, on land originally used for gardens by the Counts, as a residence for Prince Johan Maurits (1604–1679), the Dutch governor of Brazil and a close relation of the stadtholder; it was therefore a relatively new building when William was born. It was in the upper hall here, in May 1660, that a party was held to celebrate the restoration of King Charles II to the thrones of England and Scotland, and Dutch leaders rashly promised him a collection of valuable artworks as a kind of going-away present. Ten-year-old Prince William attended as a guest – but, significantly, not as a head of state.

After a fire in 1704, two years after William's death, the interior of the Mauritshuis was completely restored, but the exterior of the present building, though without the original cupola, would still be recognisable to him. Designed by Pieter Post and Jacob van Campen, it had been built in the Classical style. Post's architectural drawings survive, giving a good indication of the building's layout. The Prince William V Gallery, named after a later Prince of Orange, was constructed in 1774 and is now credited with being the first museum in the Netherlands. The whole building was purchased by the Dutch government in 1820 as a suitable place to display the royal art collection. Several works that once belonged to William and Mary can now be found at the Mauritshuis, having been appropriated by William from the Royal Collection in England. These include Holbein's 1533 portrait of the MP Robert Cheeseman, holding a falcon, and a late seventeenth-century painting of the interior of Antwerp Cathedral by Pieter Neefs the Younger. The Mauritshuis also boasts famous paintings by Rembrandt and by Johannes Vermeer, a native of Delft whose realistic indoor and outdoor scenes offer us a vivid picture of daily life in a seventeenth-century Dutch city. Vermeer's *Girl With A Pearl Earring* (painted in around 1665) is now one of the most popular exhibits.

In 1632, William's grandfather Prince Frederick Henry had extended and improved the royal apartments at the Binnenhof, and William followed his example. He and his mother had lived there modestly during his childhood, and had even been forced to give up some of their accommodation to the republican government. Later, to impress his new bride (or perhaps to impress her family), he kitted out her apartments with a magnificent painted ceiling, which was later removed from the palace and installed at Amsterdam's Rijksmuseum. The ceiling, thought to be the work of Theodoor van der Schuer, represents 'Morning' and 'Evening', appropriate to a bedchamber. There is also a record of Jacob Roman being paid a substantial sum for his work in producing elaborate wood carvings for Mary's chamber; these have not survived. However, the young couple spent very little time in the palace's grandiose environment, always preferring their country residences.

In 2021, a five-year project for the large-scale refurbishment of the Binnenhof was launched. During this period the House of Representatives – the 'Tweede Kamer' (Second Chamber) was temporarily relocated elsewhere in The Hague. The changes were deemed necessary, not only because of the age of the building but to cater for improved security and safety measures, partly linked to increases in visitor numbers. This was billed as a 'no-frills' project, at a cost of around 500 million Euros, concentrating on essential improvements rather than a historical renovation.

Public buildings in The Hague
The Old City Hall ('Oude stadhuis' in Dutch) was originally built in the sixteenth century, to replace an older castle belonging to the Counts

of Holland, but was virtually reconstructed in the 17th century. A contemporary painting by Jacob van der Ulft (1621–1689) shows how it looked when first built, while a much later painting by Jan Ekels the Elder (1724–1781) shows that the present building, the one William would have known from childhood, was more ornate, even before the interior was redecorated in the eighteenth century and the building restored in the 1880s. The tower adjacent to the building is believed to be a survival from the earlier structure, perhaps from the castle of the Counts.

The Grote Kerk ('Great Church') of St James is of a similar age to the Binnenhof. Ironically, by the time of William's birth, the 'great' church had become too small for its purpose, and the construction of a Nieuwe Kerk ('new church') was completed when William was about six years old. Most of the stained glass and the wooden pulpit in the Grote Kerk pre-date William's reign, but the funerary monument dedicated to the naval commander Jacob van Wassenaer was completed in 1667, two years after van Wassenaer was killed in battle against the English. The Flemish sculptor Bartholomeus Eggers represents the admiral as a hero even though his final battle culminated in defeat. The leaders of the Dutch Republic, who commissioned it, wanted him represented in this way in order to demonstrate that loyalty to a ruling family was not essential to heroism.

The classical style established by van Campen and Post at the Binnenhof extended to other public buildings in The Hague, such as the Paleis Noordeinde, the building known as the 'Oude Hof' or 'Old Court'. This was the home of Princess Amalia, William's domineering paternal grandmother, the widow of Prince Frederick Henry, a previous stadtholder, who had died three years before William's birth. Noordeinde is these days a 'working palace', the residence of the present royal family of the Netherlands. As such, it is seldom open to the public. Jacob van Campen, one of the architects of the Mauritshuis, was also largely responsible for the design of the Noordeinde. Its entrance, in a major thoroughfare rather than hidden behind gardens, is explained by the fact that it began life as a private house and was converted for use by Louise, the widow of William the Silent and mother of Prince Frederick Henry; it was Frederick Henry who extended it to its present form. The room that best reflects the original interior design is the 'Pieter Post Room', now used as a reception room for ambassadors and other important visitors, which contains an original fireplace. Portraits of Amalia's closest friends and courtiers hang on the walls.

After their marriage, William and Mary would prefer the Noordeinde to their apartments at the Binnenhof, allegedly because they felt it better reflected their royal status. The arrangement of the interior echoes the traditions of their time, with visitors ascending a grand staircase in order to enter the inner sanctum of the court, and passing through a series of progressively finer apartments before coming into the monarch's presence. The last of the line of stadtholders, William V (1748–1806), would leave the country for Britain during the Napoleonic Wars, but his son later returned to the Netherlands as King William I and so the palace passed back into the hands of the royal family.

Following the death of William's father, Amalia immediately tried to acquire the guardianship of the child, arguing that Mary Henrietta, at nineteen, was too young. Amalia had acted as an advisor to her husband and later as his regent, so it was not surprising that she wished to take up the reins. She was now in her sixties, a cultured and intelligent woman who was not ready to relinquish control to a teenager. She had not been born royal, but was related to Frederick Henry. As the daughter of a count, she had once been a lady-in-waiting to Elizabeth of Bohemia, a sister of King Charles I and thus the aunt of Mary Henrietta. After marrying somewhat above her station, Amalia had fallen out with her former mistress and a battle of wills had ensued, with Amalia going to some lengths to outdo Elizabeth in matters such as having their portraits painted and the acquisition of objets d'art. Elizabeth's death in 1662 finally put an end to that rivalry.

In addition to the Paleis Noordeinde, Amalia had another grand private residence in the Hague, Huis ten Bosch ('the house in the woods'). Like the Noordeinde, it had been designed by van Campen and Post, and a spectacular domed hall took pride of place at its centre. Amalia, a great collector, filled the house with art treasures, including many portraits of her late husband, who had died while it was under construction. An avenue of overhanging trees led to the front entrance of the 'house in the woods'. Gravelled walks had been created in the gardens, which Mary, a lover of both walking and nature, must have found convenient when she arrived in Holland. She would spend much of her time at Huis ten Bosch until the new palace of Het Loo was completed. It was perhaps fortunate for Mary that Amalia had already passed away by the time of William's marriage, otherwise her dominance would have been another hurdle for the new young princess to overcome.

Huis ten Bosch was the only one of the royal estates of Orange that William did not inherit immediately on his coming of age at eighteen; he had to wait until 1686. To celebrate his birthday in that year, his wife would hold an enormous party (in the absence of the birthday boy) in the central hall, which had been decorated by Amalia with paintings depicting allegories that could be related to the life of her husband. This palace, too, is one of the present Dutch royal family's official residences, following an extensive restoration during the 1950s. Located some distance from the city centre, it is not open to the public except for those invited to official events.

In 1992, a theme park was created near Nagasaki in Japan (one of the Netherlands' oldest trading partners), complete with a replica of the original palace, celebrating Dutch culture and art history. It is the largest theme park in Japan, containing 'authentic European cityscapes'. At first very successful, it went bankrupt in 2004, but was taken over and turned into a resort famous for its illuminations and live entertainment. It features canals, windmills and other structures that one might expect to see in the Netherlands as well as attractions that one would not normally associate with a Dutch city. Among other attractions, the park has introduced the world's first hotel to be staffed by robots.

Other features of The Hague
In 1616 a network of canals had been constructed, marking the city's limits, and the surviving sections continue to be an important feature

of The Hague, popular with tourists, who can take a 90-minute tour from the Bierkade. The name of this quay suggests its origins; it was the trading place for beer, which could not legally be brewed within The Hague because it did not officially have city status.

Wherever he went, there was nearly always a Dutch painter available to capture William's image and record the important events of his life. One such was Ludolf Bakhuizen, whose picture of William's arrival on Dutch shores after his successful accession to the thrones of Britain can be seen at the Mauritshuis. In it, William, mounted on a white horse, boldly confronts the viewer, a dashing figure in a plumed hat and silken robes. The reality of his appearance on landing is unlikely to have been quite so impressive. On 5 February 1691, after having been crowned king and seeing off the challenge from James II in Ireland, William would return to his home city. The occasion was recorded by the Dutch artists Romeyn de Hooghe and Jan Lujken, among others, in engravings that could be reproduced in large numbers. The City Hall was lit up. Not just one, but three, triumphal arches (designed by de Hooghe) were erected in his honour; these no longer stand.

William came to the 'Kloosterkerk' to give thanks. At this point, early in their joint reign, Mary also hoped to be able to revisit Holland, but she would never manage to do so. The Kloosterkerk, a former monastery, had changed hands a few times between Protestant sects. The mechanical clock installed in the church's tower in 1620 was the work of Huyck Hopcoper, and William's grandparents had been married in the church five years after its installation. In addition to the important occasions that have taken place there, it is the burial place of several notable historical figures, including Pieter Post and the painter Joris van der Haagen, both contemporaries of William. The Kloosterkerk remains an active Protestant church, hosting regular services as well as concerts.

Restoration England and the House of Orange
By the end of 1660, the monarchy in Britain had been restored. Mary Henrietta's eldest brother Charles, along with her second brother James, was resident in Breda in the Netherlands when the call came from the

Parliament in London for him to return and take up the thrones of England and Scotland. When the royal party set sail from Scheveningen on 2 June, the young Prince of Orange came to see them off, and his presence is recorded in some of the many works of art that depict the momentous occasion. Despite the family connection, Charles attempted to stay on friendly terms with the republican faction in Holland, and Johan de Witt, the country's 'Grand Pensionary', reassured Charles that his nephew would be looked after, even suggesting that William might command the Dutch army at some future date. Eventually, in 1671, such an appointment would indeed be made.

Accompanying the royal family on their return was a trusted advisor, the lawyer Edward Hyde (1609–1674), whose attractive daughter Anne had joined the entourage of the Princess of Orange in 1655. The princess's brother, James, had the same reputation as a philanderer as did Charles, and he was already chasing after Anne Hyde, whom he had met in Paris when Mary Henrietta paid a visit to her mother, Henrietta Maria. James married Anne secretly some time towards the end of 1659 or early in 1660. The news was only made public when it became apparent that Anne was pregnant.

Although her father was a successful lawyer and distinguished orator who would later be raised to the peerage, Anne Hyde was a commoner at the time she met James in Holland. It was for this reason that their relationship was discouraged, not only by the exiled royal family but by her own father, who felt that she had overreached herself. Hyde was even prepared to see his daughter imprisoned for her impertinence. James considered having the marriage annulled, and it was Charles II who insisted on James honouring his obligations, despite a courtier, Charles Berkeley, falsely claiming that he too had slept with Anne Hyde. Mary Henrietta, who might have been expected to be sympathetic towards Anne, was not, and on visiting England shortly after the Restoration, she showed displeasure at the idea of having her former lady-in-waiting as her sister-in-law.

The Dutch government hoped for a rapprochement with the new King of England, and proffered the 'Dutch Gift', the collection of valuable paintings and sculptures that had been promised to Charles II when he had been an exile in Holland. Some of these would be transported back to the Netherlands thirty years later, when William was king, along with other artworks that had belonged to the Royal Collection. This may have been partly an act of spite against his sister-in-law Anne, who was destined to succeed him on the throne and was displeased at their removal. However, fourteen paintings of the 26 that Anne ordered to be returned to her still remain in the Royal Collection.

The works given to Charles included 24 Italian Renaissance paintings, some by artists as notable as Titian and Veronese. These, along with twelve sculptures, had originally been part of a much larger collection acquired in Venice by the Dutch merchants Gerrit and Jan Reynst (died 1658 and 1646 respectively). Also included in the Gift were four Dutch paintings – two by Gerrit Dou and the others by Pieter Jansz Saenredam and Adam Elsheimer. Some of the works in the Dutch Gift are believed to have been damaged in the various fires that occurred at Whitehall Palace in the final decades of the seventeenth century.

While still in London, Mary Henrietta contracted smallpox, and she died there in December 1660. The same smallpox epidemic that took her life had claimed her younger brother, twenty-year-old Henry, only three months earlier, eliminating yet another name from the line of succession. The loss of his mother must have had an emotional impact on the young William, an orphan at the age of ten and having to rely on his paternal grandmother and maternal uncle for familial love and advice, and at this stage the sudden improvement in his proximity to the throne may have meant little to him. In the Protestant Netherlands, there was little of the riotous lifestyle associated with the 'Merry Monarch' in England. Mary Henrietta had specifically requested that her brother Charles take an interest in the welfare of her son, but the prince's occasional visits to his uncle did not bring them much closer, particularly with the outbreak of the Second Anglo-Dutch War in 1665. The English were the aggressors in this case, motivated by the desire to acquire some of the Dutch possessions in Africa.

The man who had been appointed William's governor, Frederick Nassau de Zuylestein (1624–1672), was his uncle, an illegitimate son of Frederick Henry. Zuylestein was married to the former Mary Killigrew, a relation of one of Charles II's many mistresses and at one time a lady-in-waiting to William's mother. Zuylestein had a son around William's age, Willem Hendrik (1649–1708), and the two youths naturally became close friends as well as being cousins. In 1666, when William was still in his teens, the political leaders of the Netherlands inevitably became suspicious of Zuylestein, declared William a ward of the state, and replaced prominent members of his household, upsetting the boy greatly.

William was sent to Leiden to complete his education, the principles of which had been laid down in writing by Rivet, and taking as his guidebook a work called *Discours sur la nourriture de son Alt Monseig. le prince d'Orange*, produced for an earlier generation of his family by the venerable Johan Polyander van Kerckhoven (1568–1646), who had been rector of the university fifteen years earlier. This was an all-embracing programme of activities that the prince had been encouraged to follow from the age of four. William was at Leiden for seven years in all, attending lessons given by the philosopher Hendrik Bornius, among others. Bornius had previously been a tutor at a school founded by the royal family at The Hague, and had been appointed by the royal court, without reference to the university's governing body.

Ten years after Cornelius Johnson, another Dutch painter, Jan de Baen, portrayed the prince in his late teens, in a fanciful Roman-style military costume, pointing to a plumed helmet presumably intended to indicate his future as a major European leader. By this time, despite his asthma and slight stature, William already had his heart set on military success.

Leiden

Leiden, a city that stands on the River Rhine, is the home of one of the world's oldest universities, founded in 1575 by William's great-grandfather, generally known to history as William the Silent (the origin of the nickname is unclear). Young Prince William arrived at Leiden in November 1659, accompanied by his mother, his grandmother and various members of his household; that same month he celebrated his ninth birthday, and the city threw him a party. The prince never formally enrolled as a student, but the university arranged an elaborate welcome that included speeches by leading academics as well as the child himself.

Leiden had its own Prinsenhof of a similar style to the one in Delft; this one was also located in a former convent, that of St Barbara. By the time William the Silent's great-grandson took up residence there, it was more or less a guest-house, offering accommodation to royal relations such as Elizabeth Stuart, the sister of King Charles I of England. Elizabeth was in exile from her husband's former kingdom of Bohemia, and needed somewhere to put her ten children, several of whom had studied at Leiden. She and her husband had been welcomed to the Netherlands shortly after their enforced departure from Bohemia.

The former Prinsenhof was situated on Rapenburg, and the building survives, though not open to the public. It has passed through many hands since 1667, when William ceased to spend any time there. The land was divided into plots, and has undergone several conversions and renovations. It is difficult now to recognise anything of the original Prinsenhof from the street.

The university itself was originally housed in a convent, then moved to the Faliede Bagijn Church, which became the present Academic Historical Museum; this can be visited by appointment only. The university's main building is now on the site of another former convent, that of the 'White Nuns', which burned down in 1616. By the time William was born in 1650, the institution was well established and was attracting Protestant students from all over Europe. It has been said that, in some ways, the Prinsenhof with its royal occupants and their tutors, was a kind of private college attached to the university.

As with other ancient universities, the buildings of the University of Leiden are scattered throughout the city. One of the oldest is the 'Gravensteen', a medieval tower that for several centuries was a prison. It is thought to be the oldest stone building in the city. In 1672 a courthouse was added, and William would have been familiar with the Gravensteen in that form. After falling into disuse in the nineteenth century, the building was refurbished for use by the university as a library store and later as administrative offices. It is not generally open to the public.

Leiden was unusual in that it also had a public library, the Bibliotheca Thysiana, which was built in 1655 to hold the collection of a lawyer, Johannes Thysius, who had died two years earlier. The collection is small by modern standards, and can be visited only by appointment, but the building is an unusual survival in the Dutch Classical style. Guided tours are available for larger groups. The library's stock is also available to bona fide researchers.

The Observatory was founded in 1633, but the building that now stands dates from 1860. The original had a tower and spire. The replacement building still contains the quadrant, an instrument built by Rudolph Snellius (1546–1613), and other astronomical equipment from the period. However, it is no longer the university's observatory, and is open to the public, along with the adjacent botanical garden, the oldest in the Netherlands. The gardens were founded by the university in the late sixteenth century, with the botanist Carolus Clausius (died 1609), from Artois in the Spanish Netherlands, in charge. By the time William was studying at Leiden, the garden had been expanded and would have had its own greenhouses. Many of the more exotic species had been supplied by the Dutch East India Company.

The university also boasted one of the earliest anatomical theatres, in which corpses were publicly displayed and dissected for educational purposes. Although the original no longer exists, the Museum Boerhaave in Leiden contains a reconstruction, based on how the theatre would have looked in 1610. The museum is located in the former convent of St Cecilia, a medieval building. A smaller building that still stands, the 'Waag' or weighing house, where local merchants came to trade and check the weight of goods, had an attic that was also sometimes used as a dissecting room. The Waag was designed by none other than

Pieter Post, that favoured artist and architect of the House of Orange; it opened in 1659.

Other buildings with which William would certainly have been familiar are the city's three surviving city gates. Two of these, the Zijlpoort (over the river Zijl) and Morspoort, are fortified buildings, whilst the Doelenpoort, which was restored in 2014, is a smaller arch topped with a statue of St George killing the dragon. This was where the city militia met, and the sculptures that adorn it pay homage to this history. The father of the artist Rembrandt was a member of the militia, hence Rembrandt's early interest in the organisation, leading to the creation of his most famous painting, usually referred to as 'The Night Watch'. Rembrandt himself had left Leiden for Amsterdam long before William arrived there to complete his education.

At the centre of Leiden, close to the Gravensteen and botanic gardens, stands the Pieterskerk, St Peter's Church, completed in the late sixteenth century. No longer in use as a church, it now contains a museum and is used for concerts and other events. Carolus Clausius the botanist is one of many famous residents buried there. The Hooglandse Kerk, dedicated to St Pancras, which had been in the process of construction long before the Reformation took hold, was eventually opened for Protestant worship. Although in the Gothic style, it was built of brick, and was extended in 1665. A point of interest is the clutch of small residential buildings that have grown up close to it over the centuries, many of which are still occupied. The interior was restored in the nineteenth century, and the building continues in use as a church. The Marekerk, opened in 1649 and thus quite a new building when William arrived in Leiden, was one of the first churches in the Netherlands designed with Protestant worship in mind, and was designed by the same city architect as the Bibliotheca Thysiana. It is one of a relatively small number of round churches in the country. Like most Protestant churches, it is open to the public for limited periods only, unless they wish to attend one of the regular Sunday services.

In 1681, Leiden-born Jacob Roman became the city's chief architect, and he would soon also be employed by William and Mary at their homes in Hoonselardijk and Dieren. The Meermansburg Almshouse, an establishment for elderly spinsters and widows, is an example of his early work. Its gardens and gatehouse can still be visited at weekends, but the apartments remain private and access to the 'Regent's Room' is limited to pre-booked groups.

Whilst at Leiden, where many of the university's governing body were politically opposed to a monarchy, William had to be kept apart from people of the wrong political persuasion; this was specified in the instructions for his education. He had also to avoid the company of anyone with anti-religious sentiments. He had brought his own teachers with him to Leiden, in order to avoid any such bad influences, and he was not officially a student of the university; hence his association with Bornius, who was likewise something of an odd man out in terms of the academic hierarchy. For the purposes of the prince's education, Bornius had access to the court library, a benefit beyond the reach of the typical student. He would return to The Hague with William and continue to teach him until 1668.

After completing his further education, William must have returned permanently to The Hague a very changed young man. Nevertheless, he remained somewhat naive as well as puritanical, and his interest in military matters gave him a no-nonsense approach to the idea of enjoying himself. A visit to the court of Charles II in 1670 found him unwilling to join in the excesses of the courtiers, until one evening he was tricked into drinking large quantities of champagne, following which he is said to have turned violent, breaking windows, and had to be forcibly put to bed. This anecdote, though very open to interpretation, offers us an alternative picture of the strait-laced youth.

Early adulthood

If we look for a reason for the comparative obscurity of William III as a monarch, either jointly with his wife, or on his own, we need look no further than his nationality. Had he been born English, or even Scottish, he would have been regarded as an acceptable king, perhaps even as a hero in view of his military record, but the Dutch continued to be regarded with suspicion by the English. During the 1650s and 1660s, they had fought two wars, mostly at sea. In 1666, when the Great Fire of London destroyed much of the city, Dutch immigrants were blamed by many, and mob violence resulted in numerous attacks on that sector of the population.

Dutch Protestants had been present in England in substantial numbers for a century, and a 'Dutch Church' had been adapted for their use from the former priory of the Austin Friars in London. Although that building was destroyed by bombing during the Second World War, it was replaced in 1950 and the church is still active. Included in the collection of surviving historic artefacts is a copy of the 'Antwerp Polyglot', a Bible printed by the French humanist Christophe Plantin (died 1589), in five languages. After their accession, William and Mary would bring a host of Dutch immigrants with them, to the delight of many and the annoyance of others.

As things stood, the titular prince of Orange was always a compromise candidate for the throne of England, despite his very real hereditary claim. Within a few months of William's birth, the provinces of the Netherlands opted for constitutional change and rejected the existing arrangement whereby he would almost automatically have assumed control of the Dutch government on attaining his majority. In return for a peace treaty with England, Cromwell's government had demanded that the House of Orange be excluded from the position of stadtholder, but an 'Orangist' party, a group loyal to the traditional ruling family, continued to exist and the youthful William became its leader in due course. In 1668 he was appointed 'First Noble of Zeeland', and other political leaders found this a subject for concern, fearing a reaction against the republican government. The popular English view of past stadtholders as 'dictators' was shared by many in the United Provinces. It was the threat of a foreign dictator being imposed on the country, in the form of King Louis XIV of France, that turned the tide.

In addition to the title of stadtholder, William would normally have inherited the title of 'Captain-General' and would automatically have become leader of his country's military forces. However, since he was unborn at the time of his father's death, the role had to be temporarily assigned to others, and soon the title was abolished altogether. Dutch fighting power was gradually reduced under the republicans. As for William, he reached the age of twenty without any experience of leading troops. Prior to becoming stadtholder, he held court, a relatively modest affair, at Delft, the former home of his great-grandfather, William the Silent, which had been little used by his own father and grandfather in the years between.

Delft

Although one of the region's largest and oldest cities, Delft had come to the fore as a place of royal residence only in the sixteenth century. The 'Delf' or canal that gave the city its name was the source of much of its prosperity, assisting in its development as a trading centre. From its foundation in the thirteenth century, it grew quickly into a major town and had a population of more than 10,000 at the time of the great fire that destroyed many of its buildings in 1536. About forty years later, William the Silent decided to make it his base.

The Prinsenhof ('Court of the Prince'), formerly a convent dedicated to St Agatha, was an attractive prospect for William the Silent because Delft was protected by city walls that had already proved strong enough to repel an army when a Spanish attack failed. The city became his capital when the Netherlands gained independence from Spain, but in 1584 a Catholic assassin, Balthasar Gérard, under orders from the King of Spain, got close enough to shoot William. Bullet-holes in a wall by the stairs mark the exact spot where the ruler was fatally injured (though in recent years a forensic examination has thrown doubt on their authenticity).

William the Silent was buried at the Nieuwe Kerk ('new church') in Delft, a Protestant church converted from an earlier Catholic place of worship. This was a departure from the earlier tradition by which the princes of Orange had been buried at Breda. It has an impressive tower with a carillon, and is open to the public, but without access to the royal tombs. William the Silent's tomb was designed by Hendrik and Pieter de Keyser and completed in 1623. Constructed in marble and bronze, it depicts the prince in armour, surrounded by figures symbolising Fame, Justice, Prudence, Religion, and Liberty. William III's father and grandfather were also buried at the Nieuwe Kerk, as have been almost all rulers of the Netherlands ever since.

The future William III was still a small child when part of the city was severely damaged by an explosion in a gunpowder store, an event sometimes referred to as 'The Thunderclap of Delft'. One of those who lost their lives in the disaster was 32-year-old Carel Fabritius, a pupil of Rembrandt. Fabritius's surviving works include 'A View of Delft', prominently featuring the Nieuwe Kerk as it looked at the time. Another Delft artist, Egbert van der Poel, painted a later view of the city showing the damage done by the blast. The Oude Kerk (old church') was affected, and has undergone many repairs and refurbishments over the years. Several notable people are buried there, including Admiral Maarten Tromp (1598–1653), the legendary admiral who had tied a broom to the prow of his ship to indicate how he would 'sweep' the English from the seas, and the artist Johannes Vermeer. Both the old and the new church host frequent musical events.

Vermeer's later painting of the city shows the city walls that still stood when William held court there. These were demolished in the nineteenth century, and only one of the original five (or possibly as many as eight) city gates still stands: the Oostport ('Eastern Gate'), with its tall twin towers, culminating in spires added in 1514, is now in private hands and houses an art gallery. Jan van Goyen's contemporary sketches of the city also show Delft's defences in their heyday, revealing how much the landscape has changed through the centuries, with the Oostport standing out as one of the few prominent buildings that survive. The present drawbridge was built between 1867 and 1903, and in recent years, a new weir has been constructed nearby, as an additional water management measure.

The style of pottery with which Delft is now synonymous originated when Italian ceramicists arrived in Antwerp in about 1500. After that city was sacked by the Spanish later in the sixteenth century, the makers relocated to Delft and other Dutch cities. Many were members of the Guild of St Luke, of which a local branch had been founded in 1611, and some took over empty premises vacated by other businesses following the 'Thunderclap'. They began copying the style of Chinese porcelain, producing a cheap alternative to expensive imports from the Far East. Delftware came in a huge range of forms, from plates, jars and tiles to flower vases.

Delftware was enormously popular by William and Mary's reign, and became even more fashionable when the princess began collecting it in earnest. The Metropolitan Museum of Art in New York City (a city founded by Dutch colonists as 'New Amsterdam' only 25 years before William's birth) has in its collection a charger dating from around 1690, depicting the new joint monarchs of England and Scotland in the traditional blue-and-white style of Delft's ceramics. Such items were also coming to be made in England, some in additional colours such as yellow and red. The Victoria & Albert Museum has one such example, showing William on his own, manufactured in Bristol towards the end of his reign.

In 1672, which would become known in the Netherlands as 'the disaster year', the country's chief administrators, Cornelis de Witt and his younger brother Johan de Witt, were brutally killed by a mob after being deposed as the republic's political leaders. Their assassination took place at The Hague's Buitenhof on a green area in front of the prison (from which Cornelis de Witt had just been released, following his arrest on a trumped-up charge of treason). It had been organised by their opponents in the Orangist party, who wanted to see William, now of age, ruling the country in place of the de Witts. The nominal role of 'Grand Pensionary' survived and was taken by Gaspar Fagel (1634–1688), a lawyer with a good reputation who was prepared to do William's bidding.

The de Witt brothers were physically obliterated from the scene despite the fact that William had already been installed as stadholder in their place and had been given emergency powers to deal with the

French military threat. It has never been proved that William was seriously implicated in the murder of the de Witts, but he certainly did little to punish those responsible. One of these, Cornelis Tromp (1629–1691, the son of Maarten Tromp), became a key figure in William's subsequent naval successes.

By this time, the country was simultaneously at war with both France and England – this time with Spain as an ally rather than an enemy. Some blamed the de Witts for the outbreak of war, and William's successes as a military leader did his reputation no harm in this political climate. At the start of his military career, he had been mentored by Prince Georg Friedrich of Waldeck, a German whose service to the Netherlands had begun in the early 1640s. In 1676, they would fall out when the headstrong William ignored Waldeck's advice and carried out a disastrous siege of Maastricht, which had been in French hands since 1673; the Dutch eventually got it back under a treaty of 1678. Waldeck remained in William's service until his death in 1692.

Earlier in the year, Louis XIV had invaded the Netherlands, and he went on to annex the principality of Orange, a region of southern France which, for historical reasons, had come into the hands of the stadtholder. Because of this relationship, it had become a haven for French Protestant refugees, something France's Catholic king could clearly not tolerate. It would continue to be fought over for many years, and William would be its last Dutch ruler. In October 1672, William's uncle, Zuylestein, who had undoubtedly been involved in the conspiracy to assassinate the de Witts, was killed in battle against the French. Shortly afterwards, William found himself in the thick of it. While Maastricht, one of his country's most important fortified possessions, was being besieged and taken by the French, he headed to Charleroi, where he had some hope of cutting off their supply lines; he was obliged to lift the siege, but Charleroi would change hands multiple times in the years that followed. Prominent among the English allies on the French side were two notable officers, the Duke of Monmouth and John Churchill, both of whom would play leading roles in the later lives of both William and his wife Mary.

Maastricht and the Dutch Waterline

The fortress at Maastricht, in a strategic position straddling the River Meuse, was of critical importance to the Dutch war effort, and was sometimes called the 'Bulwark of the Netherlands' or 'the Iron City'. France's general, the Vicomte de Turenne, quickly got the upper hand while the Dutch were otherwise occupied by political upheavals, and William was unable to access the town because the surrounding fortifications had been occupied. The French took the fortress, in the process losing the real-life Count d'Artagnan, a leader of the musketeers, who would much later become a household name as a result of the novels of Alexandre Dumas.

Parts of the original city walls, dating from the thirteenth century, can still be seen. The most impressive section of these is the Helpoort ('Hell's Gate') with its two towers, the only one of the city gates that survives from the Middle Ages, the walls having been replaced in the fifteenth century. At one time it had been the key to the Prince-Bishopric of Liège, but by William's day, it was virtually redundant. It is the oldest city gate that can be seen anywhere in the Netherlands, and now houses a small museum, run by volunteers.

Also in Maastricht, Fort Sint Pieter, a massive hexagonal fortification, overlooks the river Meuse, on the spot where the French breached the city walls in 1673. It was improved by William during the period up to 1685. It did not take its present form, however, until after his death. Not only is it located on a hill (Mount Sint Pieter) but it stands over a network of tunnels and caves, which defenders could use to great advantage to foil future attacks. In 2011, the structure was restored, and it can now be visited by the public. Guided tours of the caves are also available. During the Second World War, a bunker was constructed here for the storage of priceless artworks such as 'The Night Watch'.

Maastricht was taken by the French without further bloodshed in June 1673, while William made his way to the Dutch Waterline (*Hollandse Waterlinie*), a critical feature of the country's defences which could be used to turn back invaders by effectively making large areas into islands.

The city of Naarden (where thousands of citizens had been massacred a hundred years earlier by the Spanish) mostly consisted of a 'star fort', surrounded by bastions arranged like the points of a star. The French had taken it in 1672, but by August 1673 they had so many irons in the fire that they were severely stretched, and the Dutch saw a golden opportunity to reclaim some territory. Trenches were dug, and some unsuspecting French soldiers were captured when they strayed outside the fort. The occupants surrendered after a few weeks, creating a major success for William and a huge disappointment for his enemies.

The Waterline is now a Unesco World Heritage site, and the Nederlands Vestingmuseum, or Fortress Museum, is one of Naarden's major attractions. It deals with the history of the building and also of the Dutch Waterline, and is run by volunteers from within one of the bastions. It also hosts occasional boat trips around the moat, to view the fortifications from a different angle. The fortress would continue to be important in the military history of the Netherlands, and was still seeing action during the Napoleonic Wars.

Quick to capitalise on his achievement at Naarden, William moved on to the city of Bonn, now one of Germany's most important administrative centres. It took him just over a week to get the better of the weakened French garrison. Already Louis XIV, his army's progress prevented by the Dutch water defences, was reluctantly withdrawing troops from the country, and the loss of Bonn was the final straw. For the next four years, William would be fully occupied in staving off French incursions into Flanders. The indecisive Battle of Seneffe, that same month, was a costly one for the Dutch and their Spanish allies, but was almost as catastrophic for the French, under the Prince de Condé. Louis XIV himself would later make a personal visit to the battlefield to pay his respects to the troops he had lost.

The town of Grave, or De Graaf, had been taken by the French in 1672. After Maastricht, it was the only town now remaining in enemy hands. In July 1674, William's army finally set out to recapture it. This proved unexpectedly difficult; the town had undergone two previous sieges, and now the defences were strong. The garrison continued to hold out until October, when William's opponent, the Marquis de Chamilly, capitulated with honour, having earned the prince's respect. After his victory, William attended a service at the church of St Elisabeth to give thanks. Grave's castle, badly damaged during the siege, was demolished in the nineteenth century, but Sint Elisabethskerk still stands.

There are a few remnants of the city's defensive systems still to be seen. Part of the original double moat remains, and one of the city gates still stands. The Hampoort, located directly opposite the church, now houses the Stadsmuseum, significantly modernised. In its present form, it was built in brick in the classic Dutch style, during the years 1686–88, after the siege had reduced much of the city to rubble. At one time known as the Bossche Poort, it has been used for various non-defensive purposes over the centuries, but William's arms are still displayed above the gate.

Wijchen Castle, a medieval fortress remodelled in Renaissance style in the early part of the seventeenth century by its then owner, his great-aunt Emilia of Nassau, was William's chosen base during the siege. A comfortable residence, surrounded by a moat, it would fall into disrepair and passed through several hands before being almost destroyed by fire in 1906. In its restored form, the work of Dutch architect Frank Adrianus Ludewig (died 1940), it became the town hall of the town of Wijchen during the twentieth century. A regional museum is still housed there.

The English, jealous of Holland's dominance over trade in the Far East, had been only too ready to join in the war on the French side, but King Charles II, perhaps mindful of his close family relationship with William, not to mention the financial debts he owed to the Dutch Republic, was already negotiating a settlement. Once the de Witts were out of the picture, King Louis had been prepared to allow William to continue as ruler of a reduced Dutch state, giving up most of his territory to the two major powers, but William's subjects had reacted strongly in favour of continuation of the war. Charles II's efforts to persuade William to take the role of sovereign were rejected by the young man, apparently on moral grounds, though this was clearly what many of his supporters at home wished to see. Meanwhile, concerns about Charles's religious inclinations led to England's Parliament becoming reluctant to provide finance for the war, and before long William had made peace with Charles. Early in 1674, the Treaty of Westminster was signed, and some political factions were already calling on Charles to make William his heir in place of his brother James. William himself was not ignorant of these developments; though still in his early twenties, he was both astute and wary, with an intelligence network that stretched far and wide.

William had seen something of the world, having now campaigned in, or visited, what we would now consider to be several other European countries. He took a keen interest in the kingdom of France, but rejected the possibility of marrying Marie-Anne de Bourbon, an illegitimate daughter of Louis XIV who was more than ten years his senior. His decision not to oblige Louis in this way put paid to any hopes he had of regaining his nominal home territory of Orange in Provence. William had, however, proved his mettle in the Franco-Dutch War that began in 1672. Under his leadership, the Dutch would eventually win back all the territories lost to France.

Now that he was the unquestioned ruler of most of Holland, William took on a new official architect to replace the deceased Pieter Post. Post's successor was his son, Maurits, a talented young man still in his twenties. Maurits Post's first official commission was the expansion of Soestdijk, a house in the province of Utrecht. It had been built for Cornelis de Graeff, one of William's former governors, whose son Jacob sold it to William in 1674 as a hunting lodge. The four-year project created a new palace, which William used regularly only until he replaced it with his new palace of Het Loo ten years later. For William its main purpose was to enable him to indulge his passion for hunting. He employed Gérard de Lairesse to install a painted ceiling depicting the goddess Diana; this is preserved at Amsterdam's Rijksmuseum. In due course, William would create apartments there for his wife Mary, and the palace remained in the possession of the Dutch royal family until the 1970s. For some years it was the retirement home of Queen

Juliana, the grandmother of King Willem-Alexander. It was eventually sold on to a heritage group for redevelopment.

In April 1677, the young stadtholder led a joint Spanish and Dutch force at the Battle of Cassel near Dunkerque in present-day France; the town had become an important border outpost. It had been in and out of French hands for many years, and on this occasion one of the leaders of the French army was Philippe, Louis XIV's younger brother, who by now was married to William's cousin Liselotte. Delays in crossing a river cost William's forces dearly, and his personal courage in the face of the enemy could not save his army from an ignominious defeat. Peace talks had already begun, and William sought an alliance with Charles II to enable him to defend his country.

A few months later, in November 1677, William married his 15-year-old cousin Mary, the daughter of King Charles's younger brother James. The best-known portraits of William and Mary are those taken by Sir Peter Lely, Charles II's court painter, in around 1677, the period of their marriage. Lely was famous for his lavish portraits of English nobles. His portrait of William shows the prince as a handsome, rather dashing young man in armour, though still with those pursed lips that appeared in the portrait of him as a child twenty years earlier. Mary has a similar air of gravity, and the age difference between them is far from obvious, though a family resemblance is apparent. Mary sits gracefully, wearing a bejewelled red gown (some would say orange), every inch the queen that Lely could have anticipated she would one day become.

Chapter 2

The Stuart Princesses

Mary and her younger sister Anne were the daughters of James, Duke of York – the younger brother of King Charles II – and his first wife, Anne Hyde. The Hyde family were, of course, Protestant, but Anne's husband, as a younger son of King Charles I, had been brought up by his mother, Henrietta Maria, to favour Roman Catholicism. His elder brother, Charles II, quickly learned that the people of England, Wales and Scotland would not tolerate a Catholic ruler, and was pragmatic enough to set aside his personal preferences, while attempting to disguise those of his younger brother. Under James's influence, his wife Anne began to lean towards Catholicism too, but Charles stipulated that the children of the marriage must be brought up as Protestants.

The Duchess of York would never know that her two daughters would both inherit the throne in turn. At the time of her death, aged only 34, her brother-in-law the king was still in his prime, and in the event of his marriage to Catherine of Braganza failing to produce an heir (there were only miscarriages to show for their nine years together), Anne Hyde's youngest son, three-year-old Edgar, would be next in line for the throne after his father James, two of James's older sons having already died in infancy.

Royal Palaces – St James's Palace and Richmond Palace

Like her father and uncle, the Princess Mary was born at St James's Palace in London (the same place where she would later marry William), on 30 April 1662. At this time, she was known as Princess Mary of York, having been given her first name in honour of her recently-deceased aunt, William's mother. Her godfather was none other than that dashing Royalist commander, Prince Rupert of the Rhine (1619–82), her grandfather's cousin. Two months earlier, Rupert's mother, Elizabeth Stuart, the former queen consort of Bohemia, had died in London, having recently returned from the Netherlands, where she had been living in exile since the 1620s. Rupert, too, would remain in England for much of the rest of his life.

The city of London would change beyond recognition in the course of the next forty years. One of the first across the Channel following the Restoration, in the hiatus between the first and second Anglo-Dutch Wars, was the artist Willem Schellinks, who made the journey with a French acquaintance, as part of a European tour, leaving both a written diary and a visual record in the form of sketches and paintings, some of which have survived. His handwritten notes are now held by the Bodleian Library in Oxford.

St James's Palace, where Mary, her brother James (who died in infancy) and her sister Anne were born, originated as a leper hospital in the thirteenth century. Much of the palace we see now was built in the sixteenth century, during the reign of King Henry VIII, and is still recognisable as a Tudor building despite the centuries of occupation and change of ownership. Henry intended it as a residence for the son he hoped to have by his second wife, the notorious Anne Boleyn, and the initials 'H&A' are preserved, carved into the decoration at the Great Gatehouse.

The 'Queen's Chapel', a separate building originally designed for the use of Mary's grandmother, Henrietta Maria, was used by Dutch Protestant refugees before and during the reign of William and Mary, some of whose courtiers worshipped there. It had been redesigned by Christopher Wren after being damaged by fire in 1682.

By the time of Charles II, seven monarchs had resided at St James's; ominously, it was where the king's father, Charles I, had spent his last night alive, but it still seems to have had a place in the hearts of his sons. Cromwell's military administrators had turned it over to a barracks, but it had quickly been converted back to a residence when the monarchy was restored. It would continue to be one of the royal family's main residences until the reign of Queen Victoria, and remains the official location of the royal court – the 'Court of St James's'.

St James's is a complex of buildings clustered around four courtyards, and incorporates York House, Clarence House and Lancaster House, all of which were built in the eighteenth and nineteenth centuries as residences for lesser members of the royal family; none of these lesser buildings was standing during the lifetime of William and Mary. Concerns about security have made the palace mostly inaccessible to the general public, and this is one of the reasons it is so little sought out by visitors to London. In 2022, guided tours became available (subject to pre-booking) and, at the time of writing, it seems likely these will continue to be offered.

The Chapel Royal (not to be confused with the Queen's Chapel, which was built around a century later) still opens for two services every Sunday except in August and September. Despite some rebuilding necessitated by a fire early in the nineteenth century, most of the earlier architecture survives in its original form. The ceiling, said to have been painted by Hans Holbein the Younger (died 1543) retains heraldic symbols originally placed there to commemorate Henry VIII's fourth marriage, to Anne of Cleves, in 1540. The arms of two of Henry's previous wives are also to be seen there.

One exotic sight the Stuart princesses would have seen during their childhood was a cluster of pelicans, who frequented the parkland outside the palace. The colony still lives on the lake at St James's Park, but all of them are imports; no young have been born there, probably because pelicans normally need to flock in larger numbers before they begin to breed. The first pelicans arrived in 1664, presented as a gift to King Charles II by the Russian ambassador. It was not at all unusual for the royals to keep wild and exotic animals as pets and curiosities. Charles's grandfather, King James, had kept elephants and crocodiles in the park, and Charles's great rival, Louis XIV of France, had his own menagerie at Versailles. The Tower of London had held a collection of animals since the thirteenth century, when King Henry III was presented with three lions by the Holy Roman Emperor (they were referred to as "leopards", a probable misnomer). The zoo at the Tower was closed in 1835 and the animals transferred to a more humane environment with the creation of Regent's Park Zoo. The pelicans, despite welfare concerns expressed from time to time, remain at St James's Park for the foreseeable future.

The year before Mary's birth, her maternal grandfather, now Earl of Clarendon, acquired another residence called York House in Twickenham, where she sometimes stayed during childhood. Built in red brick, probably by the Earl of Manchester, as an extension of an earlier manor house that had been part of Henrietta Maria's marriage settlement, it still contains traces of its previous existence, including an impressive Tudor fireplace. Now the town hall of the London Borough of Richmond, the house has a chequered history, having passed through the hands of several private owners in the intervening centuries, most of whom have made changes to the house and gardens. A York House Society, formed in the 1920s, attempts to ensure that the building is looked after and continues to be used for events, including weddings and public lectures. A community garden has recently been opened.

Shortly after Mary's birth, her uncle, King Charles II, welcomed his new bride, the Portuguese princess Catherine of Braganza. At this point it seemed unlikely that the marriage would fail to produce children; Charles already had several illegitimate sons and daughters to his name, and would continue to father others for many years after his marriage took place. Mary's place in the line of succession was not, therefore, considered of great significance.

Mary's younger sister, Princess Anne, was born on 6 February 1665. Not long after Anne's arrival, James returned from a stint at sea, in his role as Lord High Admiral, to find the Great Plague ravaging London, and he quickly moved his wife and children to the city of York, where the duchess was so warmly welcomed that she would have been happy never to return south. Much of this warmth was owed to a naval victory James had recently won, off Lowestoft – against the Dutch. The family travelled north via Leicester, where they were received at Lord's Place, a fine house belonging to the 7th Earl of Huntingdon, who, though not a Catholic, would remain loyal to James through thick and thin. They arrived at York in early August 1665.

Since the reign of King Edward III, the title Duke of York has traditionally been given to the second son of a reigning monarch (or his heirs). It had first been granted to James by his father, Charles I, during the English Civil War, but he had officially been able to take it up only after the Restoration. As the title had no Crown lands automatically allocated to it, it had little practical meaning for James until his brother granted him lands in the American colonies. Nevertheless, the people of York recognised the Duke of York as one of their own, and were pleased to welcome any holder of the title.

York today is a bustling city and one of the UK's major tourist destinations. Although it contains little trace of the visit of the Duke and Duchess of York and their family, there are many buildings they would have seen and visited. They could hardly have missed the castle, with its elevated Norman keep that still dominates the city centre, or the cathedral, York Minster, that equals the castle in stature. By the time they arrived in 1665, however, the castle had seen better days. It had effectively been turned into a prison, and repairs carried out at the beginning of the English Civil War in 1642 had failed to return it to its original glory. In 1684, while the keep was being used as an ammunition store, an explosion devastated the inner parts of the building. Now known as Clifford's Tower (after the victim of one of several notable executions there), it has been substantially repaired and made safe, though the interior remains effectively a shell. Audio recordings help tell its history, and the view from the top of the tower is one of the best in York.

William and Mary's great-grandfather, James VI of Scotland, who became James I of England in 1603, had visited York on a progress in 1617, to mark the 50th anniversary of his accession to the throne of Scotland as a child. He arrived in York in April of that year. King's Manor, which nowadays houses the Archaeology Department of the University of York, is a former abbot's house, later an administrative centre, that had been used by James's chief minister, Robert Cecil. It was refurbished for the royal visit and was much improved in the 1620s. The royal arms are now displayed on the Jacobean facade, along with other reminders of the king's stay. During his stay, James also visited the Treasurer's House, now in the care of the National Trust. Built in the previous century for Thomas Young (died 1568), Archbishop of York, and located very close to the minster, it was virtually rebuilt by Young's family. However, a later owner, the industrialist Frank Green (died 1954), made an attempt to restore it to its original appearance, and this is what is seen by present-day visitors, along with Green's eclectic collection of art and antiques.

In 1667, following the visit of James I's grandson and his family, including Princess Mary, King's Manor became the residence of York's governor. After William and Mary's coup in 1688, it ceased to be used as an official residence, and the then governor, Sir John Reresby, although not an admirer of James II, was turned out for failing to support the new régime. Reresby, though forgiven by the new monarchs, died a matter of months later. Although the offices and lecture rooms are not officially open to the general public, it is possible for archaeological enthusiasts and researchers to arrange to visit parts of King's Manor.

York Castle Museum is housed in buildings on the site of the castle bailey; parts were originally a debtors' prison, construction beginning the year before William III's death. Sections of the castle's original outer wall are still visible nearby. The museum contains a series of "period rooms", beginning with a seventeenth-century dining room. Though humble by comparison with the kind of royal apartments Mary and her parents were used to, it reflects the kind of accommodation they might well have experienced while travelling the country.

In the sixteenth century, York had been the seat of a strong Catholic community, Guy Fawkes being one of the city's most notable native sons, but the Duke of York's embracing of Roman Catholicism, not long after his visit to York, did not go down well with its citizens. Archbishop Richard Sterne (died 1683), who had welcomed the future king to York, would continue to support him, but by the time of his accession to the throne, James II would be at loggerheads with Sterne's successor as Archbishop of York, John Dolben (1625–1686).

York Minster is one of the largest, oldest and most important ecclesiastical buildings in Britain. Following Dolben's sudden death from smallpox (resulting from a visit to the king in London), he was not immediately replaced. James had it in mind to appoint the Catholic James Smith (1645–1711), one of his most reliable supporters. The idea horrified the locals, a group of whom attacked Smith in the street. A local nobleman, Thomas Osborne (1632–1712), later Duke of Leeds, took from Smith a silver crozier that he had been given by the dowager queen, Catherine of Braganza; this item, associated in the minds of the people with Catholicism, is now to be seen in the Treasury in the basement museum at the Minster.

A visit to the crypt and museum underground at the Minster enables members of the public to view parts of the Roman and medieval foundations. These periods, together with the discovery of the Viking settlement of Jorvik, tend to overshadow the activities of the Stuart dynasty in York, which were nevertheless of considerable historical significance. Smith never became archbishop, and Dolben was instead succeeded by Thomas Lamplugh (1615–91), who would support James faithfully – until the point when William and Mary were proclaimed monarchs, after which he was only too happy to assist at their coronation, and thus retained his position.

At around the time when his wife and children were residing in York, James began an affair with Arabella Churchill (1648–1730), a sister of the future Duke of Marlborough. Arabella became a maid of honour to the Duchess of York, and would in time give birth to no fewer than four illegitimate children, all fathered by the duchess's husband and given the surname 'Fitzjames' in recognition of this. Her two sons by James were later given dukedoms. Another member of the Duchess of York's household was Frances Jennings (died 1731), whose much younger sister Sarah would one day become a confidante of the royal women and forge a notable career as Duchess of Marlborough. Frances also caught the eye of the Duke of York, but escaped his grasp by marrying, at the age of sixteen, a Roman Catholic army officer who took her to live in France.

By the time of her next confinement, the duchess was back at St James's Palace. Her daughters Mary and Anne, as the king's nieces, were soon thereafter given their own household at Richmond Palace, which no longer stands. Located in the area between the present-day Richmond Green and the Thames, it was built in the fifteenth century by King Henry VII after an earlier building had been destroyed by fire, and it was named for Henry's previous title, Earl of Richmond, on a site that had been royal property since Norman times. It had been the favourite residence of Queen Elizabeth I, who had enjoyed hunting deer in its grounds. Elizabeth had died there in 1603.

Although Richmond Palace has now vanished from view, some of the outbuildings – notably the gatehouse and the 'Trumpeters' House' – survive, and there are records of the palace's appearance. Once a comfortable building, one of very few to enjoy the convenience of a flushing toilet, it had deteriorated badly during the absence of the monarchy and was already in a poor condition by the time Mary and Anne moved in. New buildings were being erected to replace those that were falling to pieces.

The Richmond Museum has on display a scale model showing what the palace is believed to have looked like. Its multiple turrets, once impressive, may have been in a poor state of repair by the time Mary came to live there. The original palace gateway, dating from around 1500, can still be seen, however, and improvements partly funded by the local authority have been taken forward largely thanks to the activities of the Friends of Richmond Green, a community action group. The rooms above the gate were part of the 'Wardrobe Court'. By the time George II came to the throne in the 1720s, there was nothing much left of the palace, and George would construct the adjacent terrace of houses, now called Maids of Honour Row, to accommodate members of his wife's household.

Although the palace was closely associated with Mary's childhood, her future husband William would not be averse to spending time here during his time as king, owing mainly to the opportunities for hunting that were afforded by the extensive grounds. After Mary's death, he would use it more frequently for this purpose. Several of his close circle, including Arnold Van Keppel, later Earl of Albemarle, owned houses there, and it made a good country retreat away from the business of politics.

The Dutch artist Caspar Netscher painted Mary's portrait several times, including a miniature of her as a child, holding a rabbit. Another miniature of her, at an age somewhere between five and ten, attributed to the English artist Richard Gibson, who had been at court since the reign of Charles I, is held by the Rijksmuseum in Amsterdam. Gibson would in due course become a member of Mary's household. Clearly she had some importance as a potential heir to the throne from the time of her birth, but her status would wax and wane as her mother gave birth to each of the four sons who would die in infancy.

One of Peter Lely's earliest paintings of Mary is a group portrait featuring the then Duke and Duchess of York and their two daughters, with Anne sitting on her mother's knee and Mary standing alongside, holding a wreath of flowers. James contemplates his family in a somewhat aloof manner. Although begun in about 1668, the portrait remained unfinished at the time of Lely's death in 1680. It is now part of the Royal Collection and hangs in Windsor Castle.

Mary was barely nine years old when her mother died, a few weeks after giving birth to her eighth child – it is known that she was also suffering from breast cancer. The baby girl died just a few months later. Edgar, the youngest and only surviving son of the Duke and Duchess of York, also died that year, and this left Mary next in line for the throne after her father and any legitimate children her uncle might have in the meantime. She had not had a particularly close relationship with her mother, though she was said to be her father's favourite. Mary and Anne had been brought up mostly by a governess, Frances Villiers, whose daughter Elizabeth would become one of her ladies-in-waiting (and perhaps more). Mary's relationship with Anne probably had something of a motherly element to it, since she had, aged only three, been Anne's godmother.

Lady Villiers was by birth a member of the illustrious Howard family. Her father and her brother James (died 1688) were successively Earls of Suffolk, James having been Earl Marshal of England, responsible for overseeing Charles II's coronation ceremony in 1661. Her husband, Sir Edward Villiers (1620–89), was a friend of Sir Edward Hyde, who was Mary and Anne's maternal grandfather and retained a great interest in their welfare. One of Sir Edward Villiers' cousins, Barbara (1640–1709), was the mistress of King Charles II, and the mother of many of the king's illegitimate children. The Villiers clan, into which Frances had married, was thus as powerful as the family into which she had been born, so her appointment as the girls' governess was no surprise.

Lady Frances Villiers has been described as 'a gentle warm-hearted woman'[1] though it has also been said that she was immensely strict with her charges. The diarist Samuel Pepys was one of those with first-hand knowledge of the children's upbringing, and he was impressed with Princess Mary's talent for music and dancing. She and her sister were also noted for their big appetites, taking after their mother. As a child, Anne was sent to Paris for medical treatment – she suffered from weeping eyes – and was placed in the care of her grandmother, Henrietta Maria, widow of King Charles I. She remained there after her grandmother's death, but returned before the death of her own mother in 1671.

Recognising the possibility that Mary or Anne might some day end up on the throne, Charles II had placed Henry Compton (died 1713), Bishop of London from 1675, in charge of their education, with disappointing results. The bishop's main concern was to ensure that they adhered to the tenets of the Church of England; although strongly anti-Catholic, he was surprisingly tolerant of Dissenters. Compton was not, however, particularly learned, and seems often to have left the two princesses to their own devices. There were two chaplains in the household, who also offered religious instruction.

---

1. Roger Powell, *Royal Sex*.

Mary appears to have been more studious than Anne, and was encouraged by her grandfather. Thanks to a tutor named Peter de Laine, a Protestant exile from France, she became very proficient in the French language, which was something of a 'lingua franca' when it came to diplomatic correspondence. As teenagers, she and Anne also took roles in a masque, *Calisto*, commissioned from John Crowne (1641–1712) for performance at court – Charles II being notoriously fond of the theatre, as his parents had been. Mary took the role of Aurelia, dressed in a fabulously jewelled costume. For this performance, she was instructed in deportment and elocution by Mrs Mary Betterton (1637–1712), one of the first English professional actresses – who was almost unique among her profession at the time for having a long and happy marriage with not so much as a whisper of any adulterous affairs.

When told by Bishop Compton that it was time for Mary to be confirmed, James opposed the ceremony, complaining that his daughters had been taken beyond his control. The king was obliged to overrule him, and Mary was duly confirmed by Compton at the chapel in Whitehall Palace. A year later, Uncle Charles took both Mary and Anne to the Lord Mayor's banquet at the Guildhall. Now exposed to wider society, Mary took up playing cards, for which her chaplain would take her to task, especially when she was found doing so on a Sunday.

Other girls, including their governess's five daughters, were brought up alongside the two princesses at Richmond. One of Mary's best friends in childhood was a girl named Anne Trelawny, a daughter of Sir Jonathan Trelawny (died 1681). The newcomer joined the household at one of those times when Mary's sister Anne had been sent away for a cure. Some of these companions of youth would remain friends for a long time. Other relationships formed by Mary and Anne with their peers would become a problem later in their lives. As for Anne Trelawny, she would be removed from the household after Mary's marriage, allegedly because of William's jealousy.

The problem of the succession

Whilst King Charles was unlikely to have any more children by his queen, Catherine of Braganza, James had not given up hope of fathering another legitimate son. Two years after the death of Anne Hyde, he married the 15-year-old Italian Catholic princess, Mary of Modena, an attractive girl 25 years his junior. Mary took to her new stepmother quickly, and may have been oblivious to the fact that any male half-sibling she might acquire would push her further down the order of succession. Despite the loss of so many brothers, she did not seriously think of herself as a future queen of England and Scotland. Meanwhile, the new Duchess of York, who was so close to her in age, lavished attention on her.

Unfortunately for Mary's father James, his second wife proved to have the same difficulty as his first when it came to producing children. Of her twelve pregnancies, only two would culminate in her giving birth to a living son, and only one son and a daughter would survive into adulthood. However, Mary of Modena was only nineteen years old when the decision was made to marry off her elder stepdaughter to the Prince of Orange, and the prospects of a male heir for the future King James remained good – even though James had already become an inattentive husband and gone back to his philandering ways. The new Duchess of York soon moved into Richmond Palace with her two stepdaughters.

One of James's lovers was Arabella Churchill, with whom he had previously dallied during his first marriage. Two of Arabella's children had been born during his marriage to Anne Hyde, when Arabella was her lady-in-waiting, but the fourth was born well after his marriage to Mary of Modena. By now he had also struck up a relationship with Catherine Sedley (1657–1717), daughter of a Royalist poet and politician, who was barely older than his young wife. Deeply resented by Mary of Modena, Catherine too gave birth to James's illegitimate children: a daughter, Catherine (who later became Countess of Anglesey and eventually a duchess), and one or possibly two sons, who died in infancy. After James came to the throne, he would be persuaded to give Sedley up, and she was sent to Ireland, but swiftly returned.

Charles II, always hedging his bets, had it in mind that his niece Mary would grow up to marry Louis, the Dauphin of France, who was much closer to her in age than William. This would have meant yet another Catholic alliance, of which Parliament thoroughly disapproved, and the idea was abandoned. An advantage of marrying her to her first cousin William was that he had nearly as good a claim on the thrones of England and Scotland as she did herself, in view of his descent from Charles's sister. Mary herself did not at first find the idea of this marriage appealing.

It is believed that William and Mary first came face to face in about 1670, when he was twenty years old and she was only eight. The prince had been invited to visit his uncle, Charles II, in England, in order to be invested with the Order of the Garter. He stayed for a few months, and it would have been surprising if they had not met during his stay. If there was any reason for the reluctance both of them later showed towards the idea of their marriage, it is doubtful whether it had its origins in this early meeting. No doubt Mary had hoped for someone more dashing than the rather staid William, who by all accounts was nothing much to look at. Perhaps William's hesitation came from a lack of exposure to girls of that age, leading to a feeling of inadequacy.

In her teens, Mary grew unusually tall for a woman, a trait she inherited from her paternal great-great-grandmother and namesake, Mary, Queen of Scots. She would, in adulthood, be several inches taller than her husband William, and her enthusiasm for food resulted in a buxom figure that was again in contrast with her husband's stature; her mother, Anne Hyde, had grown extremely fat during the years of her marriage, and Mary is said to have developed a horror of going the same way. She did not share the sickly constitution of her siblings (which at least one doctor attributed to their father James having contracted a sexually-transmitted disease and passed it on to his first wife).

For several years during her teens, especially in the time between her mother's death and the arrival of her new young stepmother, Mary had enjoyed a close friendship with Frances Apsley (1653–1727), a much older girl who had been assigned to her as a maid of honour.

Frances's father, Sir Allen Apsley (1616–83), was a loyal supporter of King Charles and served as the Duke of York's treasurer. At the age of thirteen Mary was writing passionate letters to Frances Apsley, calling her 'husband'. The two used pseudonyms, just as Mary's sister Anne did when conversing with an older maid-companion, Sarah Jennings, later Sarah Churchill, Duchess of Marlborough. Pseudo-romantic relationships between women were not so unusual in the period, when girls from respectable families had less opportunity for contact with the opposite sex.

In a letter to Frances, Mary spoke of how her father had tired of his wife and looked forward uneasily to her own likely future, saying that 'in two or three years men are always weary of their wives and look for a mistress as soon as they can get them.' The men she encountered at court, including her father and uncle, were not setting a very good example. For this reason, she imagined a future where she and Frances would move into a country cottage together and spend their leisure hours growing fruit. After her marriage, Mary continued to write to Frances, but by this time she had overcome her initial misgivings about William – though she did write that she had been 'playing the whore' when she first became pregnant, suggesting that she had been unfaithful to Frances by sleeping with William. Her sister Anne continued the correspondence with Frances, who subsequently married Sir Benjamin Bathurst.

When Mary came face to face again with the adult William, in October 1677, she was disappointed. Besides being shorter than her, he had bad posture, a big nose and a weak chest. He dressed shabbily, spoke with an impenetrable accent and made no jokes. William was, however, quite taken with Mary now that she had blossomed into a young woman, and was eager to confirm the casual arrangement made with his uncle Charles some years previously. He became so determined to pursue the marriage alliance that he threatened to return home and not come back if he could not have her immediately, allegedly warning that he and Charles could continue as 'the greatest friends or the greatest enemies, for it must be one or the other'. Charles impulsively agreed, and the marriage was announced that same day.

Although Mary was less than thrilled at the prospect of her marriage, the general public were pleased to learn that she would marry a good Protestant rather than the Catholic heir to the throne of France – still England's traditional enemy. For several days, the couple stood together, welcoming dignitaries who had come to offer their congratulations. Mary's initial feelings of distaste for William appear to have changed, very quickly, to feelings of affection, but not yet; it was something of an ordeal for her to put on this public face and feign happiness. The incoming Lord Mayor of London, Sir Francis Chaplin, put on his show later in the month, and the whole royal family attended, including William. As usual, the theme was 'London's Triumphs', and the pageant was followed by feasting and further celebration. Festivities spread far beyond the capital, with the news of the marriage being particularly well-received in Scotland.

Chapter 3

Marriage

Mary and William were married by Bishop Compton at St James's Palace, on the evening of the groom's 27th birthday, with the bride in tears while her uncle the King, who had given her away, did his best to jolly her along. The ceremonial processions and banquet that accompanied the event had done nothing to reconcile her to the idea of marrying. The morning after, Mary was presented with £40,000 worth of jewels, which surprisingly did not improve her mood. They were handed over by William's representative – his best friend, William Bentinck (1649–1709), who was already a leading figure in William's household and would remain in the couple's service throughout their married life. Bentinck had begun his career as a page in 1664, had studied with William at Leiden, and had been his close confidant ever since. Could Mary have been a little jealous of this man's close relationship with her husband?

A few days later, on 7 November 1677, Mary of Modena gave birth to a son, Charles, who was made Duke of Cambridge (a title previously given to Anne Hyde's short-lived sons Charles and James). An outbreak of smallpox, which had affected Princess Anne, appeared to be on the wane, and the Duchess of York encouraged Anne, who was still recovering, to visit her just after she had given birth. The child appeared healthy, and Princess Mary was thus supplanted in her position as a future heir to the throne – it seems that William did not hesitate to show his displeasure. A month later, the little prince died, restoring the status quo. His death may have been an indirect result of his half-sister's presence at his mother's bedside; at any rate, his nurses were blamed for their failure to treat his illness in the manner thought to be correct at the time.

Despite all this, on 15 November, a ball was held in recognition of the 29th birthday of the queen, Catherine of Braganza. Her birthday balls were a regular occurrence, as the queen loved dancing. On this farewell appearance, the new Princess of Orange made a notable impact, dressed in all her finery and wearing the jewels she had received as a wedding present. The occasion was recorded by the diarist John Evelyn (1620–1706), who says that the prince and princess danced, but not whether they danced with one another.

It must have been difficult for Mary to know whether she was coming or going, and for William there would have been disappointment every time the Duchess of York became pregnant. According to some accounts, he took out his annoyance on his new wife, and it was with reluctance that she joined him on his return journey to the Netherlands. One of her final farewells was said to Queen Catherine, of whom she was very fond; perhaps Catherine, who had herself not had an easy time fitting into a foreign court, offered some badly-needed advice and encouragement.

Mary had not, however, been able to say goodbye to her sister Anne, who was in quarantine, and she was hurried out of the city by her husband to ensure she did not become infected. Smallpox had, after all, killed both William's parents in turn, and might have killed him too had it not been for the attentions of Bentinck, who had nursed him back to health two years earlier. Barely had they set out than the weather turned, holding up the royal couple's departure for a few days, and they put ashore in Kent to await the readiness of the fleet. There they were entertained by the Dean of Canterbury, and eventually boarded the 'Montague' at Margate.

Shortly after they finally left the country, Lady Frances Villiers died of smallpox, and the role of governess to the remaining royal children was taken by Lady Henrietta Hyde (1646–87), a relation of Princess Mary's late mother. The superstitious Duchess of York claimed to have had a vision of Lady Frances in purgatory, a story that did not go down well with Frances's family. Three of Frances Villiers' six daughters had accompanied Princess Mary to the Netherlands as maids of honour, and it appears that Elizabeth, who was a few years older than the princess, held a particular appeal for the Prince of Orange, who apparently took her as a mistress at some stage – despite her nickname, 'Squinting Betty'. The rumours about their relationship came to a head in 1685 when brought to Mary's attention by her father, but William seems to have managed to explain it away to his wife's satisfaction.

On arrival at the Dutch coast, William and Mary were welcomed with thanksgiving in the village of Ter Heijde, where inclement weather conditions forced them to land instead of at Rotterdam. An important naval battle had taken place just off Ter Heijde, 24 years earlier, at which the Dutch fleet had been defeated by the English, under the Cromwellian commander, General George Monck. (Ironically, it was also Monck who had later negotiated with Charles II to achieve the restoration of the monarchy.) It is doubtful whether either William or his bride had this on their minds as he struggled to carry her across the beach, which had to be negotiated on foot. Could this heroic action have been a romantic moment that changed her view of her new husband? The nearest royal residence, Huis Hoonselardijk (various spellings are used, including Honselersdijk and Honselaarsdijk) was made ready for the couple's arrival, and a few days later they made a grand entry into The Hague, in a coach drawn by six horses, their way prepared by a group of virgins scattering flowers in their path, with musical accompaniment.

Mary was brought in triumph to the Binnenhof. In the evening there was a grand firework display, and further entertainments followed. Mary found she had an opportunity to play cards, a pastime which William, despite his general lack of joie de vivre, also enjoyed. This may have been another of the things that brought them closer.

Hoonselardijk

The newly-weds spent their first few weeks at the Hoonselardijk, and gradually got used to one another's little ways. William was very popular with his subjects, as was his bride, and he began to value Mary's vivacious company at home as well as having his public position enhanced by her presence. William had already begun collecting paintings, including works by Rubens, and was pleased to find that his new wife shared his appreciation of the visual arts; she was soon giving the royal palaces a makeover.

William had spent much of his childhood at Hoonselardijk, with his mother, and it became Mary's favourite residence in her adoptive country. William touchingly requested his head gardener to ensure that flowers were blooming in every season from now on, so that he could keep his new wife supplied with regular bouquets. As well as her love for plants and a growing habit of collecting china, Mary was also able to indulge her interest in chinoiserie, furnishing her 'cabinet' – her personal display area – in Oriental fashion. Only the most honoured guests would be invited to view this.

Of Huis Hoonselardijk only the outbuildings remain now. The sixteenth-century house, on the site of an earlier castle, was first acquired by William's grandparents, Frederick Henry and Amalia. They decided to remodel the house in imitation of the Palais de Luxembourg in Paris, built earlier in that century by the French queen regent, Marie de Medici, who had made her plans widely available as a statement of her influence throughout Europe. The corner pavilions were linked by long galleries surrounding a courtyard, in the French manner, with chambers and self-contained suites of reception rooms for the prince and princess respectively in the front two pavilions. The reconstruction begun by William's parents was continued during his own reign, but later the house deteriorated and the surviving buildings, known as Der Nederhof, (the lower courtyard), originally used as stables and guest quarters, were converted into a residential home during the 1970s.

In the park attached to the house, there were four buildings that contained William's collection of exotic animals and birds, which at various times included creatures imported from the Indies, such as a 'spotted cat', an 'Indian elk' and a chameleon. Such private zoos were not exclusively owned by the rulers of great empires such as Britain, France and Spain; this collection had been begun by the prince's grandfather, Prince Frederick Henry, and there was a similar collection in William's hunting lodge at Dieren, where two camels are known to have been kept. Most, if not all, of these captive creatures had been gifts to William from various potentates. Birds might, of course, be kept for hunting purposes, and since William loved hunting, it is not surprising that there were aviaries at all the estates where he practised this pastime.

By all accounts, Mary had an outgoing personality that endeared her to her new subjects, who must have been looking forward to the time when the dour young stadtholder would finally take a wife. Her growing inclination towards plumpness was not seen as a disadvantage in Holland; quite the opposite. She became even more popular a few months after her arrival, when she was discovered to be pregnant. She carried out her duty of receiving and entertaining the nobility while William mostly occupied himself with military matters, and began taking barge trips along the canals of The Hague with a group of ladies of both nationalities. Mary was still very young, and there were enough experienced men in William's inner circle to be trusted with the more important tasks such as running the country; this would not always be the case in the future.

The royal household numbered around 200 people in all, most of them dedicated to the service of the stadtholder rather than that of his wife, who had only about 40 acolytes. Mary's household incorporated the ladies she had brought with her from England as well as her former nurse, a Mrs Langford, and her drawing-master, Richard Gibson, a collaborator of the better-known Peter Lely (who had already painted Mary's portrait). Gibson outlived Lely and continued in Mary's service after she became Queen of England and Scotland. In addition to Elizabeth Villiers, the daughter of her old governess, the ladies-in-waiting included Elizabeth's sister Anne, who soon married William's Dutch friend William Bentinck, later Earl of Portland.

Another important member of the household was Mary's new chaplain, Dr Hooper, who was disappointed not to find a private chapel available. He had been selected in order to deter the youthful princess from adopting the Calvinist practices common in the Netherlands; the marriage treaty had specified that Mary would be free to practise as an Anglican. Rather to William's displeasure, Mary quickly gave her dining room over to be used as a chapel, where she worshipped daily when in residence. Visitors from Britain were, on occasion, allowed to enter the chapel to watch her at prayer; this was a matter of diplomacy, emphasising her role as the Protestant heir who took her religious beliefs seriously. Hooper was a constant presence, always ready to read to the princess from the books he considered appropriate, while she carried on with her needlework. William came to dislike Hooper further when he discovered that the religious texts he had himself recommended for her reading had been replaced with those preferred by Hooper.

Other maids of honour included Jane Wroth, daughter of one of Charles II's most loyal supporters. Before too long, Jane was found to be pregnant by William's cousin and friend, Willem Hendrik de Zuylestein, who unsuccessfully attempted to get out of marrying her. William and Mary would fall out over the rights and wrongs of the matter, and Thomas Ken (1637–1711), who succeeded Hooper as Mary's chaplain, settled the matter by performing the marriage ceremony without William's permission. (Ken is now chiefly remembered, not for this action, but for his contribution to the Anglican hymn-book.) A furious William ensured that Ken returned to England soon afterwards.

Unfortunately, almost as soon as Mary became pregnant, William was obliged to leave for Flanders, where the French were attacking and had taken possession of the cities of Ghent and Bruges. They parted company in Rotterdam, but eventually she would be able to visit him in Antwerp and later at Breda, very close to where the fighting was taking place. By this time their marital relationship had improved so much that she wrote to a friend that the most cruel thing in the world was 'parting with what one loves and not only common parting but parting so as may be never to meet again'. On 21 March they were reunited.

Antwerp

Antwerp was a major city of the Low Countries, and it remains one of Europe's biggest ports and Belgium's largest city. For over a hundred years, it had boasted its own 'Bourse', a forerunner of the stock exchange, and it was still governed by the Spanish until the peace treaty of 1648, which granted independence to the United Provinces but closed the River Scheldt to traffic, leading to a decline in the city's fortunes. The regional governor, Alexander Farnese (1635–89), was an Italian prince, whose great-grandfather and namesake had previously governed, in a time when relations between Spain and the Netherlands were less cordial.

Because of the loss of river trade, the city's prosperity declined. The Bourse gradually ceased to function and Amsterdam became the Netherlands' main trading centre. Two major fires resulted in the construction of a replacement, which later dwindled and was merged with the Brussels stock exchang. The building that now stands on the site is the venue for an annual Trade Fair and other events. Archaeological excavations have uncovered medieval foundations and evidence for even earlier habitation.

Buildings such as Antwerp's City Hall and other masterpieces of Renaissance architecture still give us a picture of the city William and Mary knew, and the city's modern architecture gives a nod to its history without emulating the traditional style. For example, the Port Authority Building ('Havenhuis'), designed by Zaha Hadid and completed in 2016 (coincidentally the year of the architect's death), incorporates an older public building, which enjoyed legal protection because of its historic interest as a replica of an earlier building associated with the Hanseatic League. The extension takes the form of a diamond, because of the port's importance in the diamond trade.

The City Hall, designed by Flemish and Italian architects, and stands beside the main market square ('Grote Markt'). The building continues to serve in the same capacity as it has done since the 1560s. It is permanently open to the public, but the opportunity to visit some of the restricted areas is occasionally offered during 'open doors' events. Much of its interior decoration dates from the nineteenth century, but an original fireplace remains a point of historical interest.

Antwerp's 'Vleeshuis' or butchers' hall, also dating from the sixteenth century, acted as a guildhall for the city's oldest traders. Its outward appearance is little changed, but in the nineteenth century the building was sold and became a multi-purpose space occupied by various businesses. Since 1913 it has been a museum, which began as an exhibition for an eclectic collection of objects, but nowadays it concentrates on musical instruments and other music-related items.

Of the city's fortifications, a vestige remains of Fort Lillo, constructed by William the Silent. The small village that was sacrificed to a massive port extension during the 1960s is now something of a tourist attraction for those wanting to experience the 'character' of a polder[1] village. There is a small 'poldermuseum', and a convenient water bus service.

William and the pregnant Mary spent a fortnight together at Antwerp in March 1678, where William often retreated to the home of Diego Duarte, a polymath and art collector of Portuguese family. The house became known as the 'Antwerp Parnassus' because of the cultured people who gathered there. The collegiate church of St James (Sint-Jacobskerk), completed in 1656, holds the tomb of Diego's father Gaspar, as well as those of Peter Paul Rubens and other notable artists. The church's single tower was intended to be taller than that of Antwerp Cathedral, but never reached its planned height because of the lack of funds resulting from the loss of the city's prosperity.

Works by Rubens can also be seen in the cathedral, consecrated in 1521, which remains a place of Roman Catholic worship. Belgium's largest Gothic church, it was originally to have twin towers, but a fire prevented the plans ever coming to fruition, and only one tower was completed, though it is the tallest church tower in the country. Serious damage was done to the cathedral during the 'Beldenstoorm' later in the sixteenth century, and again during the French Revolution two hundred years later. New stained glass windows were installed during the nineteenth century.

The threat to Flanders from the French was of as much concern to the English as to the Dutch, because they feared for their own trade routes, and Charles II sent an expeditionary force in support of William's efforts,

---

1. Polder is the term for a low-lying tract of land, often reclaimed from the sea.

though, by the time they arrived, their presence was of little use. For the time being, Antwerp was safe enough, but an epidemic was taking more lives in the city than any aggression from Louis XIV's troops.

Mary's grandfather, the Earl of Clarendon, had by this time died, and the title now belonged to his son Henry Hyde (1638–1709), the younger brother of Mary's late mother. The new earl had been appointed ambassador to The Hague, and Mary relied on him for advice and protection in William's absence. After the reunion in Antwerp, her enthusiasm for a further meeting with her husband led the princess to take an uncomfortable coach journey to Breda, a distance of 50 miles, and shortly after her arrival she suffered a miscarriage which left her fighting for her life.

It was a case of history repeating itself, since William's mother, Mary Henrietta, had suffered a miscarriage at Breda thirty years earlier, at a similar age and in similar circumstances. Mary Henrietta had eventually had a successful pregnancy, but this was the first and probably the only pregnancy her daughter-in-law would ever experience. Modern experts have speculated that the damage done by the miscarriage caused Mary's inability to conceive a subsequent child. Her father, not anticipating that she would fail to provide him with grandchildren in due course, wrote to say that she should be 'carefuller of herself another time'.

Breda

Breda had played a major role in the lives of the Stuart dynasty, and is immortalised in British history as the location of the 'Declaration of Breda'. Located in the province of North Brabant, at the confluence of the River Mark and the River Aa, it is only a few miles from the border between the Netherlands and present-day Belgium. The name 'Breda' derives from the phrase 'broad Aa' – the section where the two rivers meet.

The Declaration of Breda, the only reason most British people are familiar with the city's name, was formulated in 1660 and contained Charles II's promises to the English and Scots to allow a degree of freedom of religion and not to take revenge on those who had fought against his father. There were naturally some exclusions from the carefully-worded statement (written largely by Mary's grandfather when he was still Sir Edward Hyde), which put the onus on Parliament to decide what to do in certain cases. Many of the surviving 'regicides' who had signed Charles I's death warrant were duly executed, and others died in prison. Likewise, Roman Catholics could not look forward to equality under the new regime.

At the time of the Declaration, Charles had been living in Breda for only a month, having previously been resident in Brussels, but he knew the city from an earlier stay, in 1650, when he had made a pact with the Scots Covenanters in an attempt to gain their support in his bid for the throne. That treaty, now virtually forgotten, had included an agreement to recognise the authority of the 'Kirk', the Presbyterian Church, but Charles's concessions had been in vain on that occasion as he and his Scottish supporters had been roundly defeated in battle by Cromwell.

His brother James had also spent some time in Breda. Being a few years younger than Charles, he had seen less of the English Civil War and had been in Brussels, awaiting permission to enter Holland, when news reached him of the death of his brother-in-law the stadtholder and shortly afterwards of the birth of his nephew William. Elizabeth of Bohemia, James's aunt, had given him the use of a house in Utrecht until such time as he could be at his sister's side in The Hague. However, his arrival there coincided with that of ambassadors from the English parliament, and he was obliged to divert to Breda to avoid them.

After a few years in France, having fallen in and out of favour with his elder brother, James returned to Breda to be with his sister Mary Henrietta, and stayed there with her for a while. One of his household, Henry Jermyn (died 1708), who shared the Stuart brothers' reputation for philandering, dared to make advances to the widowed princess, and rumours spread that they were having an affair, which did her reputation no good and was one of the causes of the friction between James and Charles.

The property of the Holy Roman Emperor since the eleventh century, Breda had been given the right to build fortifications, which survived when it came into the hands of the Princes of Orange in the sixteenth century, after the province of Brabant had been absorbed into the Netherlands. Prior to that, the House of Orange-Nassau had been lords of Breda since 1404. They were obliged to fight for it when the Spanish invaded, and it was William's grandfather, Frederick Henry, who won it back after a siege of 1637.

William's contribution was to convert the residence from a castle, with a purely defensive purpose, to something recognisable as a palace.[2] After his marriage, William decided to improve and extend the castle, a Renaissance-style building that had been converted from its medieval original by Henry III of Nassau (died 1538), but had passed into the hands of William the Silent. It was here that the Treaty of Breda had been signed in 1667, under the de Witts, handing over the Dutch colony of New Amsterdam in North America to the English, who had captured it and would rename it New York.

It was also William who installed a throne, something to which he, even as stadtholder, was not strictly entitled, but which represented a perceived change in status following his marriage to Mary. These alterations were carried out after the death of Charles II, when Mary's father still had no male heir and it had begun to seem inevitable that she would follow James to the throne of England. Dynastic portraits attesting to William's descent from the English royal family were a prominent feature of the decoration. However, he spent relatively little time in residence after taking possession of the new building.

In its present form, the castle, which stands on an island surrounded by canals, is the home of the Royal Netherlands Military Academy. Although security prevents the public from entering the complex under normal circumstances, it is occasionally possible to book a guided tour through the Tourist Office. The Spanjaardsgat or 'Spanish Gate', the only significant section of the walls still standing, commemorates the

---

2. Simon Thurley.

period of Spanish occupation and the city's eventual recapture. The Spanish Gate is an impressive sight from the other side of the canal, and can be seen at closer quarters on one of the available canal boat trips. It is nowadays the focal point of an annual jazz festival in and around the harbour area. The Valkenberg city park, formerly part of the castle complex, is still a public space. Stadspark Valkenberg takes its name from the 'valken' (falcon), falconry having been a popular sport with the historical residents of the castle, and the park is very popular with tourists and locals as a place to walk and enjoy the scenery. Parts of the old city walls are also visible here.

In 1646, Frederick Henry also founded the Orange College, a training college for youths who aspired to enter the armed forces or civil service. The Kloosterkazerne, the building which housed the college, was originally constructed as part of the Sint-Catharinadal convent complex, a thirteenth-century foundation. The renovated building is currently occupied by Holland Casino, a state-owned company that has the monopoly on gambling in today's Netherlands.

The college's most notable student was the polymath Christiaan Huygens (1629–1695), inventor of the pendulum clock and the son of Constantijn Huygens (1596–1687), who had been secretary to William's grandfather. Among other things, Christiaan Huygens would work as an advisor to the House of Orange. His involvement with the Dutch government effectively ended before William came to power, but his elder brother Constantijn (1628–1697) followed in their father's footsteps by becoming William's secretary. Christiaan himself corresponded with artists, scientists and politicians all over Europe and visited Britain several times. A few years after his final visit, during which he exchanged views with the younger scientist Isaac Newton, Christiaan Huygens died and was buried at the Grote Kerk in Breda.

Breda's Begijnhof, a kind of convent, celebrated its 750th anniversary in 2017, making it the oldest institution of any kind in the city. It came under the protection of the Nassau dynasty in the early sixteenth century. The *béguines*, as they are known throughout Europe, were laywomen who practised celibacy, and wore a black habit and distinctive pointed white headdress. The last of Breda's community of *béguines* died in 1990, but their place of residence has been preserved. The Begijnhof contains a small museum, open three days a week, where visitors can experience aspects of the *béguines*' way of life.

The Begijnhof incorporated the former chapel of St Wendelinus, which was given to them in the 16th century. The chapel that now stands at this location, within the grounds of the former convent, is dedicated to St Catherine and was consecrated in 1838, as the central courtyard was being extended. Some of the houses that now surround the courtyard and garden are occupied, reserved for single women. At the entrance to the Begijnhof is another small church, generally known as the Waalse Kerk or Walloon Church, the Walloons being the French-speaking, mostly Roman Catholic, community in Flanders. This church too formerly belonged to the Begijnhof, but passed out of their hands and is now popular as a wedding venue. Concerts and exhibitions regularly take place here.

Following the successful recapture of the city by the Dutch, Breda's Grote Kerk or Great Church, previously known as the Onze-Lieve-Vrouwekerk ('Church of Our Lady') became Protestant. In its present form, the main part of the building was begun in 1410. The 100-metre tall tower of the church was completed in 1509 and is topped with a massive cross. Visitors can climb the tower, accompanied by a guide, to obtain panoramic views of the city. The original organ, replaced in the mid-twentieth century, dated from William's lifetime.

In its 'Prinsenkapel', the church contains the tombs of William's ancestors, the House of Nassau-Dillenburg as they were known in the sixteenth century, before William the Silent (1533–1584) became William I of Orange by virtue of being the nearest heir to the province. William the Silent himself is an exception, as by the time of his death international tensions had caused him to make his home in Delft, where he is buried. This section of the church was restored in a five-year project and reopened to the public in 2003.

The vault of the Grote Kerk contains notable sixteenth-century frescoes, attributed to the Italian Tomasso Vincidor. The Prinsenkapel also boasts a triptych by Vincidor's Dutch contemporary, Jan van Scorel. The chapel underwent a five-year restoration ending in 2003, and the magnificent vaulted ceiling can now be seen as originally intended. The building is a popular venue for concerts and other events. The paved square outside the church, at one time a burial ground, is now the Grote Markt ('Great Market'); as well as hosting a street market, it is the location of many eating places.

The Stedelijk Museum in Breda is a national museum of visual culture, located in a former hostel and retirement home for the poor, the 'Oudemannenhuis', whose facade was rebuilt in 1643. The final residents left in 1954, and thereafter the building was repurposed, first as an arts centre and subsequently as a museum. It originally concentrated on showing the history of the region through art, and has been redesigned in recent years to incorporate a museum of graphic art. A permanent display, opened in 2023, explores the city's relationship with the House of Orange-Nassau.

Settling into married life

In August, William was at Saint-Denis, attempting to prevent the French from capturing Mons and Mary was alone at Hoonselardijk, being treated by physicians with asses' milk. Mary of Modena, dismayed by the news of her stepdaughter Mary's failed pregnancy, now decided that she wanted to visit Mary in her new home, accompanied by Mary's sister Anne. England's queen consort had given the Princess of Orange the playful nickname 'Lemon'.

On the military front, Mons was the most important of the Dutch cities still in the hands of their Spanish allies, with whom the French had not yet made peace. Both sides claimed the Battle of Saint-Denis as a victory, William on the grounds that the French had left the battlefield before his forces had regrouped in readiness for another attack. He arrived in Mons to find it still in Spanish hands, and a peace treaty was finally signed about a month later.

The following autumn Anne and her stepmother set off, travelling 'incognito' in accordance with the duchess's wishes. Sir William Temple

(1628–1699), the diplomat who had negotiated terms for the marriage of William and Mary, oversaw the details of the visit. Princess Amalia had died in 1675 and Temple reported back on how the 'Oude Hof', as the dowager's Noordeinde palace was known, was being cleaned up in preparation for the arrival of the duchess and Princess Anne.

By now, Mary believed herself to be pregnant again, and had begun making preparations. A nursery had already been planned, and William was looking into the possibility of enlarging 'Hof te Dieren', a hunting lodge he owned at Dieren, a long way from his capital. Unfortunately, no trace can now be seen of that building. This period had been called the 'first phase' of William's interest in architecture[3], as his focus moved from warfare to family matters. William had become aware of the significance of his royal houses as a status symbol befitting a ruler; at the same time, he was growing more motivated to ensure comfortable accommodation for himself and his wife. In this he was heavily influenced by the major architectural project being progressed outside Paris by his great rival, King Louis XIV – the Palace of Versailles. As it turned out, Dieren would gradually fall out of use after William and Mary moved their main centre of operations across the English Channel; in 1690 Bentinck checked on it and reported back that the gardens there were in dreadful state, having been left in the care of a drunken custodian.

Mary's uncle Charles had finally paid her dowry, after many years in which the Stuarts had failed to repay what they owed the House of Orange in return for its loyalty and practical assistance during the lean times, and this windfall helped William with his building programme. In short, everything seemed to be looking up. Although her stepmother found her in good health, Mary suffered another suspected miscarriage after the departure of her relatives. It is now believed that she had not been pregnant at all but suffering from an infection linked to her previous experiences, which could have been a form of malaria, a disease that was endemic in some lower-lying areas of the country such as Antwerp.

---

3. Simon Thurley.

Two years after the marriage of William and Mary, Charles II was faced with a political crisis at home that could have resulted in his younger brother James being removed from the line of succession because of his Catholic faith. In the wake of the 'Popish Plot', an imaginary conspiracy to assassinate Charles and ensure a Catholic succession, the public mood was further turned by the mysterious death of a leading Protestant MP. Several innocent men were rounded up, tortured and executed. Five Catholic lords were put on trial for their supposed involvement, but proceedings against them were eventually dropped. James and his wife were forced into a temporary exile in Brussels. Around a year after Mary of Modena's previous visit to her stepdaughter, she was back in The Hague, travelling along canals in the Prince of Orange's horse-drawn barge, and once again the 'Oude Hof' was used as guest accommodation. William's relations with his father-in-law at this period seem to have been affable enough, but it is possible that he had already been intriguing with James's opponents behind the scenes.

As a result of the growing unrest, the Earl of Shaftesbury proposed an Exclusion Bill that was supported by the Whig party in Parliament and opposed by the Tories. Every time it appeared that the bill might succeed, the king stepped in to dissolve Parliament before the matter could be resolved. Had an Act of Parliament ever been passed to exclude James, there were several names that would have been in the frame to succeed Charles II, one of whom was his niece Mary. James at the time had no male heir, following the death of his infant son Charles just as the newly-weds were leaving England, but his wife Mary of Modena was still only in her early twenties and there was every prospect that this situation would change, resulting in the birth of a male heir who would survive into adulthood. The religion in which that child was brought up would be critical. As it happened, Mary of Modena had been pregnant during 1678, but the child, a girl, had died shortly after birth. Her next pregnancy was not for another two years.

It was about this time that Thomas Ken was appointed Mary's chaplain, Dr Hooper having got married and returned to England.

Ken was sympathetic towards Mary, whilst showing signs of hostility towards William. Later, he would be one of the Seven Bishops who opposed King James, but would also refuse to take the oath of allegiance to William and Mary as monarchs. Ken would be replaced by John Covel, who was dismissed after it was discovered that he had written to the British ambassador saying that Mary was being treated as an 'absolute slave' by her husband. Mary was of course still in her teens and unlikely to challenge any of William's actions or opinions.

In 1679, Mary had thoughts of visiting her sister Anne in Brussels, where the latter was staying with Isabella, a frail younger daughter of James and his second wife, and thus a half-sister to Mary and Anne. The whole family had been sent there to be out of the public eye following the 'Popish Plot', but they were now recalled as a result of the king's illness. En route home, James asked to meet up with both William and Mary at Delft, and they welcomed him warmly. However, James was annoyed with them for having welcomed the Duke of Monmouth – whom many saw as a potential Protestant successor to Charles II, despite his illegitimacy – earlier in the autumn at The Hague. William had urged Monmouth not to set himself up as a successor to Charles, but Monmouth was headstrong and confident. James would not be placated, but he could not have foreseen that it was to be his last meeting with his daughter Mary.

In 1680, William was taking a trip to what we now call Germany, then a loose alliance of small kingdoms, principalities and duchies within the Holy Roman Empire. Celle, Hanover and Brandenburg were all states he hoped to recruit to help him fight the French. Celle was ruled by Prince George William (1624–1705), who was in his sixties and a genial host. In 1690, after William and Mary came to the throne of England, he would be rewarded for his friendship with the Order of the Garter.

Mary would later return with her husband to stay at Celle again. In the meantime, she was ill with a fever, and possibly suffering from depression. William, though not always sympathetic to her needs, feared for her life and wrote to James accordingly. Mary recovered, but James soon had a real tragedy to deal with, as his surviving daughter, five-year-old Isabella, died at St James's Palace while he was still in exile.

Even though Charles II was barely fifty years old, he had lived a riotous life, and his health was declining. After the failure of the Exclusion Bill, James was packed off to Scotland for the second time, to replace its unpopular Lord High Commissioner, taking his wife with him. After he had been allowed to return, he needed to make one more unpleasant sea journey north in order to collect his duchess. On 6 May 1682, his ship, *HMS Gloucester*, taking a course different from that recommended by the pilot, ran aground off the Norfolk coast, and the damage was such that it was necessary to abandon ship. This was another occasion when James showed his unsuitability for power by delaying, thus indirectly causing the deaths of most of the crew, who were not allowed to leave the ship while a royal personage was still aboard. Two seamen were prosecuted for negligence, but James escaped any reprimand.

John Churchill, who had recently married Sarah Jennings, was aboard the *Gloucester* when it got into trouble. Accounts of the incident vary, but Winston Churchill, in his biography of his ancestor John – one of the few who escaped in James's boat – favoured Sarah Churchill's version of events, which alleged that James had behaved in a selfish and cowardly manner, caring more about the safety of his dog than that of the crew and other passengers. Several Scottish noblemen lost their lives when the *Gloucester* went down, and the elderly royal physician almost suffered the same fate. The wreck was eventually discovered in 2007, but no human remains have been found by the divers investigating and retrieving the contents. Some of the finds have been exhibited in Norwich.

A turning point came in 1683, with the discovery of the Rye House Plot, a conspiracy to assassinate both Charles and James while they were visiting Newmarket races. Unlike the 'Popish Plot', the Rye House Plot seems to have been real, even though it never came to anything. Another group of supposed conspirators were captured and executed, including a woman named Elizabeth Gaunt – the last woman to be executed for treason in England. Gaunt's unjust and agonising death at the stake, which was carried through in 1685 after Charles's death, when James was already on the throne, was generally deplored. Many of those who were actually involved in the conspiracy escaped punishment and went into exile in the Netherlands.

One of these had been an ally of William during the wars against the French. James, Duke of Monmouth, was the oldest of the many illegitimate children of King Charles II. A personable young man of a similar age to William, Monmouth had been acknowledged by Charles and after the Restoration of 1660 was given an aristocratic wife and a dukedom. His military exploits made him popular and rumours were put about by his supporters that his mother, a wayward Welsh gentlewoman called Lucy Walter, had been secretly married to Charles when the latter was in exile in Holland. She had died in 1658, which was in some ways convenient for both Monmouth and his father. It was even rumoured that, in the absence of a legitimate heir, Charles would legitimise Monmouth, enabling him to replace the Duke of York in the line of succession. As the king's health deteriorated, Monmouth became the poster boy for a Protestant campaign to oust York as heir to the throne, and he was forced into exile as a result of his apparent involvement in the Rye House Plot.

The Rye House Plot improved James's popularity in England, but it was a different story in Scotland, where the early 1680s would later become known as 'The Killing Time' because of the authorities' relentless pursuit of the Covenanters, Protestants who attempted to uphold an agreement signed in 1638 that opposed Charles I's attempts to 'reform' the Church of Scotland. During his exile, Charles II had accepted the Covenant as an essential prerequisite to obtaining Scots support for his claim on the throne, but after his accession he unilaterally repudiated it, and James could hardly be blamed for this.

At around the same time as Elizabeth Gaunt was burned at the stake in London, two Scotswomen, the elderly Margaret Maclachlan and teenager Margaret Wilson, were drowned at the stake on a muddy shore in the Solway Firth, earning them the title of 'The Wigtown Martyrs'. Scottish Protestants had already been fed up with King Charles II; how much more discontented they were now, under his Catholic brother. In France, Protestants were being persecuted under Louis XIV as much as they had ever been during the previous century, and it was desirable for both brothers to distance themselves from that trend.

The Duke of Monmouth found his way to the Prince of Orange's court, where Mary's growing unhappiness with her father's conduct led her and William to make a fuss of James's rival for the throne. The Netherlands was, after all, the country of Monmouth's birth. Recognising the threat posed by the rebellious duke, James asked William to imprison his cousin and return him to England. William's refusal confirmed Mary's father in the belief that his two nephews were in collusion to usurp his throne. Mary being his legitimate heir, she also came under suspicion. Her father ensured that she heard of the rumours about her husband's involvement with Elizabeth Villiers; William fobbed off his wife by suggesting that his only interest in Elizabeth was the inside information she could provide about events in England and Scotland. At the time, Mary accepted the explanation, but she would later find out the truth and be very hurt by it. There may, however, have been some truth in the suggestion that William was using Elizabeth as a source of intelligence.

Although Charles II's death in 1685 was sudden, the Duke of Monmouth was ready to launch his rebellion almost immediately, and began spreading a story that King James had poisoned his elder brother. This time, he got no encouragement from William, Mary being the rightful heir to the throne if James were eliminated. Unable to muster enough support to fight off the new king's regular army on its advance from London, Monmouth was forced to flee but was quickly captured. The failure of the rebellion was the cue for a massacre of his ill-equipped army and a series of unpleasant executions ensued, by order of the 'Bloody Assizes' presided over by the notorious Judge Jeffreys (1645–1689). Though the groundswell of support for the rebellion had been inadequate, this brutal follow-up and the botched execution of Monmouth did nothing to endear the general public to King James.

Despite her youth, Mary had no intention of being 'converted' to Catholicism as her father's correspondence tried to persuade her to do.

A Scottish clergyman, Gilbert Burnet (1643–1715), was among other Protestant exiles at court in The Hague, where he had been personally invited because of his work on a *History of the Reformation*, the first two volumes of which had been published during Charles II's reign. When Burnet's outspoken opposition to Catholicism continued in exile, James tried to have him prosecuted for treason and wanted him extradited to face trial, a request denied by William and Mary. Burnet came to admire Mary greatly, and commented on her resolute refusal to be influenced by her father.

At this time Mary still expected to become Queen of England and Scotland following her father's death, however far in the future this might have seemed. It was a shock, therefore, when her stepmother became pregnant again, six years after giving birth to her last living child. Mary of Modena was still only in her early thirties and healthy enough, but her record of failed pregnancies and infants who failed to thrive did not augur well. Rumours began to reach the Hague from London that James's queen was faking pregnancy and that a 'changeling' would be substituted purely in order to prevent Mary from taking her rightful place as monarch in due course. Mary, for her part, had no real desire to wield power and had assumed that her husband William would continue to make all the decisions, just as he did at home in Holland; she was ignorant of the constitutional position. The source of the intelligence from home was her younger sister Anne, who nevertheless declined to be present at the birth of the new prince to ensure that everything was above board.

Mary wrote to Anne, asking detailed questions such as how long her father had been speaking with the Chancellor after the child was carried into another room, which of the queen's ladies had been present, and whether any of them had actually been able to see the queen's face while she was in labour. Anne apologised in her next letter for not having been able to satisfy her curiosity more fully, and referred her to Sarah Churchill for further information.

Anne herself was now married, to Prince George of Denmark, and by this time already had a history of failed pregnancies, including a miscarriage shortly before Mary of Modena entered her confinement; but at this point there was still time for her and her elder sister to achieve motherhood themselves. James's new male heir was born in June 1688, and William sent ambassadors to London in formal recognition of the changed position, to congratulate the queen but also to report back on any grounds they could discover for the child's place in the order of succession to be overlooked. One of these delegates was his cousin Willem Hendrik, who confirmed that rumour was rife about the baby's true origin. Towards the end of that same month came the events that were to prove the final straw.

Although there had been rumours over the years that he was planning to disinherit Mary in favour of an alternative, Catholic, candidate (rumours that her husband had found extremely disquieting), King James had been anxious to allay any such fears. Perhaps feeling secure now that he had a male heir, James effectively brought about his own downfall by his move against the 'Seven Bishops', one of whom was the Archbishop of Canterbury himself, William Sancroft (1617–93). Another was Henry Compton, Mary's former mentor. The seven were accused of 'seditious libel' for signing a petition requesting to be excused from supporting the king's attempt to overrule Parliament by changing the legal penalties against Roman Catholics. Even the merciless Judge Jeffreys, now Lord Chancellor, advised James to abandon the idea of prosecuting, and his advice proved sound; the four judges of the King's Bench advised the jury to acquit, which they duly did despite the fact that two of them were in the king's employment.

Utrecht-born Everard van Weede van Dijkvelt (1626–1702) was an experienced diplomat who had been visiting England regularly since the reign of King Charles II, and for the time being it was he who would often have to deal with the temperamental James when the latter came to the throne. Dijkvelt would continue to serve William as king, and would end his life in London.

Meanwhile, King Louis XIV of France continued to threaten the borders of the Netherlands, and James II would do nothing to assist William and Mary. He chose instead to stay in the good books of the

Marriage   67

Catholic Louis, which, as it turned out, was vital to his future welfare. This made William less inclined than ever to stay out of England's affairs. What happened next may be seen in the context of these events.

Het Loo

In the early years of their marriage, William and his wife longed to spend more time together. Near Apeldoorn, William had the idea of constructing a completely new palace, which was begun in 1684 on the site of an existing hunting lodge, the 'Oude Loo' ('The Old Woods'). This house was originally purchased by William as a country retreat for Mary, but he clearly enjoyed the setting as much as she did. The surrounding district, the 'Veluwe', is a hilly, forested area that in those days was conducive to the rearing of game, thus boar and deer for hunting were plentiful, and their pursuit was one of William's favourite pastimes.

To all intents and purposes, the Oude Loo or 'Jachslot' is a moated castle of significant size, and it still stands; it is the property of the Dutch state and is sometimes used by the royal family, but is not open to the public, apart from the gardens, which are open at certain times of the year. In 1985, at the age of 18, the present King of the Netherlands, Willem-Alexander, was interviewed here for national television. In that interview, the then prince revealed his unexpectedly far-sighted interest in water management. In more recent times the building has had various uses, and the indoor areas have been updated, with parts even being set aside as accommodation for Ukrainian refugees in 2022.

Despite the instability of William's relations with Louis XIV, he admired French architecture and was prepared to seek advice from members of the Academie d'Architecture on the design of this prestigious new building. It was Mary who, amid much ceremony, laid the corner-stone for the new Het Loo Palace, which was completed in 1686, and is considerably larger than the not insubstantial Oude Loo. Queen Wilhelmina of the Netherlands died here in 1962, and lay in state in the monarch's private chapel. After her death, the palace reverted to the state with the proviso that her descendants would come back into possession if the Netherlands ever abolished the monarchy.

Wilhelmina's daughter, Queen Juliana, at one time had apartments at Het Loo. Juliana's husband, Prince Bernhard, used the 'hunting room' in the same way William might have done if he had lived in the environmentally-unconscious twentieth century, and a table upholstered in rhinoceros hide continues to have pride of place in front of the painted hunting scenes. His father-in-law, Prince Hendrik, also enjoyed hunting, and displayed animal head trophies on the walls of his private rooms. Juliana's daughter, Princess Margriet, was the last of the royal family to reside in the palace proper, and moved to a house in the grounds in 1975. In 1984 the palace was converted into a museum and research library.

Inspired in many ways by the Palace of Versailles, the house was designed by Jacob Roman in the Baroque fashion, with Palladian elements, a style already somewhat dated. The grounds contain other echoes of Louis XIV's style, including a fountain representing William as Hercules, a favourite alter ego of Louis's. Romeyn de Hooghe, an artist employed by William to produce anti-French propaganda drawings among other things, also got the job of proposing suitable themes for the garden ornaments, and would have been the originator of the Hercules idea. Whilst Louis might have aspired to such physical prowess, the idea of William, with his stoop and his weak chest, emulating the muscular mythological hero, seems somewhat ludicrous.

Louis Bonaparte, briefly installed as King of Holland by his uncle, Napoleon, resided for a short period at the neglected palace, filled in the fountains and landscaped the gardens so carefully cultivated by his predecessors. The original seventeenth-century gardens were not rediscovered until the 1970s. The current managers of the house and garden mean to restore the 'unity' of house and garden that was aimed for by the original designers, as well as ensuring that the planting and cultivation now practised are both historically accurate and in keeping with that intention. Among other things, the greenhouses contain citrus trees that are known to be at least 300 years old. However, boxwood used for hedging had to be removed because of disease, and has been replaced with holly and other shrubs capable of producing a similar effect. The use of pesticides and other chemicals has been discontinued.

The present Dutch king's interest in water management is not surprising, bearing in mind the history and geography of the Netherlands. In the 2000s, it was decided that the Hercules fountain and its neighbour, the Venus fountain (constructed in Mary's honour), were wasting too much water because of leaks, following an unsatisfactory restoration that had taken place in the 1980s, and their basins have been reconstructed to bring them closer to their 1699 condition. In fact, the fountains had been constructed by Dutch engineers who channeled water from William's other estates for miles along terracotta pipes, culminating in the creation of the 'King's Fountain' or 'Koningssprong' in 1692, capable on its completion of producing a 13-metre (over 40 feet) jet that remains the highest of its type in Europe.

William made Het Loo the location of his court, creating apartments there for some of his officials. These included members of Mary's household, such as Edward Villiers, the husband of her former governess, who was now her 'Master of the Horse'. Bentinck was given spacious accommodation on the first floor, as were other court favourites and the Prince de Vaudémont (1649–1723), a French exile and valued military aide. Ladies in waiting and William's secretary, Constantijn Huygens the younger, had to climb the extra stairs to the third floor.

Nevertheless, Het Loo was always more of a retreat than a centre of government. Though the royal couple entertained important visitors there, it was not a place for large gatherings of courtiers, nor did William ever wish to be surrounded by his followers in the same way as Louis XIV was in France. After William and Mary departed for England in 1689–90, the palace did not have the same importance, although William always liked spending time there, not too close to the city. In the months before his death, he would spend most of his time at Het Loo, relaxing in his private gardens. Jacob Roman, prevented by England's 'Office of Works' from taking control of any new building projects in Britain, had continued to tinker with the design even while the king's main interest was in the new home he had built for himself and Mary at Kensington Palace, and the result was a palace that looked more imposing than was warranted by its actual size.

The Dutch were traditionally interested in plants and horticulture (even after the 'Tulip Mania' episode[4] that had ruined many people financially during the 1630s) and were aficionados of country living. The design of gardens in the Netherlands had evolved by virtue of the smallness of the country and the land available into a penchant for 'dainty' gardens like those at Het Loo. Flower beds or parterres were laid out and edged with box in such a way as to show off the rarer varieties. Dutch visitors found French gardens, even those at Versailles, disappointingly short on flowers. Both William and Mary had an enthusiasm for gardens, an interest that they brought with them to England and Scotland when they took on the throne. Dutch gardeners were already becoming popular with the English aristocracy even before the new monarchs arrived.

Mary's love of porcelain is well-attested in contemporary documents. The inventory of Het Loo's garden furnishings includes 'flat flower bottles', 'flower pyramids', and the more familiar 'flower pots'. The finds from excavations carried out in the garden have included painted Delft vases, usually with Oriental designs. Some of Mary's Delftware has found its way back to the Prinsenhof Museum in Delft, the small palace where William the Silent was murdered and his grandson William III held court before being elevated to stadtholder. Other pieces of Delftware, commissioned by the couple and bearing their arms, are on display at Hampton Court.

Lists of plants individually prepared by both William and Mary reveal a lot about their tastes. They each had their own private garden, one on either side of the main building. Mary's preferences included many plants she introduced into the Netherlands from English gardens with which she was familiar. Her lists contain the names of varieties of rose and flowering cherry, whilst William went for evergreens that could

---

4. A speculative bubble when contract prices for tulip bulbs reached unsustainable levels.

be grown in all weathers, as well as orange trees for indoor cultivation. The fashion for orangery buildings had grown up in the middle of the seventeenth century throughout northern Europe; naturally Louis XIV had one at Versailles, and the Prince of Orange could hardly go without (he already had one at Hoonselardijk, built in 1680 by Johan van Swieten). This part of Het Loo now serves as an office for the palace staff.

Although pineapples made their first appearance in Britain during the 1650s, the first pineapple houses came much later, and it was in the Netherlands that the first of the fruit was grown in Europe, at around the time William and Mary took the thrones of England and Scotland. The pineapple pictured being presented to King Charles II by his aptly-named gardener, John Rose, in a painting of the late 1670s by the Dutch artist Hendrik Danckerts, is thought to have been imported from Barbados or possibly the Netherlands, as no pineapples are known to have been successfully grown in England before the end of William III's reign – otherwise Mary would presumably have installed a 'pinery' at Hampton Court. The man later credited with popularising pineapple-growing in England was, not surprisingly, William's friend Bentinck.

The gardens at Het Loo also contained an aviary, reflecting an interest of Mary's but also a typical feature of a classical garden. Other such unusual features that could be seen at Het Loo included terraces and water cascades – rather like artificial waterfalls. There was a bowling green and even a 'labyrinth' of paths (though on a smaller scale than the hedge maze William would later install at Hampton Court). An elevated walkway was constructed to enable the gardens to be viewed from above so as to enjoy the overall effect of the intricate design.

A French landscape architect, Claude Desgots, was later employed to extend and redesign the gardens at Het Loo. Desgots had worked in England, after meeting William Bentinck, the Prince of Orange's favourite, who became Earl of Portland under the new régime in 1689. Bentinck, who was given the position of Superintendent of the Royal Gardens of England, visited Versailles on William's behalf and attempted to learn some of the gardening secrets of the ageing André Le Nôtre.

It was in his new palace at Het Loo that William would later install works of art from the Royal Collection in London, including some from the 'Dutch Gift' given to Charles II in 1660, much to the displeasure of his sister-in-law, Anne. William got into the habit of 'borrowing' art from the Royal Collection for display in his various palaces, frequently asking advice from his secretary, Huygens. Many were hung in 'cabinets', small rooms specifically designed for that purpose, where smaller works were hung very close together. An example of this kind of arrangement can be seen in a painting by Jacob de Formentrou, dating from the early part of William's reign, that hangs in the Cumberland Gallery at Hampton Court, although the room in which it is displayed was designed in the following century. Many of the works William kept at Het Loo were sold after his death.

Later in life, Het Loo would represent one aspect of the king's life that Versailles also represented for Louis XIV – a haven from public life, in which he could enjoy some privacy in which to deal with matters of state. In keeping with this preference, he had the palace designed in the style of a country gentleman's house, built around a courtyard. The main building, sometimes called the 'Corps-de-Logis', had curved colonnades on each side. After the couple succeeded to the thrones of Britain, a change was made to the design, removing the colonnades and replacing them with four 'pavilions', connected to service wings at each side. The overall effect emulated Versailles.

A noted animal painter, Melchior d'Hondecoeter, was taken on by William to produce hunting scenes for the entrance hall, and also to paint a selection of exotic birds and animals from the Far East, reflecting his country's worldwide trade. Private menageries containing such creatures were an enduring fashion among European royalty, and William had an aviary at Het Loo. Meanwhile, Mary's private apartments were decorated on the themes of love and virtue, by another Dutch master who specialised in such works, Gérard de Lairesse. There were also religious works by Gerrit van Honthorst, who had painted several members of the Orange dynasty, including William's parents. Later, another of the royal couple's favoured painters, Robbert Duval would contribute 'The Promise to Sarah', obviously inspired by Mary's deep desire for a child.

Many of the interiors that date from the palace's original construction were designed by Daniel Marot, who later worked for William on the redesign of Hampton Court Palace. Marot's hand can be seen in details of everything from furniture to gardens. He designed chimney-pieces, beds, curtains, silverware, railings, garden benches and water features. Whereas Jacob Roman was officially the Architect to the Stadtholder, Marot would begin calling himself the Architect to King William of England or 'his Britannic majesty'. By the 1690s he had become highly influential, and several of his engraved garden designs were published in 1702, the year William died.

In contrast with the hunting lodge at Dieren, Het Loo was maintained throughout William's reign, even though Mary never saw it again after leaving for England in 1689. William wanted a palace fit for a king, and Marot's work on the interior was mostly carried out after 1692. The perceived change in status is shown most clearly in the decoration of the dining room, where the impact of the elaborate painting and plasterwork is almost overpowering. Mary's quarters included mirrored ceilings, designed to enhance the display of her china collection, and an 'English gallery' was also created. The room intended for her china cabinet was repurposed as a library after her death.

Het Loo underwent various refurbishments and modernisations during its lifetime as a royal residence. During the reign of Queen Wilhelmina, whose accession in 1890 gave the Dutch monarchy a new lease of life and who abdicated in 1948, the Corps-de-Logis had an extra storey added. The result was not to Wilhelmina's liking, let alone anyone else's, because it spoiled the proportions of the building. During the 1970s, it was proposed to remove the top storey and return the building and gardens to their original appearance. Although the extra floor was removed, the wholesale changes proposed by the plan were never fully carried out. Following an archaeological excavation that revealed lost details of William and Mary's garden, a further renovation began in 2018.

The refurbishment during Wilhelmina's reign revealed seventeenth-century wall paintings, behind later overpainting, at the head of the grand staircase, and she ordered that these be restored to their original appearance, as designed by Daniel Marot. A grand staircase became a notable feature in the architecture of the period, focusing as it did on the idea of upward motion, with its attendant connotations. The paintings cover a total area of 500 square metres and, within the Netherlands, are second only to the Mesdag panorama in the Hague in size. They feature figures from around the world, reflecting the extensive explorations of Dutch traders, another idea borrowed from the Palace of Versailles. This section of the palace has been open to visitors only since 2018. The staircase leads to the Grote Zaal ('great hall'), the ceiling of which was raised from its original height, after Mary's death, in order to make the room more impressive.

The original furnishings and decor displayed in about forty of the palace's rooms date from different periods in its history, arranged in roughly chronological order. Most of these are open to the public, including the kitchens. The palace also contains a private library and a specialist museum belonging to a Dutch order of knighthood. The stable block, incorporating the coach house, still displays some royal carriages (and the official cars of later monarchs). The Dutch royal family has sometimes closed the property to the general public during the autumn, in order to use the estate for other purposes such as hunting, but the Dutch government has threatened to withdraw the subsidy it pays towards the building's upkeep unless the period of closure is reduced.

As well as walking in the gardens, it is sometimes possible for visitors to gain access to the roof, which enables the intricate garden design to be viewed from another angle. This reveals more details of the symmetrical and geometric aspect of the way the beds are laid out. In the palace's heyday, these details were often the subject of contemporary engravings, popular with the public but also a propaganda exercise for William and Mary, illustrating what a cultured couple they were in a language everyone could understand.

Following the five-year renovation, an additional below-ground exhibition space, created by excavating the central courtyard, was opened in April 2023. A glass roof brings in natural light and enables visitors to view the palace from the outside as well as enjoying the exhibits. The museum includes a permanent exhibition charting the history of the House of Orange-Nassau, as well as focusing on the parts of the palace built and lived in by William and Mary. A new 'East Route' through the building for visitors guides them through the lives of the seventeenth-century rulers, whilst a 'West Route' concentrates on the Dutch royal family of the nineteenth and twentieth centuries. Exhibits from the period of William and Mary's residence include Brussels tapestries, William's library desk and chair, and Mary's 'keukenkeldertje', a unique tiled kitchen cellar where she enjoyed making marmalade and jams from home-made fruit. The vogue for a simpler 'pastoral' life, later embraced by Marie Antoinette, had already begun.

A new chapter
On the same day that the trial of the 'Seven Bishops' ended in a débacle, seven members of England's political elite put their signatures to a letter that effectively ended the reign of King James II of England and VII of Scotland, promising Prince William of Orange cross-party support if he should decide to invade the kingdom and make his wife Mary ruler in place of her father. The seven included Henry Compton, who presumably was satisfied that, as a result of his early guidance, she was fit to be a monarch. The ringleader was Henry Sidney, later Earl of Romney, whose late brother Robert had fought for the Dutch on the orders of Charles II in the 1660s. (Many suspected Robert of having been the true natural father of the Duke of Monmouth.)

In reality, William had been privately in contact with leading English politicians for many months. He was in residence at The Hague when the invitation was delivered to him by an English admiral in disguise as an ordinary sailor. It claimed that 'the people are so generally dissatisfied with the present conduct of the government, in relation to their religion, liberties and properties ... and they are in such expectation of their prospects being daily worse, that your Highness may be assured, there are nineteen parts of twenty of the people throughout the kingdom, who are desirous of a change.' The signatories, who numbered seven, later gained the epithet 'The Immortal Seven'.

William could hardly turn down such an opportunity to present himself as the liberator of a nation oppressed by a tyrant king, but there was one hurdle to be overcome. If he invaded England, there was a risk he could be met with opposition, despite the promises of the politicians, and he might then be seen as a conqueror, a foreigner attempting to usurp the throne. The potential rewards had to be weighed up against the possible losses. The Seven had stopped short of requesting that James be deposed from the throne.

James II was aware of the movement to replace him with William, but found it hard to accept that his daughter could have anything to do with it. 'I hope it will have been as great a surprise to you as it was to me,' he wrote to her, possibly knowing that it had not but still assuming that his favourite child would come around. Her stepmother, Mary of Modena, knowing that Mary was James's favourite, was also anxious not to believe that she was party to her husband's plans. Loyal as she had always been to her family in England, however, Mary would put her husband first. The dutiful daughter had become a dutiful wife who would never have considered going against William. She no longer trusted her father; the justifications offered for the invasion had completely convinced her that he was determined to turn the country Catholic.

She did not, however, cross the Channel with William; it was considered too dangerous. It was to be expected that William's army would meet with opposition, and, regardless of whether she was heir to the throne or not, Mary had to be protected from the possibility of violence. Putting together an invasion force was stretching the resources of the House of Orange to their limits, and it was fortunate for William that James's navy happened to be at its weakest and was unable to intercept him. One admiral, a Catholic whom James had promoted, had already been dismissed after trying to impose his religious beliefs on his men. At a convenient moment, a storm blew up in the Channel, and Dutch agents spread false news that the invasion fleet had been wrecked; James was briefly taken in.

Chapter 4
A Joint Monarchy

William and Mary parted at Hoonselardijk early in November (she wrote that 'it was as if my heart had been torn from my body'), and William set sail, with a fleet of 500 ships that came from all over the Netherlands. In the hope of divine intervention, Mary attended a church service at Brielle (sometimes known in English as Brill), the port from which the fleet departed, one of many such services being held that day throughout the country to pray for their safety and success. The sixteenth-century church of St Catherine, never quite finished as planned, may still be seen.

After weathering a cross-Channel storm, William arrived safely at Brixham in Devon, the region from which the Duke of Monmouth had previously drawn much of his support. The English Navy was poorly positioned to intercept them, even if its leaders had wanted to. A Victorian statue of William, commemorating the occasion, now stands in the harbour at Brixham, a port that had been considered critical to the defence of the realm since the reign of Henry VIII. The international fighting force the prince had assembled marched into the town of Torbay, led by the prince himself on a white horse, and within a fortnight they had taken control of much of the country without meeting any substantial resistance.

Edward Hyde the younger, Mary's cousin, had been one of the first to desert King James, declining to put up a fight against the invasion force and taking a troop of dragoons over to the other side with him. When John Churchill, the future Duke of Marlborough, who had been the lynch-pin of James's military strength, went over to William's side, there was no longer any hope that James could retain his throne. Churchill was a staunch Protestant and told his critics that he was acting on his principles rather than in the hope of a reward from William. Indeed, he never would get on particularly well with the new king and queen. His defection was followed by that of James's other son-in-law, Prince George of Denmark. George's wife, Princess Anne, slipped away from the royal entourage to find safety, accompanied by two of her ladies-in-waiting: Lady Fitzhardinge, a daughter of her former governess Frances Villiers, and of course Sarah Churchill. Anne left a letter explaining her dilemma.

Another of those who deserted James was 19-year-old Henry Boyle, the son of the Earl of Burlington (1612–98) and a nephew by marriage of Charles II's advisor, Lord Rochester. Rochester, a Tory and another brother of Anne Hyde, had fallen out with James over an attempt to force him to convert to Catholicism. After James sacked him from his government position, Rochester quickly saw the need to replace the king, and abandoned James when the latter refused to negotiate with William. Henry Boyle's father, Lord Burlington, faced a similar dilemma and found his Irish estates confiscated because of his disloyalty. Another of Henry Boyle's uncles was the scientist and philosopher, Robert Boyle (1627–91). By the time of William and Mary's accession, Robert Boyle was living in seclusion because of his poor health, but he was still writing; after his death, a bequest from his will helped to finance the establishment of William and Mary College in the North American colony of Virginia two years later. As for Henry, after a few hiccups, he would become one of William III's senior ministers and given the title Baron Carleton.

Anne's decision to flee was the last straw for James, who nevertheless preferred to believe that his younger daughter had played no part in the conspiracy against him. The only real resistance to William came from an Irish contingent led by Patrick Sarsfield, who tried unsuccessfully to prevent the prince from reaching London. James vacillated for too long in an attempt to avoid battle. Louis XIV had failed to intervene in support of his Catholic fellow-monarch, and now there was nothing for him to do but welcome the exiled royal family into France and hope that in due course it would be possible for James to rally support and return to the British Isles. He could hardly have anticipated that the Catholic Stuarts would be living on his charity until he died. Early in December, Mary of Modena and her baby son arrived at Saint-Germain, and James set out to follow them a few days later. Captured by Protestant forces and protected by a Dutch guard, he was allowed by William to escape, taking ship from Rochester just before Christmas. By fleeing to France, he was playing into William's hands; it was seen as an act of cowardice and betrayal by his remaining supporters.

Even after James had fled the country, things were far from settled, and Christmas and New Year had passed before an agreement was reached about how to proceed. In the meantime William was lodged in St James's Palace. Early in February the prince grew tired of waiting, and threatened to take his army home and leave England to fend for itself if the crown was not formally offered; this did the trick, and in due course he and his immediate circle transferred to Whitehall. By the time Mary arrived in London, on 12 February 1689, to rule as joint monarch of England and Scotland with her husband of nearly twelve years, she was still only 27. In her short life, she had gained invaluable experience of how to conduct herself, first as a princess and then as the wife of the most powerful ruler in the Low Countries, and this would stand her in good stead during her all too brief career as a monarch.

The events leading to the transfer of power required constitutional changes, which were passed by Parliament only after considerable discussion. A Bill of Rights, contrary to what its title might imply, gave citizens specific rights only at the expense of the rights of the monarch. It specified that the monarch must be Protestant and was forbidden to marry a Roman Catholic, as was anyone else in the line of succession to the throne. This has been called a 'landmark document in the development of civil liberties'[1] in Britain. The unctuous wording of the oath taken by James II at his coronation was replaced with a more succinct form of words inviting the new king and queen to 'solemnly promise and swear' rather than 'beseeching' them to do what

---

1. Best.

was right. Future monarchs were required to take this new Coronation Oath, promising to uphold the Protestant faith as well as to govern in accordance with Parliament's wishes. At the same time, a somewhat misleadingly-named Act of Toleration prevented the appointment of either Catholics or Dissenters to public office and forced them to pay tithes to the Church of England. All it achieved in the way of religious toleration was to ensure that those who did not follow the Anglican path would not be physically punished.

William himself was no great supporter of the Church of England and found the religious ceremonial attending a coronation to be 'popish' in nature. He had made a point of wearing the crown and royal regalia when he first attended the House of Lords, as an indication that, despite not having been officially crowned yet, he was already king. He wore it again to Parliament before the coronation ceremony took place. The concept of 'King William's Toleration' referred to the new king's policy of attempting to please all of the people all of the time, or at any rate not to turn anyone, whether subject or foreign ally, against him. This new freedom of conscience has been credited with allowing scientists and philosophers such as Isaac Newton and John Locke the ability to progress their work without interference from the authorities. Locke had in fact predicted the triumph of a contractual form of government whereby the monarch and Parliament made a specific declaration of their mutual responsibilities. The terms under which William and Mary were accepted as the country's rulers foreshadowed the American Declaration of Independence that followed nearly 100 years later.

Samuel Pepys resigned from the royal service and never took an oath of loyalty to William and Mary, because of his personal loyalty to James II. He was briefly imprisoned, but was never charged, and escaped further repercussions by paying extra tax under the new reign. Before the coup, he had commissioned a portrait of James from England's leading portrait painter, Godfrey Kneller, and kept it in his private library. For the rest of his life he carefully avoided becoming embroiled in any Jacobite conspiracy, and he outlived his former monarch by two years. He also outlived both Mary and William – the latter by only a year. He must have died still hoping for the restoration of the Stuart dynasty in the form of Mary and Anne's youthful half-brother.

The position was settled before Mary returned to her native land. Arrangements for a joint coronation had been made by the time she arrived at Gravesend on 12 February, in a yacht called *Mary*, to be greeted by her sister Anne. From Gravesend they travelled into London along the Thames by barge, alighting at Whitehall to meet William. On arrival, Mary's evident pleasure at taking up her father's vacant throne, which extended to her being given the same apartments in the Palace of Whitehall, sleeping in the bed formerly used by her stepmother, was thought unseemly by some, notably her sister's friend, Sarah Churchill. By all accounts, the new queen inspected the palace minutely, in the way someone deciding whether to buy a new house might do nowadays. Even Gilbert Burnet, the great friend of William and Mary who was about to be consecrated Bishop of Salisbury, was somewhat critical of her demeanour.

Whitehall Palace

The Palace of Whitehall was a sprawling complex that incorporated not only the royal residence but the centre of government administration. Whitehall got its name from the white stone used for the renovations carried out by King Henry VIII in the early sixteenth century. Henry had married both Anne Boleyn and Jane Seymour at the palace, and had died there, as had King Charles II. The Banqueting House, built by William and Mary's shared ancestor King James I of England after he arrived as King James VI of Scotland to take up the joint thrones, had been improved by his son Charles I, and this is the only substantial survivor of the palace complex that William and Mary knew.

The palace was redolent with the history of William and Mary's ancestors. King Charles II had spent most of his time there during his kingship, and had moved several of his mistresses into the palace. Schellinks, who had visited not long after the Restoration, saw the King and his brother several times and watched them dining in public. Pepys, when he was in the public service as an MP and a member of the Navy Board, recorded walking through the 'privy' gardens and seeing the underwear of Lady Castlemaine (the former Barbara Villiers) hanging out to dry. After his marriage to Catherine of Braganza, Charles had his chief mistress appointed a Lady of the Bedchamber and moved her even closer to him, within the palace apartments. This enabled Barbara to influence political appointments, and she continued to hold sway until Charles's eye lit on a young French lady, Louise de Kéroualle, who supplanted Barbara in the king's affections and caused her to move out of Whitehall while Louise took her place.

Two years before the coup that removed him from the throne, Mary's father, James II of England, had arranged for a statue of himself to be erected in the 'Pebble Court', behind the Banqueting House in the grounds of Whitehall Palace. It had been commissioned during his brother's reign, from the workshop of Grinling Gibbons, and was modelled by Laurens van der Meulen and cast by his colleague Peter van Dievoet. It shows James in the guise of a Roman emperor, a style favoured by King Louis XIV of France. Although initially removed from Whitehall following the arrival of William and Mary, William later arranged for it to be replaced, and it stood in several other places, including the front of the Banqueting House, before arriving at its present location in Trafalgar Square.

Before his expulsion, James II had installed a new royal chapel within the palace, where he and Mary of Modena were free to worship according to the Roman Catholic rite. Christopher Wren ran the Office of Works, based in Scotland Yard, and was the go-to designer for all new official buildings. Wren was not a Catholic and envisaged the chapel as a multi-purpose space, which did not please his royal master; he was made to enlarge it and expand it into the Privy Garden. The chapel included decorations by the painter Antonio Verrio, the sculptor Grinling Gibbons and the Dutch sculptor known in English as Arnold Quellin; Quellin would die just as the chapel was completed. In addition to an ornate altar, the building also housed an ornate throne. The organ case, sculpted by Gibbons, is now in St James's Church, Piccadilly.

The diarist John Evelyn, though not a Catholic, attended the opening of the new chapel in December 1686, and commented that 'The throne where the King and Queen sit is very glorious, in a closet above, just opposite to the altar. Here we saw the Bishop in his mitre and rich copes, with six or seven Jesuits and others in rich copes, sumptuously habited'. James and his wife had little time to enjoy the chapel's magnificence before William and Mary arrived, and Mary disliked the chapel's ambience so much that she thought of converting it to a library. The plan was never carried through because of her untimely death and the chapel's subsequent destruction in a fire.

Another change made by James II was the construction of new apartments for his queen, which necessitated the demolition of those built by his brother for Catherine of Braganza. Catherine had been allowed to keep her apartments for a short time after her husband's death before being re-housed at Denmark House, also known as Somerset House – a predecessor of the eighteenth-century building that now stands by the Thames. As usual, it was Christopher Wren who was called upon to redevelop the site, and the building work was still in progress when Mary II arrived to take over the accommodation. Like several of Wren's team of craftsmen, Grinling Gibbons was working simultaneously on the improvements to Hampton Court, Kensington Palace and Whitehall Palace. A riverside terrace constructed for James's queen, Mary of Modena, was unfinished but was made ready for the new queen's use.

With over 1,500 rooms, Whitehall was simply enormous, the largest palace in Europe, but the new king and queen never took it to their hearts. As with Versailles in France, and to a lesser extent the Binnenhof in the Hague, it housed numerous courtiers, many of whom added to their accommodation as the years passed. William had rejected its unhealthy atmosphere and crowds of people almost on sight. Once the formalities had been completed, he preferred to stay outside London at Hampton Court.

Important functions still had to be conducted at Whitehall, however, and the new king and queen were obliged to spend time there, hosting parties on occasions such as the New Year and William's birthday.

Although she did not entirely share William's antipathy to the palace, Mary had little choice but to stay there, close to the seat of government, when William was away; it was important for her to be visible. She would later write to her absent husband, describing her anguish at having to deal with the country's affairs without him at her side. Though outwardly dignified and capable, she was clearly under great stress and missing him terribly. Her private meditations, written at Kensington, reveal that her Christian faith was considerable, but she dwelled on the possibility of her own death as a result of a possible rebellion.

In April 1691, a fire broke out in a section of the palace at Whitehall, and it damaged the adjoining buildings, many of which were mainly of timber construction. Many of the buildings destroyed were private apartments, including those formerly assigned to Charles II's mistress, Louise de Kéroualle, who had returned to France several years earlier. The state apartments (i.e. the palace's showplaces, rooms that were most elaborately decorated and furnished) survived on this occasion. Perhaps as a reward for Mary's steadfastness, William bought some new paintings for her apartments in Whitehall, the work of Jacques Rousseau, who had worked for Louis XIV at Versailles; these can now be seen in the presence chambers at Hampton Court.

Around the palace proper were additional residences belonging to those with an official position or simply in favour with the current monarch. One such had been Sir George Downing (c.1625–1684), who had worked as a secret agent for Charles II and others. Before the end of Charles's reign, Downing had acquired land at the edge of St James's Park and had hired Christopher Wren to build houses on it, closing off the access to the park so that it became a quiet cul-de-sac. This was later known as Downing Street, and the house now occupied by the British prime minister stands on the site of an earlier mansion.

Another fire at Whitehall in 1698, caused by one of William's Dutch servants accidentally setting fire to some sheets she was drying on a brazier, resulted in such extensive damage that William authorised the demolition of many other buildings in order to save the Banqueting House, as well as bricking up its windows to prevent the fire spreading.

Works by Michelangelo, Bernini and Holbein had been destroyed, while opportunist looters had broken in and helped themselves to some of the palace's contents.

Despite William's dislike of the palace, it had not been abandoned after the 1691 fire. The business of government had to continue, and the accommodation needed to fulfil the administrative functions had to be found in the few undamaged sections of the palace. There are records of a new 'Wardrobe' being constructed at Whitehall, the foundations of which have been investigated by archaeologists. This was a building around 100 feet long and had a less specialised use than that to which the term normally refers nowadays. Rather than containing clothing, it was a general storeroom for the monarch's personal possessions, with its own administrative staff. After the 1698 fire, however, the monarchy's administrative centre in London was almost completely transferred to St James's Palace, a process that was completed by Queen Anne. William's preference for Kensington had eased the gradual separation of the administrative and ceremonial functions of a constitutional monarchy.

The Banqueting House, almost the only part of the old Whitehall Palace left standing today, was the third such building to be erected on the site. Queen Elizabeth I had enjoyed social gatherings in a temporary wooden building that was decorated in a style suitable for a young unmarried queen. Her successor, James I of England, commissioned an architect called Robert Stickells to replace it with something more solid where they could enjoy theatrical entertainments, but the scenery caught fire during a 1619 performance, resulting in its demolition. Before this disaster, it had been the setting for the wedding of Princess Elizabeth (Elizabeth of Bohemia), as well as hosting a masque by Ben Jonson at which the audience had included the exotic Indian princess, Pocahontas.

The present building, designed in Italianate Renaissance style by the famous Inigo Jones, opened in 1622. Like its predecessor, it was purpose-built for formal, ceremonial occasions, including the occasional theatrical performance. Inigo Jones had employed the aptly-named Nicholas Stone as a supervisor on the building work. Stone had been employed in the Netherlands by Hendrik de Keyser, a notable sculptor

William II of Orange and his wife, Mary Henrietta, parents of William III, painted by Gerard van Honthurst in 1647. (*Wikimedia*)

Reconstruction of the anatomical theatre in Leiden, at the Museum Boorhave. (*Wikimedia*)

Mauritshuis at the Binnenhof, The Hague. (*Wikimedia*)

The Duke of York (later James II) with his wife (Anne Hyde) and their daughters, Mary and Anne, painted by Peter Lely c.1668. (*Wikimedia*)

Outer gateway of Richmond Palace, Mary's childhood home. (*Wikimedia*)

The humble resting place of William and Mary in Westminster Abbey. (*Adapted from a photograph by VCR Giulio 19 License CC BY-SA 4.0*)

The Helpoort, a surviving city gate at Maastricht. (*Wikimedia*)

The Ostpoort and drawbridge at Delft. (*Wikimedia*)

The palace of Hoonselardijk, William and Mary's first married home. (*Wikimedia*)

Constantijn Huygens, William's secretary, self-portrait dated 1685. (*Public domain*)

Queen Anne, Mary's sister and William's successor, and her son William, Duke of Gloucester, by Godfrey Kneller. (*Public domain*)

Breda Castle from an 18th century print. (*Wikimedia*)

Mary's bedroom at Het Loo. (*Wikimedia*)

Dublin Castle. (*Wikimedia*)

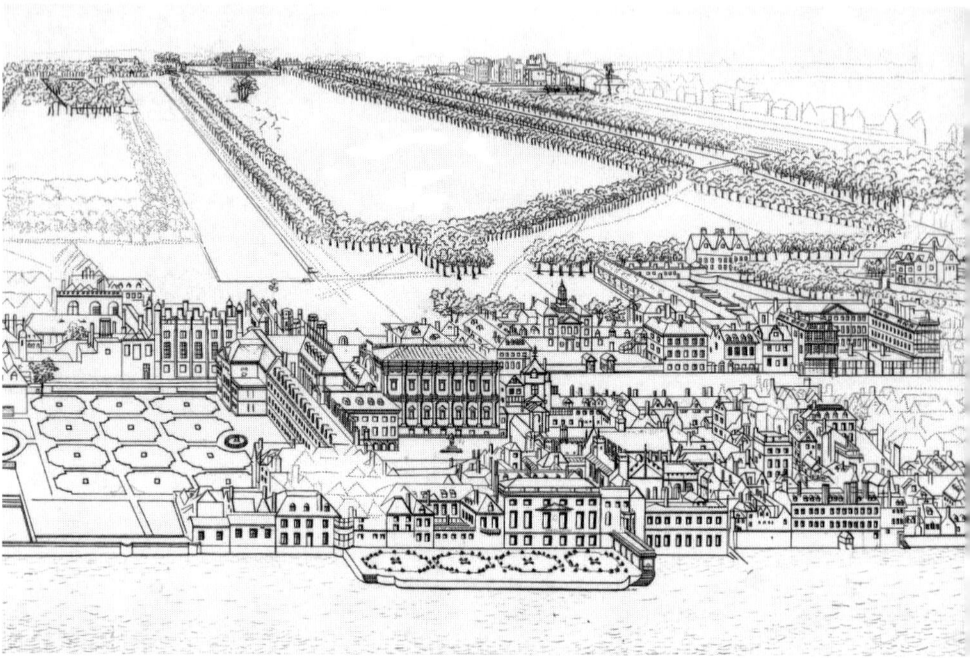

Whitehall Palace in about 1667, before destroyed by fire. (*Wikimedia*)

"Queen Mary's Steps" at the Palace of Whitehall. (*Wikimedia*)

The Battle of Aughrim 1691, by Jan Wyk. (*Wikimedia*)

William arriving at Dieren in 1691, by Pieter Schenk. (*Wikimedia*)

William Bentinck, 1st Earl of Portland, William III's best friend, by Hyacinthe Rigaud. (*Wikimedia*)

Hampton Court Palace, section reconstructed for William and Mary. (*Wikimedia*)

William and Mary's monogram, carved at Hampton Court Palace. (*Wikimedia*)

Palace of Placentia at Greenwich, prior to redesign, from an 18th-century print. (*Wikimedia*)

Royal Naval College, Greenwich, redesigned by Sir Christopher Wren. (*Wikimedia*)

Statue of William III, by Heinrich Baucke, outside Kensington Palace. (*Wikimedia*)

whose son-in-law Stone became. Back in England, he worked on the properties of numerous wealthy patrons as well as entering the king's service. Jones designed the building on three floors, with a flat roof surrounded by the distinctive balustrade we now see. It marked itself out from earlier English architecture, and Stone's decoration of the facade has echoes of Michelangelo.

In 1636, under James I's successor, the art-loving Charles I, nine paintings by the Flemish master Peter Paul Rubens were installed in the ceiling; the panels are the only surviving work by Rubens that remains in its original location. He was paid £3,000 for them, but Jones found that they did not quite fit the space for which they were intended and had to be trimmed. Perhaps luckily, Rubens sent his work to the king through a friend and thus never saw the paintings in situ. The central panel depicts the *Apotheosis of James I*; it is ironic that Charles, a believer in the divine right of kings like his father before him, should have had to pass under it to reach the scaffold where he met his end in 1649. Conservation work was carried out in 2018 on the paintings and the supporting structure later installed above them to secure them in place.

The new Banqueting House was the setting for many great occasions (though rarely, if ever, for banqueting). James I, Charles I and Charles II had all used it for the special service in which the king would lay hands on selected subjects suffering from the 'King's Evil' (scrofula) in the superstitious belief that they could thus be cured. The ritual, popular with the general public and Charles II, is estimated to have touched no fewer than 7000 sufferers in the first six months of his reign. However, it was considered to be associated with Catholicism and both William and Mary shunned the idea of participating in it, though it would subsequently be revived by Queen Anne. Another popular ceremony was the distribution of the Maundy money by the monarch, and Charles II used the Banqueting House as the setting for this occasion also, a tradition that continued until the reign of Queen Victoria.

Despite Charles II's enthusiasm for the theatre, masques were never held at the Banqueting House after the Restoration. Inigo Jones, who had designed costumes for such entertainments in the days of King

Charles I, had died during the Commonwealth period, and more importantly, the Rubens paintings were deemed too valuable to be subjected to the fire hazard presented by the brilliant torchlight required to set off the performance. Fire did so much damage to the rest of the palace in 1698 that the Banqueting House was thereafter used as a royal chapel, the one created by James II having been destroyed along with the Protestant chapel royal that Princess Anne had regularly used. Some of the marble decorations from the Catholic chapel were moved to Westminster Abbey, and later to St Andrew's Church, Burnham-on-Sea, where they can still be seen.

Wren's plans show that the queen's apartments at Whitehall Palace comprised an 'eating room', two bedchambers (one 'great' and one 'little'), a dressing room and a withdrawing room. Mary ordered the creation of a new riverside terrace, mainly for the purpose of cultivating flowers. The area was excavated during the 1930s, revealing the existence of 'Queen Mary's Steps', a staircase intended to enable the king's barge to access the building from the water. So eager was Mary to enjoy her husband's company that she rearranged the accommodation and ordered the building of a passage leading directly from William's chamber to her own. She also asked for a new robing room and a 'tea room', reflecting the trend for the drinking of the beverage, normally from fine china and porcelain vessels.

The 'Privy Garden' was one section of Whitehall Palace that Mary, at least, may have found appealing, in view of her interest in garden design. James I had installed a sundial there, which was destroyed some time during the reign of Charles II, who replaced it with a more elaborate structure, designed by the Jesuit scientist Francis Line; this reflected Charles's interest in astronomy. Complex diagrams of the sundial survive, along with a handbook for its operation written by its creator. In 1675, however, it was vandalised by none other than the Earl of Rochester, though it survived the attack; perhaps the damage is something both William and Mary would have observed in the period leading up to their wedding. The sundial survived the palace fires and was moved to another location, but its subsequent fate is unknown.

Mary spent many happy hours on the garden terrace overlooking the River Thames, which had been constructed for her use. Below was a mooring for the royal barge which Mary used for travelling on the river when conditions allowed. She could go to Windsor and other destinations by this means when it suited her. The Privy Garden itself, obviously, was not destroyed in the fire of 1698 but fell out of use along with the palace. The land was later leased to the Earl of Richmond and would be painted by Canaletto in the eighteenth century. Eventually a street called Whitehall Gardens was erected on the site. These grand houses (including the residences of at least two prime ministers) were themselves demolished during the 1930s, and the Ministry of Defence's headquarters now occupies most of the site.

The so-called 'Holbein Gate' (which has no known connection with the artist Hans Holbein, some of whose finest work failed to survive the fire) was constructed by Holbein's patron Henry VIII, and continued to stand just opposite the front of the Banqueting House until 1759, when it was demolished to ease the flow of traffic. The upper storey was occupied for a time by none other than Lady Castlemaine, during one of her periods of estrangement from Charles II; the chief mistress repeatedly removed herself from court when they quarrelled. Barbara's daughter by the king, Lady Anne, also lived there for a while.

In 1701, William gave permission to the multi-talented Sir John Vanbrugh to build himself a residence (known as Goose-Pie House), on part of the site of Whitehall Palace; this building was demolished in the nineteenth century. The young Vanbrugh had served William as a spy in the run-up to the 'Glorious Revolution' and was for some years imprisoned in France before briefly joining the Royal Navy. His two most successful comedies, *The Relapse* and *The Provoked Wife*, were both staged during William's reign, before his unexpected switch to architectural design, in collaboration with Nicholas Hawksmoor. His knowledge of France may have influenced this change, and by 1699 he was heavily involved in planning Castle Howard for one of the country's most illustrious families.

The coronation

William had commanded his wife to put a brave face on things, and after all she was widely loved for her vivacious manner, but she may not immediately have been aware of the fact that the people had not yet accepted the change of government. Some had expected a regency, which had been Mary's own preference. It had taken some months of debate before resentment of William as a foreigner and a reluctance to accept a female monarch resolved themselves into a solution that had never been tried before and has not been used since – a king and queen as equal partners in the monarchy. The day after her arrival from Holland, at the Banqueting House in Whitehall, the couple stood before Parliament, hand in hand, to hear the conditions under which the throne was being offered them, and both signed the Bill of Rights.

The Protestant's Ave Mary, a work printed in 1689 'on the Arrival of Her most Gracious Majesty, Mary, Queen of England', stands out as one of few works addressed to Mary alone; there was no shortage of public praise for the couple as an entity. This ode takes the name of the ancient Catholic hymn in adoration of the Virgin Mary, and attempts to turn it into a celebration of Protestantism, but also makes it clear that the author wants to see Mary taking an active role in ruling the country. Already it was recognised by some that there would be war, in the form of continued opposition from Jacobites and probable interference from France, and Mary would have a role to play in ensuring the country's continued stability.

There was no shortage of expert Dutch artists seeking patronage from the new monarchs, and it was Willem Van De Velde the Younger who recorded Mary's arrival in England, in oils, in a painting now held by the Royal Museums at Greenwich. William himself had not failed to recognise the potential power of the media and arranged for the *London Gazette* to print portraits of the couple in their coronation robes, from an engraving by Robert White. This official portrait was not the only one in circulation, royal souvenirs being as popular then as they are today.

Aware of the ambivalence felt towards them by many of their new subjects, the couple now took themselves out of the public eye and withdrew to Hampton Court Palace for a short time prior to their coronation, which was scheduled for 11 April, the day after Easter. Admirers did not flock to them as they might have done to other new monarchs, since the political situation was far from settled. On the very day of their coronation, they would learn that James had landed in Ireland and was building an army. Not everything was going badly, however: on the very same day, in Scotland, that country's parliament declared that James had forfeited his throne. William had been acting regent in Scotland since January, at the specific request of the Scottish Privy Council.

One reason for William's insistence on sharing the monarchy rather than handing it to Mary was to ensure that he would not be left in the lurch if anything happened to her, and this proved a wise precaution, for it meant that he could continue to rule without her. Had they had children, and had William died first, Mary could likewise have maintained control at least until their successor came of age. Although, as King of England, he was William III, he was only the second Scottish king to have been called William (the first being William the Lion in the thirteenth century), and accordingly he is correctly called William II of Scotland.

Old habits die hard, and the belief that a female was incapable of ruling the country quickly came to the fore. William, for his part, was determined not to be reduced to what he saw as the inferior role of consort; he was unwilling to accept anything less than sole rulership. The result was a complete compromise, but subtle touches in the coronation ceremonial and celebrations made it clear that the country intended to give him precedence over Mary. It would be William who sat in 'King Edward's Chair', the Gothic masterpiece commissioned by Edward I of England to house the captured Stone of Scone formerly used in Scotland's coronation ceremonies. One of the oldest pieces of wooden furniture to survive in Britain, it now rests in Westminster Abbey, carefully protected from the hands of tourists. The Stone itself has been held at Edinburgh Castle since 1996 but was temporarily returned to the Abbey for the coronation of King Charles III in 2023.

A new orb, sceptre and sword of state had been made especially for Mary, along with matching ruby rings for the couple (which apparently were mixed up during the ceremony). Although still held in the Jewel House at the Tower of London, her orb has never been used again, apart from a brief appearance at the funeral of Queen Victoria, when an extra orb was needed to convey Victoria's additional status as Empress of India. It was made by the Vyners, a famous family of London goldsmiths, who had supplied the regalia for the coronation of King Charles II in 1660. The sceptre, unlike the orb, retains its original precious stones. Mary's crown, however, had been made four years earlier for the coronation of Mary of Modena, on which James II had spared no expense. This same magnificent crown continued to be used for queens until 1831, when it was replaced by something considered less showy.

The ampulla still used at a coronation to hold the 'holy' oil (blessed earlier in the day by the archbishop) was made in 1661, in the form of an eagle, for the newly-restored King Charles II, and is thus much newer than the spoon used to anoint the monarch. The latter, however, is not known to have been used in a coronation ceremony before that of King James I of England in 1603. After the Civil War, it was sold off; fortunately, the buyer returned it after the Restoration. The anointing was probably one of the ritualistic details of the coronation that William found least appealing, but members of parliament, who were excluded from the planning of the ceremony, persuaded Christopher Wren to erect a viewing gallery from which they could see the throne, the king, and all parts of the ceremony, including the anointing.

While William was taken to Westminster by barge to prepare himself for the coronation ceremony, his wife rode in a sedan chair, already dressed in her state robes. Henry Compton, now Bishop of London, performed the coronation ceremony in the absence of Archbishop Sancroft, who, though an opponent of the previous king, had not approved of the change of government and felt himself bound by his earlier oath. Following the ceremony, a banquet took place at Westminster Hall, a coronation tradition that would continue until 1821. Westminster Hall, the oldest surviving section of the seat of the British Parliament that we call the Palace of Westminster, dates from the eleventh century and is more familiar to the public today as a result of its use for the lying in state of senior members of the royal family.

In the summer of 1689, Mary's younger sister Anne finally gave birth to a living male heir, a boy named William, who received the title Duke of Gloucester and now looked likely to sit on the throne some day. In view of Anne's previous history of failed child-bearing, this event must have given Mary renewed hope for the future. Yet before long this the two sisters had fallen out, as a result of Anne having requested a private income of £50,000 from Parliament. This was granted, but William, wanting a quiet life, sensibly agreed that this amount could be deducted from the income awarded to William and Mary themselves. Anne decided to leave her royal apartments at Hampton Court and live at a house in Kensington.

One person who exerted almost as much influence on Anne was the woman she and her husband credited with saving the life of their young son. Mrs Pack, who died later in the same year as Mary, was employed as a wet-nurse to the child, and continued to serve Anne in the more exalted station of head of his nursery. There was no love lost between her and Sarah Churchill. Nor did Sarah get on well with the boy's governess, Lady Fitzhardinge, who happened to be one of the numerous sisters of William's mistress, Elizabeth Villiers. Mrs Pack, at least, thus became an ally of Mary, and a potential spy in the 'Cockpit', Anne's residence within Whitehall Palace.

Even without this quarrel with Anne, Mary's first year as queen seems to have been rather a miserable one: 'very much neglected, little respected, censured by all, commended by none'. Much as the country had not wanted her father, many disapproved of her taking his place. Some of her enemies referred to her as 'Moll', a name that, as well as being short for 'Mary', was associated with the seamy side of life, and would continue to be so, well into the twentieth century. She was insulted by Catherine Sedley, her father's former mistress, whom she had refused to receive at court. Meanwhile, the satirist John Dryden, a Catholic convert who had been a mild critic of King James at times, was relieved of his role as Poet Laureate because of his refusal to take the new oath of allegiance. Mary came to believe that she was being punished for her actions in accepting her father's throne.

Despite his popular reputation for gravity, William was not without a sense of humour and was astute enough to recognise the value of propaganda. Accordingly, towards the end of the century, he employed Romeyn de Hooghe, one of his propagandists, to produce scurrilous images of James II and Louis XIV whilst depicting William himself as a liberating hero. The results were among the first satirical cartoons published in the British Isles.

Things gradually improved after the former King James made a serious attempt to regain the throne in 1690. James, with the experience of his 55 years, was used to exile and no doubt believed that the wheel would come full circle in due course, but he also knew that he was not getting any younger and could not afford to bide his time if he wanted to ensure a Catholic succession. It had taken the Scots a little time to accept that the new régime now governed them legally as it did England, by which time James had landed in Ireland with an army consisting mainly of French troops supplied by Louis XIV, but also including many loyalists from the home countries.

William had a lot on his plate. He was embroiled in several armed conflicts, being at war with France while the latter was simultaneously at war with Spain. In March 1689, James had landed in Kinsale and went on to Dublin, having declined to give up the throne without a fight, despite the reversals he had suffered in England and Scotland only a few months earlier.

Ireland

Ireland, where most of the native population was Catholic and there was considerable opposition to William, was the obvious place to begin an attempt to regain the throne, but James underestimated the resentment of some of those who felt he had let them down previously, as well as overestimating the willingness of the people to exchange peace for war. Some of those who had spoken up against his dethronement were beginning to have second thoughts about whether they really wanted him back.

Despite its parliament having awarded the Scottish throne to William and Mary in April, Scotland too held many Jacobites (as supporters of King James were now known). One such was John Graham of Claverhouse, who was not a Catholic but had been a staunch supporter of James, who had created him Viscount Dundee. James's campaign to regain his throne got off to a promising start in July 1689 at the Battle of Killiecrankie, where Dundee defeated government troops. At Killiecrankie, the wild charge for which the Highlanders were famous was a key factor in the Jacobite victory, but Dundee was killed and the Jacobites were unable to consolidate their position, lacking decent equipment and a charismatic leader. William's focus was always on Europe, and he never visited Scotland; he relied on his Calvinist credentials to ensure his popularity there.

The Earl of Tyrconnell, James's deputy or 'Viceroy' in Ireland, still commanded the country's sizeable army, but he needed money to continue the campaign. The city of Derry (in present-day Northern Ireland), had been lost to James when the famous apprentice boys of Derry, anticipating William's invasion of England, took the initiative and closed the city's gates to prevent Jacobite troops from entering. Derry would again be put under siege immediately on James's return.

This second attempt to besiege Derry, led by James's military commander, Richard Hamilton, was more successful, and James himself was present when it began. Having failed to breach the city walls, the Jacobite forces resorted to starving out the occupiers. The siege was lifted in August by William's supporters, under the command of Percy Kirke, who had been a stalwart defender of the former king's rule in the face of the Duke of Monmouth's invasion, a mere four years earlier. The siege had lasted 105 days when Kirke broke through the blockade of the River Foyle to bring provisions to the starving population. The Jacobites retreated without a fight.

In the meantime, James had called a session of the Irish Parliament, a body that had been inactive for nearly 25 years. An Act of Recognition was passed, declaring James to be the rightful King of Ireland, and the 'Patriot Parliament' confiscated the property of many Irish Protestants whilst negotiating terms for James's return to power. There were deep divisions among the members, with the Irish also disliking the French advisors James had brought into the country. Tyrconnell did not see eye to eye with Patrick Sarsfield, and they disagreed volubly over the need to negotiate with William.

Before James had raised enough money to mount an invasion of England, William decided his presence was required in Ireland, and reluctantly diverted resources from the war with France that was still proceeding. Embarking at Hoylake in Cheshire, at a spot now known as 'King's Gap', he landed at Carrickfergus in June 1690, with an army of about 15,000 English, Dutch and Danish soldiers and financial support from the English Parliament; he had as yet little confidence in troops from the home nations. It was impossible for the new king to be in Ireland for the whole of the war, since he had other military obligations in Europe, and he needed to act quickly. Arriving in Belfast, he issued a proclamation, promising the Irish that 'all who behave themselves as becomes dutiful and loyal subjects may enjoy their liberties and possessions under a just and equal government'.

With the Presbyterian church on his side and two Irish regiments absorbed into his army, William headed for Dundalk, pushing back any potential opposition, whilst James dithered and ignored his advisors when they suggested moving further south and awaiting French reinforcements. The Williamite army gathered near the village of Loughbrickland. While watching developments from a position near the ford, William was wounded by shrapnel, but his followers took heart from his resilience.

The enemy snipers are thought to have recognised William on the banks of the river by his pronounced stoop. However, his physical shortcomings did not prevent him spending the whole day riding up and down the lines, encouraging his troops. He was impatient to engage James's army. Among his troops were the Blue Guards, a Dutch elite infantry unit snazzily dressed in Nassau blue coats with yellow or orange trim. An important part of William's military capability, they were never popular with his parliament, who would refuse to finance them after 1699 – though they continued to serve the country well in the next decade, under the leadership of John Churchill.

Instead of taking the advice of his French-appointed deputies, who suggested a strategic withdrawal designed to wear William out, James insisted on giving battle as soon as possible. The River Boyne was, he thought, likely to offer protection against the possibility of William capturing the city of Dublin. The Jacobite army was drawn up at the village of Oldbridge, where a modern visitor centre has been established.

At the Battle of the Boyne on 1 July 1690 (11 July according to the modern calendar), the two rival kings led their troops out and the smaller Jacobite force was defeated. William lost his deputy, the 74-year-old Duke of Schomberg, who was shot and killed while riding across the ford to attack the enemy on the opposite bank of the River Boyne, but casualties in general were relatively small. Nevertheless, rather than regrouping, James once again decided to escape back to France. He rushed to take ship at Waterford, a decision that ensured his bid to regain the throne was not taken seriously in Ireland again.

Dublin

Some readers may be surprised to learn that the Battle of the Boyne was William's first major victory in the field. Even among his admirers, he was noted more for his courage and decisiveness rather than his military brilliance. It must have been an enormous confidence-booster. Ireland's Protestant leaders quickly got together to welcome him.

William now occupied Dublin, and was received with ceremony at St Patrick's Cathedral, where he listened to a congratulatory sermon from Dr William King, a Protestant clergyman of Scottish extraction, shortly to be appointed Bishop of Derry and later Archbishop of Dublin. The city at that time was the second largest in the British Isles, a centre of power and a cultural hub. Centred on the castle (the largest building in Ireland), which had been the seat of British/English administration for centuries and would continue to be so until 1922, it was not very different from other cities in the kingdom, with a surge in industrial and commercial development, dependent on often inadequate infrastructure. Dublin Bay and the River Liffey were vital transport routes made narrow by treacherous sandbars. Sir William Petty, a polymath who had served under several régimes and died the year before the Dutch invasion, was the first President of the Dublin Philosophical Society, founded in 1683. Petty carried out statistical surveys of the population that are extremely valuable to today's historical researchers.

At the time of the Battle of the Boyne, it was barely forty years since Oliver Cromwell had entered Ireland via Dublin and aroused hatred among the Irish by attacking Drogheda and massacring the inhabitants. He had proceeded to introduce repressive laws directed against the Catholic population, and had brought in Protestant settlers from elsewhere. As well as incomers from the British mainland, there were refugees from the wilder parts of the country where disorder and violence still reigned. The Catholic Irish had been delighted by Cromwell's death and expected better treatment from Charles II, but were severely disappointed. St Patrick's Cathedral was a symbol of Charles's re-establishment of the Protestant Church. Archbishop Oliver Plunkett, executed in 1681 and later canonised by the Roman Catholic church, had been an innocent victim of the 'Popish Plot' hoax. Plunkett's mummified head is now held in Drogheda as a sacred relic.

Under Mary's father, King James II, things may be said to have improved slightly for the Catholic population. When Richard Talbot, the Catholic Earl of Tyrconnell, became Lord Deputy of Ireland, and later Lord Lieutenant, he disarmed the Protestant militia and appointed Catholics to important positions. He later warned James of the likelihood of William invading England, and moved quickly to raise an army, but was thwarted by the lockout at Derry.

Only small parts of Dublin's medieval castle, first erected by King John of England in the fourteenth century, survive today, notably the

Record Tower, the only one left of the four original corner towers. The Dark Pool ('Dubh Linn'), on a tributary of the Liffey, next to which the castle was built, formed part of the moat. In 1684, the castle was so badly damaged by fire that it had to be largely rebuilt. It continued to house a garrison but was not yet the regular residence of the Lord Lieutenant of Ireland. The next Lord Lieutenant, Mary's uncle the Earl of Clarendon, went on with the programme of redevelopment that had already started under his predecessor, and work began on new state apartments, though the project was underfunded.

The Irish Horse Guard had been housed at the castle at the time of their establishment in 1662, but these were moved to a new location near Wood Quay and eventually disbanded by James II on his accession to the throne. At the same time, the Royal Irish Dragoon Guards were created. Although their formation was prompted by Monmouth's Rebellion, they now fought for William, both at the Battle of the Boyne and overseas. Another cavalry regiment, the Royal Irish Hussars, was raised in 1693 in Derry by Henry Conyngham, an erstwhile supporter of King James.

The building work on the castle would go on well after William's death, with almost all remnants of the medieval structure being obliterated. At the time of his occupation of Dublin, the Record Tower was known as the 'Gunner's Tower'. A hundred years later (by then known as the 'Wardrobe Tower'), it was earmarked for demolition, but the authorities relented, probably because it was in use as a prison. As its present title would suggest, the Record Tower became the repository for archives that have now been deposited in the National Archives elsewhere in Dublin. For a while it also housed the museum of the Garda Síochána, Ireland's police force. This has been moved to another part of the castle and is still open to the public.

The private chapel to which the Record Tower originally gave access is not the Chapel Royal that stands today, which was opened only in 1814, for use by the Lord Lieutenant, and was used by King George IV on his visit to Ireland. It was designed by Irish architect Francis Johnston in the Gothic Revival style. It has been deconsecrated and reconsecrated, but is no longer used for worship. The interior remains an impressive sight.

In 2022 the castle celebrated the centenary of its role in the events of 16 January 1922, when the government of Ireland was handed over to the Irish people by the British government, after many years of violence and arguments. It was the revolutionary leader Michael Collins who took control as head of the provisional government. A few months later, Collins was assassinated by a former British army officer turned IRA extremist.

St Patrick's Cathedral, built in the twelfth century and extended over the years, had been in a very poor state of repair since the early seventeenth century, so much so that Cromwell's troops had used it for stabling horses. Under Charles II, it had been repaired and improved, and had been the spiritual home of French Huguenot refugees during the 1660s. A new roof had been completed in 1671. The structure had been strengthened with buttresses and a new west window was installed. This has since been replaced with 'St Patrick's Window', dating from the nineteenth century, which neither James nor William could ever have seen. No seventeenth-century glass survives.

The Lady Chapel, known for many years as the 'French Chapel' because of its association with the Huguenots, is dedicated to the Virgin Mary, and was extensively restored in the nineteenth century along with the rest of the cathedral. A further restoration project was carried out in 2012. The chapel contains a chair reportedly used by William when he attended the celebratory service in the cathedral.

During his occupation of Dublin, shortly before William's arrival, King James had attempted to turn the clock back and make the cathedral a centre of Catholic worship, as it had not been since before the Reformation. William King, then the cathedral's chancellor, was an avid supporter of the new régime, and as a result was temporarily imprisoned in Dublin Castle. In November 1690, while Bishop William Lloyd was preaching directly to William and Mary in England on *A Discourse of God's Ways of Disposing of Kingdoms*, to justify William's war in Ireland,

King would be found preaching a further thanksgiving sermon in St Patrick's Cathedral.

Jonathan Swift, the cathedral's future dean, was in his early twenties and had been living in England, where he worked as a secretary. In 1690, he briefly returned to Ireland, but did not stay long, eventually returning to his homeland in 1694 as a priest in Carrickfergus, where William had landed before the Boyne. Swift's memorial is now a prominent feature of the cathedral interior. Although not appointed until after William's death, he lived through the joint reign and met William in person through his role as secretary to Sir William Temple. After leaving Temple's service, Swift approached William directly in an attempt to gain preferment; he failed to impress the king.

St Mary's Pro-cathedral, the headquarters of the Roman Catholic church in Ireland, did not exist in the Dublin William saw. Even today, it does not hold the status of cathedral, having been erected long after the city's two cathedrals – St Patrick's and the Cathedral of the Holy Trinity – were appropriated by Henry VIII's Church of England. The Cathedral of the Holy Trinity, now known as Christ Church Cathedral, is even older than St Patrick's, but the original building collapsed into its weak foundations during the reign of Elizabeth I. The evidence of the damage is still obvious. The collapse destroyed the original tomb of Richard de Clare, known as 'Strongbow', a Norman earl largely responsible for the conquest of Ireland by Anglo-Norman forces. It was replaced, but Strongbow's reputation in today's independent Ireland is not what it once was.

Buildings that had been erected alongside Christ Church were used by James II for a parliament, and he held a mass in the church itself, leaving behind some candlesticks and a tabernacle. Ironically, it was not long afterwards that William donated a gold communion plate, for use in the Protestant rite, in thanks for his victories over James; this is still on display, along with James's gifts. Some repairs had already taken place by the late seventeenth century, but it was not until the nineteenth century that Christ Church was extensively restored, and further repairs took place in the 1980s. The crypt, the largest in the British Isles, has been subject to some undignified uses over the centuries, but now hosts an exhibition of the church's treasures, including the mummified bodies of a cat and a rat, of unknown age, and the preserved heart of the twelfth-century saint, Laurence O'Toole, which was stolen in 2012 and remained missing for six years but is now back at the cathedral, despite being essentially a Catholic relic.

In recognition of his role as a 'liberator', a statue of William was erected in Dublin in 1701, near Trinity College. In keeping with its purpose as a reminder of his role in maintaining the Protestant religion by force of arms, it depicted him on horseback in Roman dress. The population of Dublin remained predominantly Protestant well into the eighteenth century. The mayor of Dublin behind the erection of the statue was Bartholomew Van Homrigh, a Dutchman who had been a merchant in the city since the reign of Charles II. By 1710 it had been damaged by students from the Tory faction. In 1798, the year of a rebellion against British rule, it was attacked again. A second failed rebellion, in 1803, made it a target for republicans and Catholics alike, and the practice of processing to the statue on William's birthday was abandoned in 1806. Daniel O'Connell, a Catholic, became Lord Mayor in 1841, but allowed the statue to stay, and it remained in existence (though in a poor state of repair) until 1928, when it was destroyed by an IRA bomb. The statue that now stands in its place on College Green is that of the writer and campaigner Thomas Davis (1814–1845), a more inclusive figure.

On this occasion, Drogheda, the town so savagely punished by Cromwell, surrendered without a fight. William's army was encamped in what is now the Dublin suburb of Finglas. From here, part of the force advanced to Athlone and the other, under William's command, towards Kilkenny, where he arrived on 19 July 1690 and was lavishly entertained by James Butler, 2nd Duke of Ormonde. Ormonde was an unreliable ally, who had supported James II until the last moment and would eventually return to his Jacobite roots.

Waterford was taken in late July, and at around the same time William received the surrender of the Jacobite Earl of Dover, Henry

Jermyn, who retired to his English country estate under an amnesty. Nevertheless, even after the success of the Boyne, William was probably not feeling entirely triumphant, having received news that his fleet had been defeated by the French at the Battle of Beachy Head on 10 July, with the loss of several ships and resultant panic in the south of England. Abandoning his plan to sail home because of the continuing naval threat, he went on to besiege Limerick, where many Jacobites had retreated after the Boyne. At first trying an all-out assault which met with little success, he abandoned the attempt, having lost large numbers of men. The town remained a Jacobite stronghold until the following year, when his troops returned and managed to negotiate a less costly surrender, in the wake of the Battle of Aughrim, at which the Jacobites had been soundly defeated by a multi-national force. It was Sarsfield who negotiated the treaty that ended this phase of the war.

William himself was not present at these major actions of 1691, leaving a combination of Scottish, English, French and Dutch commanders to handle matters on his behalf. The wide-ranging theatre of war required him to delegate to his leading supporters, and he did so efficiently. He left Ireland in early September and on arrival in England went straight to Windsor, where the queen was waiting for him. Administering the country in his absence, Mary was mortified at the outcome of the Beachy Head encounter, especially since she had already earmarked the man most responsible, the Earl of Torrington, for dismissal from his position as First Lord of the Admiralty.

Despite being joint monarch, Mary had been obliged to take the title of 'regent' during her husband's absence in Ireland, denoting her lesser status in the eyes of the government. A 'Council of Nine' (all men, naturally) had been appointed to act as her advisors: the dukes of Devonshire and Dorset, the Marquess of Carmarthen, the Earls of Marlborough, Nottingham, Orford, Pembroke and Peterborough, and Sir John Lowther. Her natural tendency to defer to her husband in all things had caused Mary's abilities to be overlooked, but the time had come for her to flex her royal authority and she did so with a dignity that led to changes in public opinion and, more importantly, increased the respect shown to her at court.

The defeat at Beachy Head had caused widespread panic and alarm in parts of England; the town of Teignmouth in Devon was torched. Torrington, who was already nicknamed 'Tarry-in-Town' for his reluctance to act decisively, had in fact been against the idea of engaging with the French at sea, but Mary's council had outnumbered him and he may have taken a defeatist attitude. At his court-martial, he blamed a lack of communication for his failure and laid the blame largely on the Dutch contingent. Xenophobia ensured his acquittal, but William never forgave him. As for Mary's Council, they almost came to blows when discussing who should succeed Torrington as commander of the navy. Mary's suggestion of bringing in Sir John Ashby, one of the heroes of Beachy Head, as joint admiral of the fleet, was met with disdain by some of her councillors but was nevertheless accepted. She indicated afterwards that the Dutch people had been 'kinder' to her than the English had been so far.

While Mary was struggling with affairs of state, her husband had not exactly been having an easy time of it, though military campaigning came more naturally to him than governing did to her. The young Duke of Savoy, Victor Amadeus, now sent an envoy to congratulate William on his recent victories. The duke had become tired of his dependence on the French and was seeking support in his continuing struggle against the dominance of Louis XIV. William had little choice but to promise his assistance.

With this in mind, William called a parliament in England, requesting finance to pursue his wars in Europe. Parliament, impressed as much by Mary's proven calibre as by William's performance in Ireland, voted to raise the necessary funds by confiscating the Irish estates of Jacobite supporters (though in fact William gave away many of these gains to his supporters). He also proposed the expansion of the navy and the building of new ships, the money to be obtained by additional duties on items such as beer.

A Joint Monarchy   105

Although James had been temporarily fought off, the war in Ireland would not come to an end until the Treaty of Limerick, signed in October 1691 after a three-month siege of the city, offering toleration to Catholics and pardoning Jacobites who changed sides. It also allowed the so-called 'Flight of the Wild Geese', the evacuation of the Jacobite army to France; the number of people who left is estimated at 20,000. Sadly, the Parliament of Ireland later went back on the terms of the treaty, spurred on by the actions of the new pope, Innocent XII, who recognised James as the country's lawful ruler.

In the interim, William himself had not only travelled the length and breadth of Ireland, but had found time to continue his campaign in Europe and make his first visit to Holland in more than two years. He had informed Parliament of his intention, and closed the session with a warlike speech. Encountering a January storm in the English Channel, he was obliged to land in a small boat, which was almost overwhelmed by the rough seas, and was greeted on shore by a former servant and escorted, via Hoonselardijk, to The Hague, where he made his triumphal entry. His speech on arrival equalled the one he had given in the English Parliament, in terms of its success in obtaining promises of financial support.

William's arrival in his homeland was greeted with enthusiasm. Among other paeans of praise, he received a 20-line poetic tribute from Bernard Mandeville (1670–1733), a young Dutchman who came to England in 1691 to learn the language and remained there for most of his life, taking up residence in London. Mandeville would become renowned as a physician, philosopher and writer, best known for his *Fable of the Bees*, a controversial treatise published in 1714 under Mary's sister, Queen Anne.

After the celebrations, William's first serious task was to hold a conference with some allies: Frederick, the Elector[2] of Brandenburg; Maximilian Emanuel, the Elector of Bavaria; the Governor of the Spanish Netherlands; and many other rulers from the minor German

---

2. Rulers who had a vote in the selection of the Holy Roman Emperor were known as "Electors".

kingdoms. William stated his intention of using more British troops to address the threats to Flanders. Brussels was a target for the French, and Mons was under siege again. William's attempt to relieve the siege ended in failure. At first the campaign seemed to be going well, but his efforts were hampered by the inefficient preparations of his Spanish allies. After Mons was given up to the French in April, he returned to The Hague.

Wanting to see his wife again after his three-month absence, the king arrived in London from the Netherlands to find the Palace of Whitehall on fire. Mary had been sleeping there, and had had a narrow escape. It was neither the first nor the last fire at the palace. The Stone Gallery, which overlooked the river, survived, but everything between it and the river was damaged beyond repair. After the event, some felt that the resulting destruction of a few of the older buildings was an overall improvement. William had always preferred Kensington, where he and Mary were able to spend some time together.

Little daunted by the recent setbacks in his European war, William was soon back on the Continent, setting sail on 2 May from Harwich. In June he made a heroic intervention as the French attempted to take the city of Liège in present-day Belgium, the capital of an important buffer zone. Although badly damaged by artillery fire from the vicinity of a nearby Carthusian monastery, but the citadel – built only twenty years earlier – withstood the attacks and the city was saved from capture. A commemorative medal held in the British Museum's collection shows a local landmark, the 'Perron' or column of Liége with the attack on the city in the background. On the obverse, William, in the guise of a Roman emperor, holds a standard decorated with a Christian symbol and the cap of Liberty. William's military prowess offered many opportunities for such propaganda, unlike the somewhat patchy record of his father-in-law. Nevertheless, as soon as he left for his palace of Het Loo, intending to spend the winter in England, the army he left behind was soundly defeated at Leuze by a smaller French force.

Abel Boyer, an Anglo-French writer who was briefly tutor to Princess Anne's surviving son, the Duke of Gloucester, later wrote a biography of King William in which he praised Mary's capabilities. The queen's 'Council of Nine' was meeting twice a week in his absence, and had to deal with the continuing Jacobite threat, represented by people like Viscount Preston, who had been arrested on his way to France with secret papers in his possession. With William's written permission, Mary issued a reprieve after the trial, retaining Preston's property as security. It was claimed that she had been swayed by pity for his wife and children.

In return for his freedom, Preston gave up information about other Jacobite sympathisers. Mary's own uncle, Henry Hyde, who had succeeded to the earldom of Clarendon, retained some loyalty to James and was one of those who had declined to take an oath of loyalty to the new monarchs. For many months, he was imprisoned in the Tower of London because of his association with Preston. Mary eventually relented and allowed him to retire to his country estate. Henry's brother Laurence, the Earl of Rochester, although he initially shared Henry's misgivings and had tried hard to persuade James to take steps that would have allowed him to keep his throne, quickly backpedalled and took the oath in order to retain his position.

Although the queen retained nominal authority in her husband's absence, members of her council were sometimes reluctant to allow her to exercise it, particularly on matters relating to the armed forces, without an assurance that William would approve. Nevertheless, one aspect of her 'regency' was the duty of reviewing troops – in the absence of William's army, this tended to mean the militia, whose chief role was to defend the country against foreign invasion. She was also faced with the problem of the nonjuring bishops and other clergy, those who had failed to swear the oath of allegiance to herself and William. Some died, others changed their minds when it became clear that the new regime was there to stay. Six bishops had to be replaced, and Mary had to deal with this knotty problem, which she must have found particularly painful in view of her devotion to the Protestant faith.

Although the disposition of ecclesiastical honours was supposed to be carried out by William only, the removal of William Sancroft from his position as Archbishop of Canterbury because of his refusal to swear the oath of loyalty meant that a new archbishop had to be appointed as a matter of urgency, and Mary selected John Tillotson, who enjoyed William's confidence as well as her own and had a reputation as a reformer. Tillotson's attempt to eliminate corrupt practices from the Church of England would meet with limited success.

When Tillotson was resident at Lambeth Palace, on the other side of the River Thames, Mary could travel by barge to visit him and seek his advice. As had been her habit in Holland, she enjoyed travelling on the water and would use the opportunity to enjoy musical performances from her own private ensemble, who often travelled with her. Another of her favourite river journeys was to the Apothecaries' Garden at Chelsea, now the Chelsea Physic Garden, where she consulted with the botanist, Samuel Doody, and viewed some of the exotic species.

William's military initiatives in Europe were faced with stalemate, as he was consistently unable to tempt the French commanders to give battle, but Mary continued to defer to him, firmly believing him more capable than her of dealing with any crisis, despite the low opinion she had of some of the members of her Council of Nine. Gilbert Burnet, having spent the summer close to her, noted how she put a brave face on any adverse circumstances, whilst Boyer commented that 'never was so great a capacity for government joined with so little appetite to it'. It is clear, nevertheless, that she grew in confidence over this period. There were even times when she wrote to William privately on matters she did not discuss with the Council (as indeed he sometimes wrote to her in strict confidence). In her attempts to administer the realm effectively, she had the support of Daniel Finch, Earl of Nottingham, a sensible and pragmatic Secretary of State who recognised her authority.

Within a year of his previous defeat, Mary's father was again threatening to return to England with an invasion force. Early in 1692, the queen discovered that John Churchill, now Earl of Marlborough, apparently irritated by her refusal to grant him the Order of the Garter, had been in contact with James, seeking a pardon in the event of the former king's return to the throne. She promptly dismissed Marlborough, whom

William had never quite trusted. There was reputed to be a plan to assassinate William and abduct Mary. Worse was to come: Mary came into the possession of forged documents implicating Marlborough and several others in a treasonous plot, and she acted swiftly to have the proposed culprits arrested. Marlborough was briefly consigned to the Tower, and some of his powerful supporters were highly critical of the action taken against him.

This resulted in a serious rupture in the relations between Mary and her younger sister Anne. When Mary demanded Sarah Churchill's dismissal, Anne flatly refused, and in response to threats from the queen, both Anne and Sarah decamped to Syon House, where they were guests of the Duke and Duchess of Somerset. Anne's husband, Prince George of Denmark, got the cold shoulder from William as a result of Anne having rejected overtures from the king. What Anne did not know was that her friend Lady Fitzhardinge was checking up on her at William's behest.

Following the quarrel over the status of the Churchills, Anne fell seriously ill, and for a time her life appeared to be in danger. Mary relented enough to visit her, but there was no real reconciliation between the sisters. Marlborough's arrest was the final straw. Even in William's absence, he was blamed for the temporary downfall of the Churchills, with Anne referring to him as a 'Dutch monster'.

In the meantime, Arnold van Keppel, a Dutch soldier and long-standing friend of William's, began to receive additional favours from the king, and their relationship would grow ever stronger in the years following Mary's death, with Keppel being created Earl of Albemarle in 1697. Portland became envious of the younger man, and William became scrupulous in his attempts to treat these two bosom friends with equal favour.

While William was deciding what to do about Ireland, there was trouble in Scotland. The Scottish government, still independent of the English Parliament, had bargained with the chiefs of the clans, James's potential supporters, by paying them to swear the oath of allegiance to the new monarchs, but most had not got around to it. The Earl of Stair, who served as Secretary of State for Scotland, had threatened reprisals against anyone who still had not signed by the beginning of 1692. A regiment was sent, led by a member of the Campbell clan, to attack the MacDonalds, who were among the offenders. They sealed off the glen, snatching property and killing 30–40 people. The Massacre at Glencoe has passed into legend, but few people today understand what it was all about.

It took some time for the news to travel. William had signed the orders for the attack himself, but successfully delegated the blame to Stair. It was not until 1695 that a pamphlet by a Jacobite sympathiser, titled *Gallienus Redivivus, or Murther will out*, was widely circulated in London, accusing the king not only of responsibility for the massacre but of culpability in the murder of the de Witts twenty years earlier. William ordered a Commission of Inquiry into the circumstances of the Glencoe event, which naturally exonerated him of blame for the massacre. Stair was dismissed, but his career was far from over. Coming not long after Mary's death, these developments did nothing to increase William's popularity, especially in Scotland where times were hard. The 1690s being a period of severe famine in parts of the country, Jacobite feeling remained strong, especially after the abortive attempt to set up a Scottish trading company in what is now Panama, the 'Darien scheme', where William's reluctance to assist would only add to the resentment felt by the Scots.

The former King James had unwittingly assisted his enemies and made his restoration almost impossible by broadcasting the fact that, on his return, he intended to take revenge on those who had opposed him. In 1692, the French supplied the ousted king with an invasion fleet, but he now faced Admiral Edward Russell, a stalwart supporter of the new régime who had been one of the seven signatories to the invitation made to William in 1688.

It was as a result of two further naval battles, this time with a more successful outcome, in May and June 1692, that Mary decided to reward the Royal Navy by the construction of the Greenwich Hospital. Off the French ports of Barfleur and La Hogue, the Dutch and British navies had come together to inflict major damage on the French fleet, which lost fifteen ships of the line. The larger allied force had, however, suffered considerable human casualties.

In August 1692, while Mary was holding things together at home, William was at Steenkerque in the Netherlands, attempting to get the better of the French army that had taken the city of Namur. Here he made a surprise attack on the Duke of Piney-Luxembourg, with some success. Unable to claim a decisive victory, he arranged an orderly retreat, leaving the French to deal with their own casualties. British troops were now an integral part of William's army, reflecting not only the change of government but the country's role in a 'Grand Alliance' against the French, fighting alongside the Holy Roman Emperor, the Swedes, the Spanish and the Portuguese. It was not until mid-October 1692 that William arrived back at Kensington Palace. His address to Parliament was politely received, but his habit of rewarding his Dutch followers had not helped his popularity.

By the end of 1692, the incoming Poet Laureate, Nahum Tate, was referring to Queen Mary II in the same breath as Queen Elizabeth I[3] as well as crediting her with the navy's victory at La Hogue. The following year a victory medal was struck to commemorate the occasion. So gracious was Mary's response to Parliament's expressions of gratitude that she was suddenly the nation's darling, no longer viewed as an unnatural daughter but as a loyal and dutiful wife, and at the same time far more approachable and empathetic than her husband.

Two years earlier, in August 1690, she had made herself popular with the common people by receiving a deputation of sailors' wives at Whitehall. The women were complaining that their husbands had not been paid for their naval service. It seems that Mary, defying her advisors, insisted on seeing their representatives personally and promised prompt payment of the money owed to them. Thus she won over many of her previous critics, and would continue to do so.

---

3. *A Present for the Ladies.*

Even Dryden deigned to write the preface to a work by his friend, William Walsh, *Dialogue concerning Women, being a Defence of the Sex*. Walsh praised Mary's record to date, focusing on how she 'managed affairs with that dexterity which is very rarely found in those who are the most ambitious of command', the more so because she had come up against Louis XIV, at a time when she 'had nothing but the Universal Hearts of her Subjects to defend her'. She was, in fact, the 'most illustrious example' of the best qualities of her gender.

Mary's reputation as a monarch has been largely eclipsed by the events of her younger sister's reign. Anne seems, at least in the present day, to have had a more eventful personal life than Mary, with her supposed lesbian affairs with Sarah Churchill and, later, Sarah's cousin Abigail Masham being of particular interest to the modern generation. Furthermore, in her twelve-year reign, Anne presided over further constitutional change, as well as yet another succession crisis, an indirect result of her multiple failed pregnancies and five lost children, of whom by far the longest-lived was the Duke of Gloucester, who died at the age of eleven.

Mary was, however, every bit as active as a monarch as was Anne, who relied heavily on the advice of people such as the Churchills and, later, Masham. Anne also got caught up in squabbles between the Whig and Tory parties. Mary, although she always deferred to William, appears to have enjoyed a less complicated relationship with her Council of Nine.

Greenwich Hospital

The fifteenth-century Palace of Placentia, incorporating the Queen's House constructed for Anne of Denmark in the early seventeenth century, to plans drawn up by the late John Webb, had been badly damaged during the Commonwealth and was little used after the Restoration. It was gradually demolished and redeveloped as a naval 'hospital' in response to the earlier establishment of the Chelsea Hospital for soldiers by King Charles II. The latter, designed by Sir Christopher Wren, was not completed until 1692, when the first pensioners were admitted and an opening ceremony was carried out by William and Mary in February of that year.

Plans for the new buildings at Greenwich were created by Wren and his assistant Nicholas Hawksmoor, and included a refectory, an infirmary and a chapel. The work was paid for from a variety of sources (including confiscated smuggling fines) and expenditure approved by Parliament under the 1695 'Act for the Increase and Encouragement of Seamen'. That Queen Mary II had taken a personal interest in the development of the plans is shown in the presence of the grand avenue that splits the frontage into symmetrical 'quadrants' so as not to obstruct the remarkable view of the river from the balcony of the Queen's House. She would not live to see the project to fruition, but her husband would ensure its completion as a tribute to her.

In the Grand Square that separates the four main buildings of the complex stands a statue of King George II. The original plan had been for a statue of William, but it remained unfulfilled until John Michael Rysbrack was commissioned to repurpose the stone. Rysbrack would, however, create likenesses of William at other locations, including an equestrian statue at Queen Square in Bristol. It was a straight swap – Bristol had been intended to show off a statue of George II, but the new arrangement reflected the city's support for the 1689 Crown and Parliament Recognition Act that had brought William and Mary to the throne. (Queen Square is named after Mary's younger sister, Anne.) An early nineteenth-century statue, modelled on Rysbrack's, now stands in St James's Square.

The four courts would eventually be named for King William, Queen Mary, Queen Anne and King Charles. The lower section of the Painted Hall in King William Court, originally intended as the hospital's refectory, contains magnificent Baroque wall and ceiling paintings, the work of Sir James Thornhill, which were begun in 1707, long after the deaths of both Mary and William but are nevertheless dedicated to their memory. The ceiling includes a portrait of the couple seated together in Heaven. Thornhill was heavily influenced by the work of seventeenth-century Italian artists Antonio Verrio and Louis Laguerre, both of whom had been active during the joint monarchy of William and Mary.

Although not dating from their reign, the Painted Hall is unsurpassed as an example of contemporary painting in the UK, and has also been referred to as an early example of architecture being made to complement interior design[4]. The entrance, designed by Wren and Hawksmoor, makes an almost unprecedented use of light through its large windows. In recognition of its naval origins, it was in the Painted Hall that Admiral Nelson's body would lie in state a century later. Sometimes called "Britain's Sistine Chapel"[5], it reopened in 2019 after a thorough restoration.

The original Greenwich Hospital would go through several subtle changes of use and eventually became part of the Royal Naval College, Greenwich, in 1873. It remained so until 1998, when it was opened to the public. UNESCO has made it a World Heritage Site, calling it the 'finest and most dramatically sited architectural and landscape ensemble in the British Isles'.

The Queen's House, the first building in the country to be designed in the Palladian style, remains at the centre of the complex. Used by Henrietta Maria only from its completion in 1635 till the outbreak of the Civil War in 1642, the house contains little of its original decoration but several of the paintings purchased for it by Charles I can still be seen at other locations in London. The Dutch painter Willem van de Velde, with his son of the same name, had been using part of the building as a studio, at the invitation of Charles II, but this arrangement lapsed around the time that Mary began taking an interest in the building complex. Rather than painting the landscape around them, the van de Veldes were retained on a pension to produce scenes of naval warfare.

The marble floor of the Great Hall was designed by Inigo Jones to complement the geometric design of the ceiling, and the hall is a cube, a forerunner of Jones's design for the Banqueting House in Whitehall.

---

4. Simon Thurley.
5. http://www.ornc.org/Pages/News/Category/painted-hall-conservation (Old Royal Naval College website)

The 'Tulip Stairs', a spiral staircase with a wrought iron balustrade, was the first self-supporting staircase to be built in Britain, and is counted a masterpiece of seventeenth-century architecture. The house's progressive architecture represented the classical qualities of harmony, detail and proportion, in complete contrast to the ruins of the Palace of Placentia that still stood close by. Much of the suburb of Greenwich was designed to blend in with it.

Despite its name and the fact that it was still being used for official purposes, Mary chose not to use the Queen's House as a residence. It later became part of the Royal Hospital School and in the twentieth century was incorporated into the National Maritime Museum. In 2016 it reopened after a lengthy refurbishment, and now acts as a gallery for the museum's substantial collection of marine paintings and portraits.

Kensington Palace

William suffered from asthma, and the polluted atmosphere in the city of London was causing him considerable discomfort when resident at Whitehall – where he never kept a permanent lodging. Initially he thought of moving his whole court to Hampton Court Palace, but this idea proved unpopular with courtiers because of its distance from the centre of administration. His eye then fell on a mansion built by Sir George Coppin in 1605 in the quiet outlying village of Kensington. The house had passed quickly through Coppin's hands and those of the Earl of Nottingham, from whose son, Daniel Finch, William purchased it. Finch was currently Secretary of State and keen to keep on the right side of the new king, of whose accession he had been less than supportive.

Before settling on their new residence, the couple briefly rented Holland House, a Jacobean mansion which was largely destroyed by aerial bombing during the Second World War. Its east wing survives and Holland Park, its former grounds, is now used for multiple purposes. The location was handy for central London, more so than Hampton Court Palace, which William had begun to favour. William and Mary moved into Kensington Palace on Christmas Eve, 1689. Mary, tall and in good health, had no difficulty in travelling on foot between Whitehall and Kensington, a distance of around two and a half miles, and she regularly did so, as recorded in her diaries.

A private avenue was eventually constructed to make it easier for the royal couple to travel between the two palaces. It was lined with around 300 glass lamps for illumination at night, a luxury unavailable to the rest of London's residents. The ever-reliable Sir Christopher Wren, who had been given the task of expanding 'Nottingham House' into a royal palace, was instructed to build a shed for storage of the lamps, which continued to be used during the reigns of later monarchs.

In the summer of 1690, Mary wrote to her husband, expressing great excitement at the prospect of seeing him on his return from Ireland and asking for his opinion as to whether he would like to move into Kensington Palace straight away, even though his apartments still smelled of paint and her own were not yet ready. Nevertheless, she says she will 'be very willing to suffer any inconvenience for the sake of your dear company'. There was still scaffolding up on the outside of the building. Though William's letters to Mary from this period have not survived, hers suggest that he regularly complained about the slow progress on the building work at both this palace and Hampton Court. We also get the impression that he did not write to her nearly as often as she wrote to him.

Wren was economical in his design for the palace: rather than demolishing and rebuilding, he simply added an extra wing or 'pavilion' at each corner of the original building, with the King's and Queen's apartments diametrically opposite one another, resulting in the rather understated structure that can be seen today. Although credited to Wren and his assistant Hawksmoor, it has been suggested that Jacob Roman, may have had a hand in the design, since William was in the habit of actively discussing his building plans with his team wherever in Europe he happened to be at the time – in Roman's case, back home in the Netherlands. Still an official residence of several members of the royal family, Kensington Palace is partly open to the public and is managed by 'Historic Royal Palaces', an organisation that also has responsibility for the upkeep of Hampton Court Palace, the Banqueting House in Whitehall, and several other important buildings.

A fire in 1691 did considerable damage to one section of the building, enabling Wren to rebuild the 'King's Staircase' in marble to make it worthy of William, at the same time setting it apart from the humbler staircase in the Queen's apartments. A guard chamber was also constructed at this time. The new monarchs both had a say in the design of their respective apartments, and the Queen's Gallery, one of the early additions, was lavishly furnished and decorated with exotic artefacts and hangings from around the world. Mary was particularly fond of oriental porcelain, a collection of which can still be seen. Although this was her private space, the apartments included a panelled dining room where she and her husband could eat together. The bed that is now displayed in the Queen's Bedroom is the very one in which Mary's stepmother, Mary of Modena, had given birth to Mary's half-brother, James, Prince of Wales, in 1688. Grinling Gibbons was again called into service to produce the carved mirrors that can be seen in the Queen's apartments.

Since Mary had a supervisory role in the building project, with William spending so much of his time abroad on campaign (but not forgetting to request progress reports), it is not surprising that her personal apartments at the palace were begun before her husband's. The staircase in the first of the corner pavilions was already being altered in 1692, as she relayed opinions and instructions between her husband and the architects, but her own apartments are preserved much as she left them.

Other VIPs resided within the palace. As they did at Het Loo, William's favourites occupied private apartments. Both Bentinck and Van Keppel, who was beginning to supplant him in the king's favour, had their own spaces, close to the king's private quarters. Even while Mary lived, William was generously paying for the bill for the furniture in Van Keppel's rooms. In 1699, when Bentinck resigned from his state duties, his apartments were given over to Van Keppel, who had since been raised to the peerage as Earl of Albemarle. Shortly afterwards,

Bentinck gave up his role as administrator of the royal residences to the Earl of Ranelagh.

The King's Gallery was not completed until 1695 and was extensively remodelled by one of William's successors, King George I, as a display area for the royal picture collection, but William used it for other purposes too. His secretary, Huygens, recounted how he had walked there with William and had been requested to improve the way the pictures were displayed against their background of patterned green velvet. Now decorated in red and gold, with wall paintings by William Kent, an architect favoured by George II and Queen Caroline, it still features Van Dyck's portrait of *Charles I at the Hunt*. William also had a 'cabinet', a smaller room for the display of paintings, in which he kept works by Holbein and Van Dyck, among others. The gallery has been reorganised to such an extent that it is now mostly impossible to say which of those held there during William's reign are still on show today.

The fireplace dates from William's reign and the dial that can still be seen above it – accompanied by a map that shows Britain and France as being the same size – was connected to a weather vane on the palace roof, which could be used to check wind direction when planning naval campaigns. William was also an aficionado of the barometer, and the Royal Collection holds several barometers and clocks made for him by the innovator Daniel Quare, who built the first portable barometer in 1695. In this room the king did much of his military planning, and later in life would play wargames with his nephew and namesake, the young Duke of Gloucester, the great future hope of the country's Protestants.

The Duke of Gloucester seems to have had a good relationship with his aunt and uncle, even after the estrangement between Mary and her sister Anne. He was allowed to visit them independently, and the fact that his own nursery was in the Kensington district made this more feasible. The child was in poor health throughout his life, and the location had been selected because it was thought that the cleaner air would benefit him. He was only five years old when Mary died, and two years later William would personally bestow on him the Order of the Garter. William subsequently threw a lavish birthday party for the young duke, at which his parents were able to watch him walking in procession to St George's Hall with the other knights.

Kensington Gardens, now a 265-acre royal park open to the general public, began life as part of the palace's private gardens. There was little or no development in the surrounding area until a century later. Flowing through it is the 'Long Water', ending in the Serpentine, an artificially created lake. This would have been unknown to William and Mary; it was introduced thirty years later on the orders of Queen Caroline, wife of George II.

Most of the public art in and around Kensington Gardens dates from the nineteenth and twentieth centuries, and it was the Victorian era that made the greatest impact on this landscape. A statue of William that stands outside the palace was cast in Germany and given to King Edward VII of the United Kingdom by his unloved relation, Kaiser Wilhelm II, in 1907. William, looking very upright and haughty, is again without his horse, and wears contemporary dress, looking to modern eyes rather like Captain Hook's pantomime costume. A very similar statue by the same designer, Heinrich Baucke, once stood outside the Berlin Palace in Germany. This was lost when the palace was largely destroyed during the Second World War.

As at Het Loo, the palace possessed an orangery, but the building that now stands was designed after William's death by Nicholas Hawksmoor for his successor Anne. However, the carvings by Grinling Gibbons that are also to be seen in the Orangery can be dated to the reign of William and Mary, since Gibbons did not carve in wood after 1700. Gibbons left coloured drawings of some of his work in the queen's apartments, suggesting they originally had gilding that has worn off with time.

Like her sister, Anne would die at Kensington Palace. Successive rulers did not spend as much time at the palace, but a succession of minor royals occupied apartments there, including Princess Victoria before her accession to the throne in 1837. Several of the apartments and outbuildings continue to be occupied by junior members of the British royal family. Until 2022, it was the official residence of the Duke and Duchess of Cambridge, who moved to a home in Windsor after being created Prince and Princess of Wales. The King's and Queen's apartments have been open to the public since 1899.

The Diana Memorial Playground was added to the park in 2000. It is very popular with children and is free to enter; consequently, there is a restriction on the numbers admitted at any one time. The playground was designed with accessibility in mind, and its presence demonstrates once again how Britain's royal residences are not frozen in time, but can develop and change through the decades. In July 2021, a statue of Diana, Princess of Wales, was unveiled in the Sunken Garden; it was commissioned by the princess's two sons, William and Harry.

William III's return from fighting in mainland Europe, late in 1692, was short-lived. His welcome presence was marked by thanksgiving dinners and the royal couple paraded through London. In February 1693, one Robert Young was tried for his role in the fabrication of the 'Flowerpot Plot', which had briefly caused havoc in the previous year, during William's absence, by throwing suspicion on such names as the Earl of Marlborough, the former Archbishop Sancroft, and Thomas Sprat, Bishop of Rochester. Young got off lightly with a turn in the pillory[6]. In March, certain abuses by William's Irish government came to light, and there was increasing demand for action to be taken against Catholics. William's way of dealing with the problem was to head back to mainland Europe, and he arrived in The Hague at the beginning of April.

In July 1693, at the Battle of Landen (also called the Battle of Neerwinden), William was defeated by the French, who received reinforcements at a critical moment. William himself had three narrow escapes when bullets tore through his clothing and hair, but once again most of his army escaped with their lives, a notable exception being his Dutch cousin, Count Solms. Henry Sidney, another of the 'Immortal Seven', who would soon be created Earl of Romney, was appointed to a senior military position in Solms' place. Despite several military

---

6. The pillory differs from the "stocks" in that the victim's head and hands are enclosed in the framework, rather than the feet.

setbacks during the campaigning season, William simply would not lie down and accept defeat. He was back beside his wife at Kensington Palace, all in one piece, on 30 October.

At the end of the year, William took it upon himself to try to build bridges with the Pope. He wrote to Innocent, claiming that he had never planned to make himself King of England, but that James II's autocratic conduct had led to his downfall, whilst William had tried his best to persuade his father-in-law to save himself from the wrath of his people. He even claimed that he was prepared to renounce the throne and leave it to James's male heir, if only France's aggression could be stemmed.

Prince Louis of Baden visited the king and queen at around the same time, and was officially entertained, in great style, at Whitehall Palace, remaining in the country for about six weeks. It was during this period that the royal couple's Secretary of State, the Earl of Shrewsbury, was raised to a dukedom, in spite of repeated accusations of treason against him. The new duke was known to have been brought up a Catholic and was believed to be in regular contact with the former King James. Soon he would be quietly allowed to retire on health grounds.

Having closed down the English Parliament in April 1694, as he was about to depart for Holland on yet another military expedition, rough weather prevented William sailing from Gravesend or Harwich, and consequently he was able to celebrate Mary's thirty-second birthday with her in London. Henry Purcell, organist of both Westminster Abbey and the Chapel Royal at St James's, had composed another birthday piece for her, as had become his annual habit. This final ode in the series, with words by Mary's great admirer, the Poet Laureate Nahum Tate, was titled 'Come, Ye Sons of Art'. William and Mary spent a night together in Canterbury before he finally embarked on 5 May at Margate.

William's enlarged fleet was enjoying some success at last: the port of Dieppe was bombarded, followed by Le Havre. William's troops crossed the River Scheldt and took back the town of Huy, on the River Meuse in present-day Belgium. Little else was achieved before his return. In November, he landed in Kent and met Mary at Rochester, and they travelled together to their home at Kensington Palace. That same month, John Tillotson, the Archbishop of Canterbury whom Mary had favoured, died in his mid-sixties. Both Mary and William felt the loss keenly, having valued his support and advice since his appointment. His replacement, Thomas Tenison, would soon have an even sadder duty to perform for the queen.

Economic and financial revolution
Despite the vicissitudes of Dutch politics, that country had enjoyed enormous prosperity during its so-called Golden Age. In most European countries, a family's wealth was demonstrated by the amount of land they owned. Because the wealth of the Netherlands originated from trade rather than agriculture, people's most valuable possessions were their house and its contents. Hence the explosion of 'Golden Age' culture, with most households owning items like paintings and musical instruments that would have been considered a luxury by the equivalent classes in Britain, and workshops being set up by artists and craftsmen to fulfil the demand for such items. William and Mary were great patrons of the visual arts in particular.

The thrones of England and Scotland represented an additional opportunity for the House of Orange to extend its property portfolio as well as its status on the international stage. A financial revolution had taken place in the Netherlands, closely linked with seafaring and trading successes. The Dutch East India Company, founded in 1602 by a merger of leading Dutch merchant companies, was thriving under government control. They took their lead from their British equivalent, a trading cartel that enjoyed a monopoly on the goods under their country's control.

The Dutch cornered the market in spices such as nutmeg, mace, and cloves, setting up and maintaining trading posts in Indonesia, taking much of their business from the Portuguese merchants who had preceded them in India, China and Japan. By the time William came of age, the company owned nearly 200 ships, had 50,000 employees, and ran its own 10,000-strong private army. Although war in Europe gradually enabled other countries to make inroads into Dutch territory, a sophisticated economic system had developed to take advantage of their gains, and the 'Wisselbank' (the 'Exchange Bank') of Amsterdam would be at the forefront of the changes that led gradually to the establishment of the Bank of England in 1694. The Bank of Scotland would follow a year later.

William and Mary's accession to the three thrones of Britain would help to popularise the new financial institutions, with a resultant boost for the economy of the home countries. The existence of banks and insurance companies, in particular, would be critical to the industrial revolution of the eighteenth century. Lloyd's of London came into existence during the brief reign of James II, taking its name from Lloyd's coffee house where it began, and in 1691 it relocated to Lombard Street, the traditional banking district, close to the future headquarters of the Bank of England.

Progress was helped along by the rebuilding of much of the City of London following the Great Fire of 1666. The medieval St Paul's Cathedral had been destroyed, and work began in 1675 on a breathtaking new design by the up-and-coming Christopher Wren, who had recently been knighted by King Charles II. Craftsmen from all over Europe flocked to work on the edifice, which took nearly thirty years to complete and opened in 1697, with William III on the throne of England and Mary already dead. It was not declared officially complete until 1711.

In addition to St Paul's and the 51 other London churches rebuilt by Wren, Hawksmoor and their team, Wren was responsible for The Monument, a 62-metre column marking the spot where the Great Fire was believed to have started; it was completed in 1677, the year of William and Mary's marriage. His Temple Bar Gate, a replacement for the old Temple Bar which represented the official entrance to the City of London, was removed in the nineteenth century because it interfered with traffic. After spending over a century on a private estate in Hertfordshire, it was returned to the capital in 2004 and now stands in Paternoster Square near St Paul's. Constructed of Portland stone, it is adorned with statues of Charles II, his father and his royal grandparents, in celebration of the restoration of the monarchy, and was already in place before Mary left for the Netherlands to marry William. Thus a new London was already taking shape by the time of their accession.

The Custom House, which stood on the north bank of the Thames at 'Sugar Quay' near the Tower of London, dated from the previous century; the name of the quay referred to the cane sugar that was being imported from the Caribbean. The replacement building designed by Wren and opened in 1671 was later replaced again and the site ceased to be used for collecting import duty in the nineteenth century. A reminder of its original purpose is the modern building owned by a major sugar manufacturer. A new Custom House was built a little further up the river, constructed during the trading boom of the early nineteenth century, part of which survives and is due to be converted for alternative use.

The original Royal Exchange, a financial trading centre based on the 'bourse' at Antwerp, had been founded in the 1560s, and its destruction in the Great Fire led to traders seeking an alternative meeting-place. Jonathan's coffee house in Exchange Alley, off Lombard Street, London, would be the birthplace of the Stock Exchange in 1698. A new Royal Exchange building was opened in 1669, but the present building – which no longer has a key role in Britain's financial system – is early Victorian in date. Fortnum & Mason, one of the country's oldest department stores, founded as a grocery only five years after William's death, appropriately has a branch at the Royal Exchange now.

The drinking of tea and coffee was becoming fashionable. Tea had been widely available in the British Isles for only about thirty years, popularised by Charles II's queen, Catherine of Braganza; its wider availability was largely thanks to the efforts of the British and Dutch East India Companies. Along with the drinking of such beverages came a growing interest in the manufacture of china, an industry that had grown in Holland since the acquisition of a Portuguese trading ship loaded with porcelain from the Far East in 1602. The Elers brothers were Dutch silversmiths and potters who moved from London to Staffordshire around 1690 to take advantage of the availability of good-quality local clay and coal to fire the kilns.

The making of pottery had been commonplace in the district we now know as Stoke-on-Trent for several centuries, but it was mostly coarseware for domestic use by local people. The Elers brothers helped develop new methods of glazing, and used a cast to produce teapots in imitation of the popular Chinese red pottery. By the end of the century, master potters like the Wedgwood family would be in the process of transforming 'the Potteries' into a thriving industrial centre. Pewter, long the favoured medium for drinking vessels, soon began to go out of fashion.

The development of the trade in ceramics contributed to the prosperity of the nearest major port, Liverpool, which thrived on imports of tobacco and sugar from the Americas. In 1673 a new Town Hall was built, standing on pillars over the Exchange, and in the fifty years after Mary's death, Liverpool's population quadrupled. Sadly, much of the city's growth was funded by the slave trade, as reflected by the exhibits at the International Slavery Museum at the Royal Albert Dock. In 1699, before the first of today's commercial docks was even planned, the *Liverpool Merchant* took 220 enslaved Africans to Barbados in the West Indies, and this was only the beginning.

Coffee houses like Jonathan's had begun to spread across cities like Oxford, London, and Dublin, thanks to familiarity with the culture of the Middle East and the growing availability of the drink in Europe. A French gentleman, visiting long before his country's revolution, called the coffee houses the 'seats of English liberty'[7], largely because newspapers were available for public consumption. These 'penny universities' had become a feature of daily life by the time William and Mary came to the throne. Their existence was a boon for cultural figures such as John Dryden, who favoured Will's coffee house in Bow Street. (Dryden's fellow satirists Jonathan Swift and Richard Steele were less complimentary about Will's.) The invitation to intellectuals to congregate in such places had its drawbacks; several of the regulars at Jonathan's were implicated in one of many plots to assassinate William.

'Mrs White's Chocolate Club', founded in 1693 in Mayfair by an Italian entrepreneur, developed into the present-day White's (now

---

7. Abbé Prévost, *Séjour en Angleterre*.

located in St James's Street), a men-only club whose members include several royals and former prime ministers. White's sold theatre tickets and later became a popular gathering-place for hardened gamblers and Tory supporters. The Kit-Cat Club, founded about 1696, supported the Whig party and had several meeting-places, including the Fountain Tavern, which stood on the site in the Strand now occupied by the exclusive restaurant Simpson's-in-the-Strand. Early members of the latter included John Vanbrugh, the playwright William Congreve (1670–1729), and the future prime minister, Robert Walpole (1676–1745).

Less salubrious was the growing fashion for gin, which had followed William and Mary from Holland. Gin, or 'Jenever', was naturally preferred to brandy, which was more expensive and its supply restricted because it had to be imported from France, a country with which England was frequently at war. Often adulterated with turpentine, cheap gin was manufactured at home and became increasingly popular from the 1690s onwards, especially with the poorer classes. Gin-shops had become ubiquitous by the 1720s, when Parliament began passing legislation to reduce consumption because of a perceived increase in drunkenness and crime.

Satire, arising out of political rivalry, was already becoming commonplace in Europe, but newspapers as we know them today were still in the process of development. In the Netherlands, the "coranto", printed in a columnar format, had been in existence since the 1650s and was modelled on earlier German newspapers. It was in these early mass media outlets that printed advertising began, developing from simple 'lost and found' notices by pioneers like Abraham Verhoeven (1575–1652), an Antwerp publisher who gave notice of his own new releases in early news-sheets printed on his press. By the end of the century the practice of drinking imported non-alcoholic beverages had spread to other countries and it soon crossed the Atlantic to the British colonies. In 1690 a London merchant, Samuel Price, issued a broadsheet claiming that the drinking of coffee, tea and chocolate carried health benefits and advocated that they be purchased for consumption at home, not merely as an aid to conversation in clubs and coffee houses. These commodities could of course be purchased from Price's premises in Newgate Street.

In Scotland, the *Mercurius Caledonius* hit the streets in 1660, whilst in England, the *Oxford Gazette*, later renamed the *London Gazette*, first appeared in 1665, in a pamphlet format. *The Daily Courant*, which began publication in 1702 – the year of William's death – with a *female* editor, at first published only overseas news, financed by advertisements, and was the first daily paper printed in London. An *Edinburgh Gazette* was launched in 1699 and an *Edinburgh Courant* followed in 1705. In Ireland, news-sheets had been in existence since the 1640s, but the first proper newspaper is said to be *The News-Letter*, first printed in Dublin in 1685 on behalf of the 'Leather Bottle' tavern, presumably for the perusal of customers.

Scotland and Ireland had their own senior educational institutions. Trinity College, Dublin, founded under King James VI (later King of England also) in 1592, was the alma mater of Jonathan Swift. Swift had moved to London during the political turmoil of 1688, but returned there to take up a church appointment (after having unsuccessfully petitioned King William for something better) and would eventually take up the post in Dublin for which he is best-known. In Scotland, there were five ancient universities, and a Chair of Mathematics was established at Glasgow in 1691. Aberdeen already possessed a Chair of Medicine that was one of the oldest in the world. Scottish universities were open to 'Dissenters', and it would become common for English youths from Nonconformist families to travel north of the border to complete their education, equipping them to play a full role in commerce and industry, as well as leading the movements towards social change. Meanwhile, the Merchant Company of Edinburgh established 'hospital schools' for boys and girls, and Perth Academy was officially founded in 1696.

These developments were key to an intellectual revolution that had played its part in William and Mary's accession and would continue to influence every aspect of British life during the next century. Thanks to the stability offered, albeit briefly, by the reign of the new constitutional monarchs, the country was given the breathing-space necessary to thrive by embracing progress.

Chapter 5

King William the Widower

In December 1694 Mary fell ill. Anticipating death, she went through her private papers methodically, reportedly in the course of a single evening, burning anything that might turn out to be an embarrassment and preserving the rest in neat order. These include the diaries and memoirs that give us valuable insights into her personality. Within a few days she had been diagnosed with smallpox, the killer disease that had already taken several members of her family, and the doctors could do little for her. Having never suffered the disease in her youth, she would have been aware that she was at risk from the epidemic that was raging in London at the time.

Although the sisters had fallen out over Anne's friendship with John and Sarah Churchill, Anne was desperate to see Mary during her last illness, but was kept away from the sick room because she was once again pregnant. As was so often the case with Anne, the pregnancy ended in a miscarriage, about a month later. Within a year, she would be pregnant again, for the twelfth time.

Mary died on 28 December, aged 32, at Kensington Palace, attended by her doting husband, who had arranged for a truckle bed to be moved into her chamber in order to be close to her; he knew there was little hope of recovery. When a deputation from Parliament arrived a few days later, he acknowledged them politely, but briefly, thanking them for recognising 'our great loss'. Mary is said to have requested him, on her deathbed, to give up his mistress Elizabeth Villiers. Though he did so, the association had made Elizabeth a wealthy woman, as William granted her the Irish estates of James II, which should have been inherited by Anne. Later she married the Earl of Orkney, apparently happily.

Mary's funeral, which took place nearly four months after her death, was one of the most lavish ever recorded up to that time, costing a massive £50,000. William disliked ceremony and ritual, but his personal wishes could not override those of his subjects, and perhaps he too felt that Mary deserved every possible tribute. This was the first public funeral of a reigning monarch since 1625, and the opportunity was taken to revive older traditions, with an emphasis on the permanence of the monarchy as represented by both the English Mary and the incomer William.

Music for the service was written by Henry Purcell, who was around the same age as the late queen. Less than year later he, too, was dead, probably of pneumonia, and the *Funeral Sentences* and *Music for the Funeral of Queen Mary* that he had written for the royal occasion were performed again at his own funeral. The 'funeral sentences', added to by the youthful William Croft for the burial service, have been performed again at many royal funerals, including that of Queen Elizabeth II in 2022.

Numerous poems and other written tributes to Mary were produced by contemporary authors, such as an obsequious *Essay on the Memory of the Late Queen*, written by Gilbert Burnet, by now one of King William's trusted advisors. Joseph Addison, future co-founder of *The Spectator*, then only 24, ventured to address *A Poem to His Majesty*, in which he praised William's military exploits but paused to comment on the great loss of 'Maria' and how British hearts are wounded and 'tears burst out unbidden' at the sound of the late queen's name. Addison received a substantial financial reward and political advancement, and held a pension from William until the king's death; the writer would himself die at the early age of 47 and be buried, like Queen Mary, in Westminster Abbey.

William, by all accounts, was distraught at the loss of his wife, who had proved such a useful deputy as well as an emotional support in difficult times. During her final illness, he had written to a close confidant: 'You can imagine what a state I am in, loving her as I do.' In retrospect, he told Burnet that she had not a single fault. In an uncharacteristically sentimental mood, he tenderly preserved her wedding ring, and for the rest of his life he wore a mourning bracelet holding a lock of her hair. For several weeks after her death, he declined to involve himself in the administration of the realm, turning away courtiers who arrived with official papers needing his signature. Eventually his friend Bentinck (who knew what it was to lose a wife, Anne Villiers having died six years earlier) removed the king from the atmosphere of solemn mourning at Kensington Palace and took William to stay with him at Richmond.

The queen's embalmed body, brought from Kensington Palace to Whitehall, lay in state for five hours each day over a three-month period at the Banqueting House, which was approached by those wishing to pay their respects along corridors hung with black. The catafalque was guarded by men-at-arms, and the queen lay on a bed of purple and gold, in a coffin draped with an embroidered canopy, with her crown and the other symbols of monarchy arranged at the head and feet. Her ladies in waiting worked in half-hour shifts to stand sentinel at each corner. During the last two weeks, the ordinary public were allowed in, and queued in freezing weather to gain admission. The coffin was railed off so that no one could approach within five feet. The Union flag as it then stood (representing the union of the crowns of England and Scotland) was prominently featured. The flags of Ireland and France were also on display. The joint coat of arms that had been devised for the couple on their accession was seen for the last time. One of those who reported back on the scene was Celia Fiennes, the daughter of a politician and granddaughter of a viscount; Fiennes left a famous memoir of her travels through England on horseback.

The official mourners were mostly female. Elizabeth Seymour, Duchess of Somerset, the highest-ranking peeress, was designated chief mourner, since Anne was still recovering from her miscarriage and not well enough to fulfil the role. The duchess was a close friend of Anne's, and had taken the princess's side against William and Mary, when they quarrelled over Anne's closeness to John and Sarah Churchill. Now Anne was full of regrets for the time spent at loggerheads with her sister.

The funeral procession moved from the Banqueting House to Westminster Abbey along a black-trimmed walkway designed by Sir Christopher Wren to prevent the rabble from joining in. The procession included hundreds of people, mostly officials and people of high rank, and is thought to have lasted several hours. Three hundred women, mostly chosen for their relationship to men who had served the queen in the army and navy, walked at the head of the procession. Further back came the members of Parliament, dressed in black, and the House of Lords, in their traditional scarlet robes, an important statement showing their continued support for the surviving monarch. For the time, it was the largest funeral procession ever held for an English monarch.

A set of contemporary prints made in the same year record the occasion in some detail. Now held in the London Metropolitan Archives[1], the six pictures form a panorama, and were executed by Romeyn De Hooghe and published by the Dutch printer Pieter Persoy, presumably with the Netherlands market in mind as well as the British. Not having been able to see for themselves, most of the Dutch population would have been curious about the pageantry associated with a royal funeral in London, as well as wanting to show their respects to their popular princess.

Mary was buried at the Abbey, with the Archbishop of Canterbury, Thomas Tenison, officiating. The praise for the dead queen that naturally featured in his sermon was tempered by a suggestion that her death was a punishment for the nation's wrongdoing. He ensured he could not be thought to be referring to William, whom he also praised. The queen's wax effigy was left on display following the burial. Mary is one of several queens laid to rest in the Henry VII Lady Chapel, where her remains still lie in a vault, close to those of her mother, Anne Hyde. The magnificent tomb that was designed and planned was never built, and the resting place of William and Mary is now marked only by an engraved stone slab.

Clergymen throughout the land took the opportunity to preach sermons praising Mary. William Fleetwood, the rector of the London

---

1. London Picture Archive, record 34923.

church of St Austin and later a bishop, said: 'She took away the scandal and reproach that long had lain upon the court, the want of good example in a prince,' adding that she 'so behaved herself as best becomes a humble supplicant before the throne of his adorable all-powerful majesty' – and he was not referring to William either. Mary's piety had indeed been notable from her youth. William Wake, another London rector and a future Archbishop of Canterbury, regretted that she had not lived longer, pointing out how 'that firmness of constitution which she enjoyed, accompanied with a yet early and vigorous youth, seemed to promise us that we should be many years blessed under the influence both of her authority and of her example.'

Mary's father, who was still alive in exile in France, did not go into mourning for his daughter, and even forbade his followers to do so. He considered her a traitor who had 'sinned against the commonest and most indispensable law of nature…' – in obeying her husband, she had failed to obey her father. At his small court in Saint-Germain, she was still referred to as 'the Princess of Orange' rather than Queen of England and Scotland.

There was no need for an official transfer of power, since William and Mary had, at least nominally, been joint monarchs, and William remained on the throne. In her time of need, Mary had valued the Earl of Nottingham's support so much that she had stood godmother to one of his children the year before her death. William did not have as high an opinion of him but prized his honesty. Still a newcomer to British politics, he favoured the Whigs and Nottingham, a Tory, had eventually been ousted, a move that had upset Mary greatly, causing her to withdraw somewhat from her involvement in political matters.

Those who had anticipated rebellion following her death had overestimated the strength of Jacobite feeling. In recent years, Mary had come to inspire the loyalty of her subjects, and William profited indirectly. Being seen to grieve so intensely, he had obtained public sympathy at a critical moment. Without Mary to act as a deputy when he was out of the country, he appointed a group of 'Lords Justices' in place of a regent. These included the Archbishop of Canterbury and several members of Mary's former Council of Nine.

From his base in France, the former King James wasted little time in attempting to take advantage of the English people's supposed dislike of William. Following the 'Lancashire Plot' scare of 1694 (which turned out to be an invention), an assassination attempt was planned by James's supporters, over a year after the funeral; there would have been no use in assassinating the Dutchman while Mary lived and could potentially rule alone. The plotters' strategy was never put into action, after information had been leaked to the Earl of Portland a day or two earlier than the planned date in February 1696. James, who had amassed a fleet at Calais, in readiness for his own return, was forced to abandon his opportunistic attempt at a comeback.

Nine men involved in the conspiracy were subsequently arrested and executed, ranging in rank from the baronet Sir John Fenwick, the lawyer Sir William Parkyns and the Scottish army officer Sir George Barclay, to several commoners; a few others escaped death but died while serving long prison sentences. A notable name among those condemned to death was Ambrose Rookwood, a great-grandson of his namesake who had been executed for his part in the Gunpowder Plot ninety years earlier.

Following Mary's death, William became reconciled with his sister-in-law Anne, though their relationship remained distant, and he allowed her to visit him at Kensington Palace to offer her condolences. She received privileges previously denied her, such as apartments at St James's Palace, and was even given the jewels that had belonged to Mary. The Act of Settlement named her as next in line for the throne in these circumstances. It was acknowledged that she would take precedence in the order of succession over any children William might have by a second wife, in the unlikely event that he remarried. This was something that he never seriously considered. Remarriage might have proved unpopular, unless he could have found an English princess who would make an acceptable replacement – and there wasn't one.

William had carried out large-scale rebuilding and alterations to Hampton Court Palace in the early years of his reign, and these continued until Mary's death in 1694. In those early years, it was mostly with Mary that Wren dealt. Wren's son recalled that his father often had to report progress to the queen while William was away, and that she went to the palace in person to inspect the work, in order to be able to offer William an update. Although the memories of his late wife must have been painful to him, they were even stronger at Kensington, and William continued to prefer Hampton Court as a residence. Following her death, he withdrew more and more to the palace outside London, where access to the king was strictly controlled.

Hampton Court Palace

Hampton Court Palace was already an imposing building, more than 150 years old, when William and Mary arrived in Britain as the country's new monarchs. Originally built in the grand Tudor style by Cardinal Wolsey, and much expanded after it came into the hands of Wolsey's master, King Henry VIII, it is immediately recognisable by its magnificent gatehouse. Wolsey built the palace at a total cost of 200,000 crowns (around £50,000), which has an estimated value of around £25 million today. He gifted it to the king in 1528, fearing for his future after his failure to obtain Henry's divorce from Catherine of Aragon. Henry immediately began to expand it, enabling the completed building to host some thousand courtiers and support staff.

The gatehouse is not, however, quite as William would first have seen it, having been reduced in height by nineteenth-century alterations. Displayed at either side of the towers that flank the gatehouse, and elsewhere within the palace, are roundels containing the sculpted faces of classical figures, once thought to be those of Roman emperors but now believed to include Alexander the Great and other classical heroes. These are attributed to the Italian Renaissance sculptor Giovanni da Maiano, and were extensively restored in 2011. All have been subject to relocation, some several times, over the centuries. Two are believed to have been brought to Hampton Court from the Holbein Gate at Whitehall when it was demolished in 1759.

After entering through the Great Gatehouse, visitors arrive in the Base Court, where guest accommodation was provided in centuries past. The royal family had a more protected position in an inner courtyard, the 'Clock Court', accessed by means of another gateway only slightly less grand than the main entrance and comparable in style. The astronomical clock that can be seen in what is sometimes called 'Ann Boleyn's gateway' (luxurious apartments were planned for the upper floor, which the unfortunate queen was never to enjoy) was constructed in 1540, and shows matters of interest such as the date and time of day, the phases of the moon, and the time of high water at London Bridge – a useful detail since travelling into London meant taking a barge along the Thames. No doubt William found the plethora of information as fascinating as his sixteenth-century predecessors had.

The comparatively insignificant-looking Tiltyard Tower is the only one now standing of the five towers that were present in Henry VIII's lifetime. However, in 2015, the foundations of one of the vanished towers were discovered by archaeologists, helping to throw light on the original layout of the tiltyard, a space used for jousting. The function of the towers was to provide entertainment and refreshment for guests. Later, they were used only for storage, one even coming into temporary use as a pigeon-loft.

By the 1680s, many important historical events had taken place at Hampton Court: the birth of the future King Edward VI, the death of his mother, Jane Seymour, and the arrest of one of Henry's later wives, Catherine Howard. A conference was held here by King James VI of Scotland when he arrived to take up the throne of England as James I, and it was also here that some of Shakespeare's plays, including *Macbeth*, are thought to have been premièred; in fact, the Great Hall is the only surviving 'theatre' where Shakespeare's work is known to have been performed during the author's lifetime. King Charles I was held prisoner at the palace, and his son, Charles II, created a scenic canal, now called the 'Long Water' (not to be confused with the water feature of the same name in Kensington Gardens), in honour of his new bride, Catherine of Braganza.

Shortly after their installation on the British thrones, William and Mary began a redesign and rebuild of the Tudor palace. The plan was to demolish the whole structure, and Christopher Wren's design was initially based around a domed building, but ideas were gradually modified until a plan that incorporated much of Henry VIII's palace was arrived at. There was a setback almost as soon as construction began, when a wall collapsed, bringing down the ceiling and killing several members of the workforce. Similar things were happening at Kensington Palace because of the pressure on the team of architects and builders to finish the job quickly, which explains the use of bricks rather than stone. The need for a construction force to work in two places at once did not help.

The appearance of Wren's new buildings was unmistakably influenced by the Palace of Versailles, but the use of pink bricks with Portland stone features for contrast distinguishes the Fountain Court as something specific to Hampton Court. Although Henry VIII's private apartments were lost in the reconstruction, the Great Hall was preserved, with new apartments for the king and queen overlooking the gardens they both loved. Wren's groundbreaking design included roof trusses that made use of iron rods to suspend the floors of the new apartments he was creating for the royal couple.

The gardens at Hampton Court were the largest anywhere in England, and William and Mary were in total control of their planning. The French garden designer, André Mollet, who had been in the service of William's grandfather in Holland and had worked at Hoonselardijk, was employed by Charles II on the construction of the Long Water, but Mollet had died long before William and Mary were married. It was Daniel Marot who designed the spectacular Great Fountain Garden, located at the East Front of the new palace. Marot had been summoned to England by Mary shortly before her death, and stayed for several years. Marot planted two avenues of oak trees, and installed thirteen fountains, most of which were removed by Queen Anne. Not everyone was fond of the Dutch style; an English critic of Anne's reign complained about the gardens 'being stuffed too thick with Box, a fashion brought over out of Holland...'[2] The remaining fountain is now the central focus of the garden, surrounded by intricate flower beds, comparable with those of William and Mary's reign.

On first taking up residence at Hampton Court, Mary had remarked on its clean air, but had complained of the lack of 'conveniences'. In the new build, the queen's private apartments, which she would never have time to enjoy fully, overlooked the Fountain Garden. William's overlooked the Privy Garden, devoted to his particular tastes and located on the south side of the palace. Disappointed with the view, he ordered the level of the garden to be lowered so that he could see the river. This continued to be his private haven until his sudden death in 1702, at which time the gardeners made a lengthy inventory of their work, apparently in order to ensure they were paid. Thus it has been possible to reconstruct the garden as it looked at that time.

Jean Tijou, another Huguenot refugee, was employed to make the wrought-iron gates and railings there, doing similar work at Kensington Palace and St Paul's Cathedral. His work at Hampton Court included the golden screens that decorate the approach to the palace from the river, as well as the balustrade of the King's Staircase used by William to reach his private apartments. Tijou's son-in-law, Louis Laguerre, painted the Labours of Hercules in exterior window spaces on the new wing of the palace, once again referencing William's steadfastness and determination to overcome all obstacles that stood in his way.

No features of the Tudor gardens were retained, but a new garden was created in 2009 to mark the 500th anniversary of Henry VIII's accession. Its features included painted wooden figures of heraldic beasts, echoing the ten Tudor statues that flank the bridge leading into the Great Gatehouse. Known as 'The King's Beasts', they include a lion, representing England, a dragon representing the Tudors' Welsh ancestry,

---

2. Stephen Switzer, 1715.

and others representing family connections, including a unicorn and a panther, symbols of the Seymour family.

'Queen Mary II's Exoticks' is a collection of historic plants maintained at Hampton Court in recognition of the queen's taste in garden design. Though not grown from the original specimens, they are based on plants she is known to have nurtured here, collected by botanists from locations all over the world, including places as far afield as Africa, South America, and the Far East. Mary's plant collection was displayed in an area that had been occupied by fishponds during Henry VIII's tenure of the palace, which she had identified as the warmest section of the gardens. She employed a Dutch carpenter called Heindrik Floris to build her greenhouses, probably among the first ever constructed in Britain, fully equipped with furnaces and flues. Leonard Plukenet (1641–1706), a British botanist, was appointed by Mary to care for her collection, as well as for the thousand orange trees she acquired. The Pond Gardens, where Mary displayed her trees during the summer months, are now a popular feature of Hampton Court, preserved in the style of a Dutch sunken garden. Even Oxford University supplied Hampton Court with seeds from species held in its impressive physic garden. Queen Anne and her immediate successors continued to maintain Mary's exotic plants. During subsequent reigns, however, the collection went out of fashion and was gradually dispersed. The concept was revived by the palace's gardening team during the 1990s.

After Mary's death, William ordered the demolition of the greenhouses, and replaced them with a formal orangery, designed by the versatile Christopher Wren. Here he also installed a series of fifteenth-century paintings by Andrea Mantegna, *The Triumphs of Caesar*, which Charles I had purchased and Oliver Cromwell had obligingly preserved. William had a drawing room and dining room within the orangery building, which he used for entertaining friends. The 'Hampton Court Beauties', a series of paintings now displayed in the dining room, were commissioned by Mary from Sir Godfrey Kneller, court painter since the reign of King Charles II. Later, William would order the construction of a separate banqueting house where he could dine informally with his closest companions. The 'Little' Banqueting House, seating up to fifty guests, is now a popular wedding venue. Its ceiling was painted by Verrio and depicts Minerva with her entourage.

The eight portraits acquired for the orangery dining room represent the most beautiful and distinguished of the court ladies, including Lady Mary Bentinck, daughter of the Earl of Portland. At the time of the queen's death, Lady Mary was only in her teens but was already married to the Earl of Essex. It was the queen's mother, Anne Hyde, who had originally commissioned Sir Peter Lely to paint the 'Windsor Beauties', ladies of Charles II's court (including one or two royal mistresses), and the idea of commissioning this new set or portraits may be seen as both an imitation of and a rejection of the Windsor Beauties, which are now themselves also displayed at Hampton Court. Ironically, one of the virtuous Hampton Court ladies, Frances Whitmore, was the niece of Margaret, Lady Denham, one of the Windsor Beauties, who had been a mistress of James II and possibly also of Charles II.

The Maze that is now one of the most famous visitor attractions at the palace is believed to have been begun by William but was completed in the reign of Queen Anne, who appointed Henry Wise to the position of royal gardener. Wise also worked at Kensington Palace and, although he was English, was heavily influenced by Dutch and French garden design. It probably replaced an earlier, less substantial 'labyrinth' from the Tudor period. The Hampton Court maze is one of the best-known in the world and has spawned replicas on several continents. By modern standards its design is relatively simple, and it should be remembered that it was intended as an entertaining puzzle, not as a fearsome challenge.

The famous 'Great Vine' – whose grapes can now be purchased by the general public as souvenirs – had not yet been planted; this was a mid-eighteenth century arrival, planted on the orders of King George III who, though he enjoyed gardening, did not care to live at Hampton Court. It does, however, grow on the site of the earlier greenhouses, at least five of which are known to have existed since Mary originally installed them in the 1690s.

The interior decoration at all William and Mary's homes reflected the queen's love of flowers and plants. Not only were the popular 'still-life' paintings displayed on the walls, but Mary, a great lover of Delft pottery, had vases designed and made to order. Vases with spouts ('portable gardens' as they are described in inventories of her possessions), some in pyramidal shape, were widely copied. Her collection of Delft was on show in a pavilion called the 'Water Gallery', originally a landing-stage for boats, which overlooked the River Thames. In it were displayed many vases and flower pyramids, and it was admired by the writer Daniel Defoe, who worked for a time in William's secret service. Defoe called the Water Gallery 'the pleasantest little thing within doors that could possibly be made'. After Mary died, however, he would express his disapproval of her habit of collecting porcelain, which he felt had contributed to a craze for imported china that threatened British manufacturers. The building also contained a private bathing-house and a dairy. Celia Fiennes, visiting a year after Mary's death, mentioned Kneller's paintings in the Water Gallery and said that 'the Queen took great delight in it'. By 1699, however, the building had been demolished.

Nowadays the Tudor kitchens at Hampton Court are a popular attraction, sometimes the location for colourful re-enactments of sixteenth-century events such as Henry VIII's Christmas festivities. William and Mary's additions to the palace, however, included a different, and much smaller, kind of kitchen – the so-called 'Chocolate Kitchen', where William's chocolate maker, Solomon de le Faya, prepared the expensive drink for the royal couple.

Towards the end of William's reign, he commissioned William Talman, Wren's deputy at the Office of Works as well as his great rival, to redecorate the state apartments at Hampton Court. Talman's patron was the Earl of Portland, one of the king's most favoured courtiers, but the benefit from this lasted only as long as William lived, following which the irascible Talman went back to his former pastime of designing country houses for wealthy nobles. The work carried out at Hampton Court included the addition of tapestries based on a set of 'cartoons', original designs by Raphael that William had found in storage. Tapestries were an essential in any large house, not only for their artistic effect but for their insulating properties. John Vanderbank Senior, a Huguenot immigrant, was the foremost tapestry weaver in the country, and the owner of a workshop that supplied the royal family; many copies of the designs would be made there for wealthy patrons. Copies of the Raphael cartoons can still be seen in the specially-designed gallery at Hampton Court, the room where William was accustomed to host meetings of his Privy Council, but the originals are now on permanent loan to the Victoria & Albert Museum.

A fire in 1986 damaged the King's Apartments. It broke out in a 'grace and favour' apartment occupied by a general's elderly widow, who died as a result of the incident. The King's Audience Chamber, also called the Privy Chamber, was severely affected, though its oak panelling and the carvings above the fireplace escaped destruction. The staircase is adorned with Antonio Verrio's fancifully unhistorical mural, *Victory of Alexander over the Caesars*, and Verrio's signature can still be deciphered on the panel at the top of the stairs. The succession of rooms leading through the audience chamber and eventually to the inner sanctum – the King's Bedchamber – were designed to be more and more impressive as the visitor progressed through them in the expectation of seeing the monarch himself.

First came the Guard Chamber, hung with a collection of weapons and looked after by the Yeomen of the Guard. Those seeking an audience would have to pass a security check before entering the Presence Chamber. This contained the throne, which stood on a Turkish carpet under a great canopy. Even if the king was not present, everyone who passed the throne was expected to bow to it in accordance with royal protocol. The king's dining room came next, and William would sometimes dine in front of spectators. The opportunity to view this event was considered a major privilege for those present. Traditionally, the fact that the king was eating was symbolic of his good health and thus the stability of the monarchy.

In 1701, Godfrey Kneller completed an equestrian portrait of William, intended to be hung in the Presence Chamber, where it can still be seen, as a celebration of the king's achievement in bringing peace to Europe. It is accompanied by a quotation from Vergil, alluding to the coming of a Messiah-like figure to rule the world. William could perhaps have anticipated that he would not have long to enjoy it, but the vision of heavenly approval – in the shape of several Roman deities – may have been a comfort to a man who had spent most of his early life fighting, without any great result. His sister-in-law Anne expressed dislike of the painting; she may well have felt that William was getting intolerably conceited.

In the Audience Chamber, VIPs such as ambassadors would be greeted by the king and perhaps invited to look down from the windows into his Privy Garden. The Withdrawing Room next to it was a more private space, where the king might hold more intimate conversations with members of his government. The chosen few might have been allowed to attend a 'levée', the ceremonial dressing of the king as he arose from his night's sleep. Even in the reigns of more flamboyant kings, this occasion had borne little resemblance to the average person's morning preparations. William, in fact, preferred to put it off until later in the day when he was fully dressed, and to see his subjects in person in the Withdrawing Room, where those in favour, such as his friend Bentinck, might be found drinking chocolate, the king's favourite beverage, with him.

Beyond this is the King's Bedchamber, where he came each morning to get dressed in readiness for the duties of the day, and where he prepared for bed; his actual bedroom was a smaller adjoining room where only his personal servants could normally follow. This has a ceiling painting depicting Mars and Venus, again by Verrio. Beyond this point very few people would ever venture. It was the king's most private retreat, with direct access to the Queen's Apartments and also to his collection of art treasures. In 1700, perhaps anticipating that he would spend most of the rest of his life at Hampton Court, he had a number of works transferred here from his 'cabinet' at Kensington Palace. The royal family ceased to live at Hampton Court Palace in about 1760, following the death of King George II. The palace has been open to the public since 1881, during the reign of Queen Victoria, by which time no monarch had lived there for well over a century and many changes to the seventeeth-century buildings had taken place.

An early visitor to William and Mary's Hampton Court was Isaac Newton, who was introduced to King William by Christiaan Huygens at an audience in July 1689. William was interested in any advantages science and technology might be able to offer his government, and had long been aware of Huygens' abilities, whilst Newton, having published his *Principia Mathematica* two years earlier, was still forging a career.

The Royal Society, founded in 1660 by King Charles II as the 'Royal Society of London for Improving Natural Knowledge', had come into its own, and one of its leading lights was Robert Hooke (1635–1703). Hooke was a correspondent of the pioneering Dutch scientist van Leeuwenhoek, who had already been visited at home in Delft by William and Mary. Henry Oldenburg, the society's first secretary, was German by birth and had been imprisoned in error as a spy during the Anglo-Dutch Wars.

The seeds of the society had been sown by a group of scientists and natural philosophers at Gresham College, where public lectures were often held, and continue to be held to the present day. The Royal Society's founding members included Christopher Wren, who was of course well-known to both William and Mary, having already held high academic office when they were mere children. William Brouncker (1620–1684), the Royal Society's first president, had designed ships for the Royal Navy. His successor, Joseph Williamson, already an MP at Westminster, became a member of the Irish Parliament after the Battle of the Boyne, and was primarily an antiquarian rather than a scientist. Williamson continued as a diplomat throughout the reigns of William and Mary, but William disliked his condescending manner.

William's progress of 1695

A royal progress was an activity common to many British monarchs. As with national and international tours taken by today's royal family, it enabled them to meet their supporters, as well as being seen by the common people, at little or no expense to themselves; those eager to curry favour would offer the use of their own residence and provide accommodation and refreshment to the royal entourage for the duration of their visit. What had begun centuries earlier as a way of ensuring that the country's government met in the location most convenient to its ruler had become a form of ceremonial, since the king's administrators rarely needed to follow him around the country. Sometimes combined with the kind of triumphal entry that William had experienced on returning to the Hague in 1691, it was more like a cheap holiday for the monarch. In William's case, it in some ways represented a welcome respite from his official duties, especially after Mary's death.

Several years after being crowned king, William III had visited several parts of Britain but had still not been on a formal progress. The loss of the one person he could trust to do his bidding must not only have affected his appetite for war, it must have made him feel less like a British monarch; barely six years of permanent residence in a foreign country was hardly enough to overcome the habits instilled in him by his birth and upbringing.

In May 1695, less than six months after Mary's death, William arrived in Holland, to join the allies in another siege of Namur, which began in July, supported by English, Scottish and Dutch troops. Soon, the French began bombarding Brussels in revenge for the earlier attacks on St Malo and Dieppe, and William reached an uneasy agreement with Louis XIV that there would be no further such attacks. This did not mean calling off the siege of Namur. Eventually, on 5 September, the French were forced to vacate the city. This was one of William's most notable successes as a commander, and a day of thanksgiving was declared throughout England. William returned to Kensington Palace in late October, to an enthusiastic welcome.

This must have seemed like the best possible time for a royal progress, and William duly travelled to Newmarket, a town favoured by several of his predecessors (especially that great lover of horse-racing, Charles II). On 17 October, William participated in a hunt, one of his regular pastimes. He had an official residence at Newmarket, where a royal hunting lodge had been built by King James I in 1605; it had been destroyed during the English Civil War. William instead stayed at a house in the high street, which Charles had repurposed with the help of the architect William Samwell. Of this house nothing remains, though part of the original 'Palace House' still stands, now home to the National Horse Racing Museum.

For political reasons, William had tended to favour Oxford over Cambridge. Soon after his arrival in England in 1688, he had visited the city of Cambridge to find himself being welcomed by none other than Mary's former chaplain, John Covel, who became Master of Christ's College and Vice-Chancellor in 1688, retaining the former position until his death. On Mary's death, Covel had sent him poems in her memory. On this repeat visit, William once again received the compliments of the university, before moving on to stay for a few days at Althorp in Northamptonshire, then as now the home of the illustrious Spencer family.

Robert Spencer, at that time Earl of Sunderland, had been an enthusiastic supporter of James II but had quickly changed sides, and he now offered William a week's hospitality, in a residence where he displayed his impressive art collection, which no doubt attracted the culture-loving king. While at Althorp, William paid a call on Earl Montagu, his Master of the Wardrobe, at Boughton House; this was a new residence, built by Montagu in the 1680s in the style of Versailles, with a series of state rooms designed specifically to impress William and Mary. Here the king is known to have greatly admired, and perhaps coveted, the art collection. He is quoted as saying 'Twas no good for one to set one's heart on any of them'. Some of these artworks can still be viewed, on occasions when events allow the public to visit the house.

It is said that William was inspired by Boughton's state rooms when planning the developments at Hampton Court Palace. A Huguenot artist, Louis Chéron, designed their ceilings. As Master of the Wardrobe, Montagu had access to some of the most skilled architects and craftsmen, including Daniel Marot. He also owned tapestries made at Mortlake from designs based on Raphael cartoons. The house and its contents now belong to one of Montagu's descendants, the Duke of Buccleuch. The second duke, a grandson of the ill-fated Duke of Monmouth, had been born in the January before William's visit; he and his father, who eventually inherited the house, would later create additional avenues and water features in the gardens, which have since been restored.

William now moved on to Castle Ashby, the home of the Earl of Northampton. The king was 'very well pleased with the place', according to one of his retinue, mainly because of yet more opportunities for hunting and riding. While there, his influence on the earl persuaded the latter to plant four avenues of trees in the Dutch fashion; two of these survive. The Great Chamber, where the king had dined, was later renamed the King William Room. The house is now privately owned, and the property is not open to the public except when events are hosted in the grounds.

On leaving Castle Ashby, William travelled via Stamford, where he had expressed an interest in seeing Burghley House, the home of the Earl of Exeter. He did not stay over, as the earl – who had never confirmed his allegiance to the new regime – was not present. Burghley House, the family home of William Cecil, who had been one of Queen Elizabeth I's most trusted advisors, remains one of Britain's most visited stately homes. It is famous too for the annual Burghley Horse Trials, as befits an estate that interested such a great horseman as King William. Perhaps an even greater motivation for the visit was Lord Exeter's art collection. Antonio Verrio, the Italian artist well known to William, had taken up residence at Burghley about ten years before the king's visit, having fallen out of favour with James II, but he would soon return to work for William III.

The royal entourage moved on quickly to Belton House, owned by the High Sheriff of Lincolnshire – whose family, the Brownlows, would remain there until the 1980s, when they donated the property to the National Trust, enabling today's public to visit 'the perfect English country house estate'. Arriving on 29 October, the king was lavishly entertained. The Marble Hall and Chapel Drawing Room showcased contemporary decor, much of which was updated in later centuries. Belton still holds art works by Kneller, Vanderbank and the Dutch master Melchior d'Hondecoeter, not to mention a collection of Oriental porcelain from the early 1700s.

William travelled on next day to the city of Lincoln, to attend a service at the cathedral and to stay at Welbeck Abbey with another of his favoured aristocrats, the Duke of Newcastle. He was in the process of smoothing over Newcastle's hurt feelings as a result of an earlier failure to elevate him to the highest rank. The (now very wealthy) duke was without heirs, and his estate would eventually pass into the family of William's foremost favourite, the Earl of Portland. William was putting himself about, though not to the extent of meeting the general public except in the most formal of situations.

The duke was not entirely thrilled to be receiving a royal visit that promised to set him back financially. However, he entertained the king with 'great magnificence', to the tune of an estimated £5000 in expenditure. Welbeck Abbey – a former monastery – was only one of the duke's houses, and not the most impressive. Although his ancestor had been a noted horseman, one of the originators of the discipline of dressage, it was not this duke who built the riding school in the grounds of the Abbey, but his successor, Portland, after the troublesome William Talman had failed to carry through Newcastle's original plans for a rebuild of the house.

Welbeck Abbey remains in the hands of the family of the Dukes of Portland to this day, and guided tours of the state rooms are available at certain times of year, displaying works by Kneller and Cornelius Johnson. The Portland art collection is held in a separate museum. The 5th Duke was noted for his eccentricity; a recluse, he had a network of underground tunnels built on the estate. Following his death in 1879, his successor found many of the family's collected paintings stacked in the house in a random arrangement, many without frames, and spent years getting the collection back into some order.

During his stay at Welbeck, William went out hunting with the Earl of Kingston, whose more famous daughter, the future Lady Mary

Wortley Montagu, was a mere six years old at the time. Kingston was the owner of Thoresby Hall, which would be destroyed by fire in 1745. The replacement building has been converted to a hotel in the twenty-first century. The king's next port of call was Bradgate House, home of the Earl of Stamford and the possible birthplace of Lady Jane Grey. Only ruins now survive, since a replacement house was built two miles away, during the nineteenth century, but the remains of the old house can be visited at certain times, along with 'Old John', a folly built by a later earl.

By early November, William was being entertained at Warwick Castle, where he celebrated his 45th birthday. A hundred gallons of punch are said to have been provided for the royal party. He was aware of the great fire that had swept the town the previous year, and wanted to offer an indication of his sympathy for the displaced population. The castle belonged to Lord Brooke, who had recently refurbished some of the interiors. Warwick is one of Britain's most impressive, and extensive, surviving castles, and is today owned by a company that specialises in entertainment and tourism. It is one of the country's most popular visitor attractions. Much of what a visitor will see is as it was when William III stayed here, but likewise much has changed, and the atmosphere of a seventeenth century country house is hard to recapture.

The royal entourage went on into Oxfordshire, where William visited the Duke of Shrewsbury at Eyford House, one of his minor residences, which both men favoured for its secluded Cotswolds location; it has long since been replaced by a more modern house. The next port of call was Burford Priory, another residence created from one of the religious establishments closed down by King Henry VIII during the Reformation and remodelled in the Jacobean style. There the king was welcomed by the Earl of Abercorn, Charles Hamilton. A few years earlier, Hamilton had successfully appealed for the inheritance of his late brother, Claud, who had been a staunch supporter of James II, and he had only recently taken up his place in the House of Lords. Not long after William's visit, a former steward was found murdered in the grounds; Hamilton himself was charged with the murder, but was found not guilty. Burford Priory is now in private hands – those of members of the famous Murdoch family.

Cornbury Park, the home of Mary's uncle, Henry Hyde, was on the royal party's route, but Hyde had fallen from grace and William's main reason for visiting was to take a look at the property on behalf of one of his Dutch favourites, or perhaps with some idea of buying it himself. It had been built in the Dutch style by Mary's maternal grandfather, the Earl of Clarendon, but her uncle was in financial difficulty and had recently sold his art collection. Cornbury Park remains in private hands as a working estate and is not open to the public.

The king did not stay overnight at Cornbury Park, but moved on to Woodstock, and from there he visited Oxford, where he was met by a deputation from the university, who were determined not to be outdone by their rivals at Cambridge. They presented him with lavish gifts, such as a pair of gold-fringed gloves, but the visit was cut short because of rumours of an assassination attempt which was supposedly due to take place at the official banquet to which he had been invited, to be held at the Sheldonian Theatre (quite recently built to one of Christopher Wren's early designs). Oxford was anxious to cast off the reputation for Jacobitism that still clung to the city, but William hurried back to Windsor within a day. Returning to Kensington Palace, he wrote that he was 'very pleased with my journey…having met with a great deal of affection of the people everywhere'.

Towards the end of November, the king addressed the English Parliament with praise for the country's armed forces and their recent performance at Namur. The speech went down well, even though it was accompanied by yet another request for funds. When Parliament began discussing how to raise the money, Isaac Newton, who had served as an MP for the University of Cambridge and within a few years would be Master of the Mint, offered his expert opinion that the best solution was a revaluation of the coinage, and this duly took place.

At Whitehall Palace in 1696, the king met the leaders of the army in response to public accusations of corruption. They were ordered to report to the Horse Guards building in Whitehall, where William and his council laid the law down to them about a growing tendency to extort money from members of the public. The Horse Guards building had been constructed on the orders of King Charles II in 1663 and was not the building that now stands on the site, which replaced it in the mid-eighteenth century. Horse Guards had increasingly become an administrative centre following the fires at Whitehall.

The recently-promoted Duke of Leeds, who as Marquess of Carmarthen had been one of the 'Immortal Seven' and an advisor to Mary, had blotted his copybook by getting involved in the affairs of the East India Company and allowing himself to be accused of accepting bribes. Although the accusation was never proven, the duke lost the confidence of the administration and was soon obliged to retire from government. He would, however, entertain Peter the Great and his entourage during the emperor's visit to Britain in 1698.

William's recent progress through the kingdom had not taken him as far as Wales or Scotland. His failure to recognise the significance of these outlying parts led him into the unwise decision of bestowing on his favourite, the Duke of Portland, the lordships of Denbigh, Bromfield and Yale in north Wales. A swift response came from the outraged Welsh gentry, in the form of outspoken opposition from Robert Price, MP for Weobley, who originated from Denbighshire. His speech was later published under the title *Gloria Cambriae; or the Speech of a Bold Briton in Parliament against a Dutch Prince of Wales*. This was one of several occasions when William was forced to defer to the wishes of Parliament, in recognition of the monarch's inability to wield absolute power. Not long afterwards, William's secretary, Constantijn Huygens the Younger, resigned from the king's service, tired of being overworked and underpaid and having his advice (on matters other than art) ignored; Huygens died the following year.

In the part of the world that we now call the United States of America and Canada, 'King William's War' would continue even after hostilities in Europe had ended. Though he was never actually present at any of the battles in North America, William's subjects had been sucked into the war by events in Europe, notably the row between Louis XIV and the

Holy Roman Emperor, Leopold, which would culminate in the War of the Spanish Succession that again brought John Churchill to the fore as a battle commander. In 1689, Churchill had already been rewarded for his actions in helping to bring about the Glorious Revolution with the earldom of Marlborough, which would later be converted to a dukedom by Queen Anne.

In 1697 the Peace of Ryswick was signed at Rijswijk, to give it its correct spelling. Rijswijk was at the time the location of a palace called 'Huis ter Nieuwburg' ('House at New Borough'), designed by Jacob van Campen for Prince Frederick Henry. Formal gardens had been created in the 1630s, on the French model. After William's death, the palace passed through various hands but was increasingly neglected until its demolition in 1790. The importance of the treaty signed there was, however, not forgotten: a monument (the 'Needle of Rijswijk') was built on its centenary.

The treaty brought to an end the Nine Years' War that had started at the time of William and Mary's coup, and in latter years had been fought between France and the multi-national alliance that William had led. Under its terms, King Louis XIV, now in his sixties and no longer hungry for military success, would recognise William as King of England, leaving his rival, James, out in the cold. Other participants were equally worn out and their prosperity damaged so much that they appear to have been glad to abandon the fight. There were, however, secret clauses in the treaty.

The childless William had offered to allow his late wife's half-brother, James Francis Edward Stuart, to succeed to the throne in the event that no other male heir presented himself. At the time, William's sister-in-law Anne had one surviving son, the Duke of Gloucester, who at that time was about eight years old, James's son being a year older. The idea of allowing the unofficial 'Prince of Wales' to succeed seems to have been encouraged by none other than one of William's alternative heirs, Sophia of Hanover, who was nearly seventy, twenty years older than the king himself. Sophia was a granddaughter of King James I of England/VI of Scotland. She had lived at The Hague and knew William well, and she visited him at Het Loo shortly before the treaty was signed.

William had never achieved the level of popularity a more sociable man might have hoped for. In 1697 another two assassination attempts were discovered. Multiple executions took place, and the youthful Duke of Gloucester made a point of announcing his loyalty to the king. Gloucester had now been given his own household and income by Parliament, which was a cause of some friction between William and his sister-in-law, despite the rapprochement that had occurred since Mary's death. Gilbert Burnet was selected to superintend the boy's education, whilst the Earl of Marlborough was appointed his governor. This was a clever move, designed to neutralise Marlborough's supposed tendencies towards Jacobitism.

William had spent much of 1697 in Holland, continuing the campaign against the French, but mostly on a defensive footing. On 16 November he made a triumphal entry into London, with a throng of attendants, to be met by the Lord Mayor on St Margaret's Hill in Southwark, where the formalities in many ways echoed those that had taken place when Charles II was restored to the throne in 1660. William declared a day of national thanksgiving on 2 December, which he would himself celebrate with a firework display at the home of the Earl of Romney (one of the 'Immortal Seven') in St James's Square.

Another pleasant event marked a milestone in William's reign. The rebuilding of St Paul's, London's prestigious cathedral, was almost complete, and the first service could be held. The official opening took place in early December. Since he hated ceremonial, it is perhaps not surprising that the king stayed away, even though the ostensible purpose of the service was to celebrate the Peace of Ryswick. William left it to Bishop Compton to preside over the consecration. John Blow, the choirmaster of St Paul's, was given the task of composing special music.

In the following year, William hosted a visit from Russian dignitaries, led by the Tsar, Peter the Great. William had first met Peter in September 1697 at Utrecht in the Netherlands, shortly before the treaty was signed. The emperor and his entourage officially arrived in

England in January 1698, though rumours of Peter's incognito visit were already circulating. They stayed for three months, and entertaining them all proved expensive – they ran up a bill of £300 for the damage they did to a house in London that belonged to John Evelyn. Having arranged for Peter to have his portrait painted by Sir Godfrey Kneller, William became impatient for the Russians to move on, tolerating their continued presence mainly because both countries were eager to expand and improve trading links.

On his return from the Continent, William's demands for money had been rejected by the English Parliament, who had anticipated a reduction in the defence budget following the success of the peace negotiations. William suffered some loss of face, but Parliament took note of his threat to leave the country permanently, and eventually agreed to maintain an army in Ireland and to support William's expanded navy.

For some years, William's Scottish subjects had been attempting to set up a colony called 'New Caledonia' in what is now Panama. This is now remembered as the Darien project. The colony's failure was due in no small measure to a lack of support from the king, who feared arousing the antagonism of his Spanish allies. The debts incurred by the Scots would lead indirectly to the 1707 union, as a result of which the Scottish Parliament would be closed down. In recent years it has been hard for the Scottish nation to forgive this slight, but the responsibility cannot reasonably be laid at William's door.

At the same time, William was facing political opposition at home, for a number of reasons. Sir John Somers, one of the king's leading supporters, had been elevated to the peerage in order that he could serve as Lord Chancellor, but fell from power, not only because of another corruption scandal but because of a personal connection with the notorious Captain Kidd. William was forced to demand Somers' resignation, and the latter withdrew temporarily from political life (though he continued as President of the Royal Society!)

The Earl of Galway, a French Huguenot who had given valuable service in Ireland and was serving in the role of Lord Justice (effectively a viceroy), was another who fell foul of the continual accusations of corruption. William wrote to him from Hampton Court in May 1700, stating that he did not blame him for any of the administrative complications that had occurred but that he felt obliged to appoint another in his place – for this unenvied honour he had selected the Duke of Shrewsbury. Shrewsbury refused to go to Ireland, while Galway was only too happy to retire, though he would eventually return to the military life. Two months later, William was off to Holland again, having spent much of the summer at Hampton Court for a change.

Immediately after the Duke of Gloucester's eleventh birthday banquet, the boy contracted a fever, which was diagnosed as scarlet fever. He died five days later, and was buried in Westminster Abbey. William, who had not long arrived in Holland, wrote to Marlborough that the news 'pierces my heart with affliction'. He later discovered that his sister-in-law Anne had written to her father in France, asking his forgiveness because she saw her son's death as a punishment from God for her disloyalty. William visited Anne when he returned to England at the end of 1700, and ordered a period of mourning, but he was back again at Het Loo when the news arrived of the death of his father-in-law, the former James II, in September 1701, at the age of 67. William's own health was poor, and he was within a year of his own death; he had already made his final art purchase at an auction in Amsterdam. Despite the callous manner in which James had responded to Mary's death, a message of forgiveness from the former king seems to have made a great impression on William, to the extent that he wore mourning clothes for a time, though he did not expect the same of his courtiers.

A month before James's death, the English parliament had passed the Act of Settlement, which specified that the thrones of England and Ireland could in future only be held by Protestants who were in communion with the Church of England; it provided for circumstances that had not been covered by the Bill of Rights in 1689. Somewhat surprisingly to us today, James had spurned overtures from William about the possibility of adopting the 'unofficial Prince of Wales', James Francis Edward Stuart, as heir to his thrones, an idea that Queen Anne would also later consider. James saw that his son, now aged 13, would have been required to convert to Protestantism in order to succeed to the throne, and would never agree to this. Following the former king's death, Anne would receive a letter from her stepmother, Mary of Modena, reminding her of what the former queen consort saw as the familial duty of the future queen regnant, but Anne had no power to alter the order of succession.

The Act of Settlement confirmed Sophia and her descendants as the heirs to the throne in the event of the death of Anne. The possibility that Sophia, who was 35 years older than Anne, would not survive her was clear. Other potential claimants had been passed over in favour of the one who had the most impeccable Protestant credentials. Sophia, however, had a mature son, who would one day take his place on the throne as King George I of Great Britain. William had already welcomed George's son, the future George II, to Het Loo, in the company of his grandfather, the Elector of Hanover, and the visitors were present when the news of James's death arrived.

Another succession crisis, elsewhere in Europe, would put paid to William's hopes of retiring peacefully. King Charles II of Spain died in November 1700, aged 38, and the absence of an heir led to the War of the Spanish Succession, an event most British people know little of beyond the name they heard at school. It was critical for Europe, however, since one of the leading claimants to the Spanish throne was Philip of Anjou, a grandson of King Louis XIV of France, and this was not something William could allow to happen without a fight. The future of both Britain and the Netherlands was at stake, and both countries had long since committed themselves to supporting the claim of Leopold I, the Holy Roman Emperor, an Austrian prince who ruled extensive territory in Hungary, Bohemia and Croatia, as well as in his homeland.

William addressed the States-General of the Netherlands when war appeared inevitable, and in September 1701 he signed the Treaty of the Hague, firmly allying himself (and the countries he ruled) with Leopold. Louis had given him little choice when he decided to recognise the claim of James II's son to the thrones of England, Scotland and Ireland after James's death. The youth would never succeed in sitting on those thrones, and is known to history as 'The Old Pretender' (in contrast with the son he would have in 1720, whom we remember better as 'Bonnie Prince Charlie'). Both the Old and the Young Pretenders would live long lives but die disappointed men.

William returned to England for the winter, the future uncertain and his own health worse than ever. But he was no housebound invalid. On 21 February 1702, the king went out riding, either in the park adjacent to his palace at Hampton Court, or possibly in Richmond Park, and sustained a rather nasty fall when his horse stumbled and threw him. Legend has it that the cause of the stumble was a molehill. William broke his collar-bone.

Even though he was no longer young, William did not die of the injuries he incurred in the fall. His collar-bone was set by a military surgeon named Ronjat, and the king was taken to Kensington Palace to recuperate. Here he was attended by his personal physician, Govert Bidloo, moonlighting from his job as a professor of anatomy at the University of Leiden. Perhaps because both doctors were nervous about their responsibilities, there was apparently some dispute as to whether the treatment given by Ronjat had been adequate. The king's scheduled visit to Parliament had to be cancelled, because his knee had swelled, making it difficult for him to walk.

It has been suggested that William caught a chill while lying on a couch in the draughty palace, and the resultant fever eventually, in conjunction with his already weak chest, turned to pneumonia. The most senior physician in England, Thomas Millington, was called in. That pneumonia was the actual cause of death seems to have been confirmed by a post-mortem examination held on 10 March. Whatever the cause of his death, William lived for more than two weeks after his riding accident, and continued to conduct the business of state during that period. One of his last acts was allegedly the signing of a bill charging 13-year-old James Stuart, the 'Old Pretender' to the Catholic claim on the throne, with high treason.

William's deathbed companions were his faithful friend Bentinck, now Earl of Portland, and his newer favourite, the Earl of Albemarle, who had returned from Holland post-haste with a military update. Archbishop Tenison and Bishop Burnet were both present. Anne was now queen. She was already wearing black following the deaths of her son and her father, and now changed to purple in recognition of the king's passing.

Although the thrones of England, Scotland and Ireland passed to Anne with few complications, the title 'Prince of Orange' and the role of stadtholder of the United Provinces were another matter. Anne did not have any claim on these, and William's closest male relative in the line of succession was 14-year-old Johan Willem Friso, the son of William's first cousin. The teenager was already stadtholder of Friesland and Groningen, the provinces over which his father had ruled. The remaining provinces decided to do without a stadtholder for the time being. As it happened, Johan Willem himself died within nine years, drowning when a ferry sank, at the age of 23. He too left a posthumous son, who would become William IV of Orange and later marry into the Georgian line of the British royal family. Johan Willem's descendants now sit on all extant European thrones.

William III's funeral, on 12 April, was a private and low-key affair, especially when compared with that of his wife Mary. It took place at midnight, and the funeral procession from Kensington was led by an open chariot, in which the king's wax effigy was placed; the coffin was added when the procession reached Westminster. William was buried alongside his wife, in the Henry VII Lady Chapel at Westminster Abbey, where his mother, Mary Henrietta, also lies. The people of England and Scotland demonstrated no great sorrow at the news of his death.

A wax effigy was later created by a Mrs Goldsmith, 'the famous woman for waxwork' as she was called by the *Daily Courant*, in the same style as that of his wife Mary. William's was not used for his funeral, but both his and Mary's effigies are now on display in the Queen's Diamond Jubilee Galleries, and are thought to be those made by Mrs Goldsmith, whose husband ran a business 'at the sign of King William and Queen Mary in the Old-Jury', in the historic City of London. They were acquired by Westminster Abbey in 1724, when they were being displayed to the public for profit by the gentlemen of the choir. How closely they resemble the king and queen is impossible to say, but it seems likely that Mrs Goldsmith had occasionally seen both monarchs in person. Wax effigies of monarchs were by no means a new idea, and might be put on public display almost before the monarch's body was cold in its grave.

The royal couple are represented in their coronation robes. Also now on display in the Galleries at Westminster Abbey is the chair in which Mary sat at her coronation, smaller than the ancient Coronation Chair used by William and all other monarchs since the thirteenth century, which is also to be seen there.

According to popular report, the horse William had been riding when he died was 'White Sorrel', which had originally belonged to Sir John Fenwick, one of the Jacobite conspirators executed in 1697 for his involvement in the first of that year's assassination attempts. The horse had been acquired when Fenwick's property was confiscated, and its role in William's accident was considered a supreme irony. However, it was the mole, the 'little gentleman in black velvet', that the Jacobites regarded as their lucky mascot.

The fanciful Jacobite toast remained in use for centuries, even after the failed Jacobite rebellions of 1715 and 1745, which had little to do with William and more to do with the selection of opportune moments in history at which the Stuart dynasty might have had a chance of recapturing the thrones of England, Scotland and Ireland. None of James II's legitimate children have left any present-day descendants, and his distant relations who can claim descent from the House of Stuart have long since ceased to make any claim on the throne of the United Kingdom.

Legacy

Bearing in mind that William lived to the age of 51, whilst his wife died at 32, and that he was already a national leader in the Netherlands before he met Mary and continued to rule England, Scotland and Ireland for several years after her death, it is hardly surprising that history has a lot more to say about him than it has about her. Mary, often confused with Mary Tudor (Mary I of England) and/or Mary, Queen of Scots (Mary I of Scotland), not to mention her stepmother, Mary of Modena, receives little recognition in the present day for her undoubted historical significance.

In Sellar & Yeatman's 1930 humorous fake history of England, 'Williamanmary' is treated as a single monarchy through which England was 'ruled by an Orange'. We may laugh, but the book actually throws an interesting light on the way history was and is taught in British schools.

Mary's premature death naturally produced mountains of laudatory works about her. Gilbert Burnet, her friend and mentor, wrote his *Essay on the Memory of the Late Queen* almost immediately. Although it enumerates her good qualities, it is really more of a religious work than a biography. In contrast, her first biographer, Grainger, who was writing barely a year after her death, had little that was not complimentary to say about her. There have been other biographies over the years, but in general Mary has not been anywhere near as popular a subject as William. American writer Nellie Waterson wrote *Mary II, Queen of England* in 1928, and the novelist Hester W Chapman produced a biography with the same title in 1953.

Other early historians tended to overlook Mary's role in government. Oliver Goldsmith, in his *History of England, from the Earliest Times to the Death of George II*, published in 1771, almost completely ignores her existence, mentioning her only briefly as William's wife. His chapter on their reign is titled simply 'William III'. Goldsmith was born in Ireland in 1728 and thus would have known people who remembered both William and Mary. Naturally, the focus of his interest is largely on William's activities in Ireland, of which Goldsmith, being a Protestant, would have approved.

Two nineteenth-century historians, Agnes Strickland and Arthur Trevor, both of whom lived through the final years of the Hanoverian dynasty that began on the death of Queen Anne, recorded their views of William in no uncertain terms, even though neither could have known him personally. Strickland, the daughter of Suffolk gentry, was a novelist as well as a writer on history. In her voluminous work on the *Lives of the Queens of England*, she repeatedly expresses pity for Mary, having to live with such a disagreeable, penny-pinching husband. Since Agnes took the credit for work mostly done by her sister Elizabeth, we may assume that the sisters shared this view. Trevor, on the other hand, in his biography of the king, unsurprisingly describes William in terms that are diametrically opposite to those of the Strickland sisters, making him out to be a paragon of courage, tolerance and every other admirable quality. Such one-sided views are fairly typical of Victorian attitudes to history, and cannot be taken at face value. William and Mary's own words and actions, as they are preserved in official and unofficial documents and correspondence, are our only reliable means of assessing their characters.

William's attitude towards his wife, though it may at times have fallen within the modern definition of 'controlling behaviour' (not surprising in a reigning king), was clearly far from that of an abusive husband. He was, however, a politician as well as a military commander, and some of his actions in these environments do not bear intensive scrutiny. Mary apparently chose to defer to him because she felt herself unready for an active role in government; this was forced upon her at an early age and she seems to have worked well with her counsellors and earned the admiration of her subjects.

William's posthumous reputation, however, remains deeply tarnished in the eyes of some of the Irish, forever associated with the humiliating defeat of an anointed king but even more despised for his role as the architect of religious unrest in their island. The activities of the Orange Order, primarily in Northern Ireland, are a living reminder of a time in history when it was legal to discriminate against Catholics. Even in the twenty-first century, some members of the order take pleasure in parading their perceived superiority over non-Protestants by marching through districts mainly occupied by Catholics in towns such as Portadown. In recent times, that march has been hijacked by neo-Nazis, leading to worse violence and almost putting an end to the peace process that both Protestants and Catholics had worked so hard to achieve.

In the midst of all this, 'King Billy' is both loved and hated by people who know virtually nothing about William's life. The colour orange, symbolic of the Protestant victory, is used to mark out the followers of the Orange order, many of whom are unaware of its origins. The song 'Lilliburlero', with lyrics written by Whig MP Thomas Wharton as a criticism of James II well before the events of 1689, to a melody attributed to Henry Purcell, quickly became popular as the Glorious Revolution gained momentum and continued to be a popular song even years later, when the lyrics were no longer meaningful. Numerous alternative versions of the song have been written over the years, including a French version called 'Marche du Prince d'Orange'. The BBC, perhaps unwittingly, gave it the status of a song of liberation when they began using it on radio during the Second World War.

The anniversary of the decisive Battle of Aughrim began to be celebrated on 12 July 1796, nearly a century after William's death, and was associated with violence and social division from the beginning. William had not been present at Aughrim, a battle immortalised in a contemporary drawing by the Dutch artist Jan Wyck, who specialised in depicting military scenes and who was actually in Ireland to witness the Williamite successes. Wyck, along with his compatriot Dirk Maas, had been commissioned by William to record the campaign on canvas. Ironically, Aughrim is sometimes called 'Ireland's forgotten battle', perhaps because it has been overshadowed by the Boyne; that could be partly because William and James were both present in person at the Boyne, justifying the label given to the war in the Irish language: *Cogadh an Dá Rí* ('War of the Two Kings').

On the 300th anniversary of William's arrival in England, the Westminster Parliament debated a motion in honour of what the then Conservative government saw as a triumph for democracy and freedom. Although this was endorsed by the Opposition, there were dissenting voices who pointed out how little the 'Glorious Revolution' had affected the balance of power or improved the lot of ordinary people. Moreover, many felt it had led to the Troubles in Northern Ireland. For the Netherlands, by contrast, the events of 1688–89 were of little historical significance. Things could have been quite different if William and Mary had left an heir.

Even in the twenty-first century, the 12 July commemoration (now merged with that of the Battle of the Boyne) continues, with bunting, parades and marching bands to the fore. William's image, traditionally shown on a white horse, sword in hand, crossing the River Boyne, is at the heart of the celebration, which spread from Northern Ireland to the cities of Glasgow and Liverpool which also had large Catholic populations. It is even echoed in countries that did not exist at the time of William's victory, including Australia and Canada, whilst the Orange Order has spread all over the world, even to some African countries, but remains strictly a Protestant organisation.

As if to illustrate how the significance of William's passage through Ireland has been misunderstood, a painting that takes pride of place at Stormont, the headquarters of the Northern Ireland government, was examined by art historians Bendor Grosvenor and Jacky Klein as part of the BBC TV series, *Britain's Lost Masterpieces*. The painting was for many years assumed to represent William's victorious entry into Belfast, and for some time it adorned the office of the Reverend Ian Paisley. It was controversial because it included an image of the Pope, apparently blessing William, and a rosary in the hands of one of the minor figures. In 1933, following the purchase of the painting from the collection of the late Marquess of Curzon (a former Viceroy of India but apparently with a less than good grasp on British history), a group from the Scottish Protestant League vandalised the painting in protest at the depiction. It was repaired and touched up, but historians have now definitely established that it is in fact a representation of St George, and the figures in the crowd are members of the Guild of Crossbowmen of Antwerp in the Spanish Netherlands.

It would not be fruitful to dwell on the topic of this type of symbolism in a book about William and Mary, since the present-day commemorations have very little to do with the Glorious Revolution and everything to do with the tragic divisions between religious communities that began long before William was born. William and Mary themselves, though divisive figures in the context of the politics of their time, were neither universally popular or universally unpopular as individuals. They left behind a more positive legacy in contrast to that just discussed.

Search for 'William and Mary' online or in an index today and you may well be taken to results you were not expecting. The College of William & Mary, founded in 1693 by letters patent issued in the names of the monarchs, is one of the oldest tertiary educational institutions in the English-speaking world and has claims to be the first university in the United States. It was granted the title of university in its original royal charter, and completed its transition from a school in 1779, at the instigation of Thomas Jefferson. Situated in Williamsburg, Virginia (renamed after William when the town became capital of the colony), it came into being after a long campaign by the colonists, finally brought to fruition by James Blair, who would be the college's first president. Blair, a Scottish clergyman, made the case with the assistance of John Tillotson, Archbishop of Canterbury, who would die the following year, not long after Queen Mary herself. Blair held the presidency until his own death fifty years after the founding of the college. In 1695 work began on the Wren building, so called because it was supposedly designed by the royal architect, Sir Christopher Wren. If there is such a thing as a 'William and Mary style' of architecture, this surely conforms to it.

By 1699, Williamsburg had become the capital of the colony of Virginia, and had expanded greatly. 'Colonial Williamsburg', a living history museum in a district of the city, boasts of being the largest such museum in the world. It contains a number of period buildings, mostly reconstructed, such as the Capitol building, a courthouse, a tavern, and the Governor's Palace. The architecture of the latter, like that of the college, is Dutch-influenced, much like the style of building that was popular in Britain at the time. Although the colony was settled shortly after the Restoration, even the original buildings date from the early eighteenth century, a few years after the deaths of William and Mary.

However, archaeological excavations have uncovered the remains of several of the earliest buildings, as well as contemporary artefacts.

There are numerous other settlements called Williamsburg in the United States, most of which did *not* take their name from William III. However, King and Queen County in Virginia, founded in 1691, is certainly named after William and Mary. There are no settlements specifically named after Mary; any places in the United States with 'Mary' in their names, notably Maryland, are likely to have been named after other queens of the same name, of whom there is no shortage, Britain alone boasting half a dozen[3].

Whilst William and Mary did not care to cross the ocean to visit their colonies, they understood their importance and did not ignore them. Jamaica and other islands in the Caribbean received rich furnishings and other reminders of their status from the Crown. William's reputation for meanness did not prevent him from supplying portraits of himself and Mary, as well as escutcheons and other symbols of royalty. The couple also sent gardeners to places such as Virginia to obtain suitable botanical samples for use in Britain. When received and successfully grown, these would remind visitors to the royal palace gardens that the monarchs' realm was not limited to the British Isles or even to Europe.

Although William's posthumous reputation suggests he was not particularly well-liked by his subjects for most of his reign, he was celebrated after his death by the erection of several statues. These were mostly created during the Georgian period, when he became symbolic of the Protestant dynasty that had 'liberated' the country from Catholicism. The first two Georges were spectacularly uncharismatic men, and thus it was felt necessary to remind their subjects how they came to be on the throne.

Indeed, this was the case with one such statue whose subject was chosen to replace the original concept of a statue of George II. Even so, it shows William looking far more dashing than he ever did in real life,

---

3. Mary of Guelders, Mary of Guise, Mary I of Scotland, Mary I of England, Henrietta Maria, Mary of Modena, Mary of Teck.

and wearing classical dress. The equestrian statue was cast in bronze in 1733, by Jan Michiel Rijsbrack or Rysbrack, a notable Flemish sculptor, born shortly before Mary's death. It stands in Queen Square, Bristol. For the local Whigs, it was a memorial to the city's support for the coup of 1689. (Jacobites may have preferred to see it as a reminder of the manner of William's death.)

At around the same time, statues of William were erected in Glasgow and Hull. The creator of the Hull statue, Peter Scheemakers the Younger. Hull's version, like Rysbrack's, is an equestrian statue with William in a Roman toga, but is heavily gilded and has become a well-known landmark in the Market Square in the centre of the city. Its inscription describes the king as 'our Great Deliverer'. When William set out for England in 1688, it had been anticipated by the authorities that his fleet might land at Hull and make its way up the Humber. The Catholic governor, the second Baron Langdale, was the victim of a coup by local Protestants, who imprisoned him in his own citadel. This was the incident the people of Hull chose to remember, even though William had not actually graced them with his presence.

The statue in Glasgow, similar in style but without the gilding, was financed by James Macrae, an administrator who had spent many years at sea. It has been vandalised several times over the years, with the local Protestant population still blaming Catholics for the damage. Its existence seems to have done nothing to dispel historical bad feeling between the two communities in the city. The market town of Petersfield in Hampshire also has an equestrian statue of William, the work of John Cheere (1703–1781); this was commissioned in 1750 by Sir William Jolliffe, the local MP, and is thought to have originally been gilded. On the occasion of one general election, the statue was tarred and feathered. In the centuries since, it has become 'a popular local landmark' (to quote the Leader of Hampshire Country Council) and was restored during the summer of 2023.

During the Victorian period, William and Mary had not completely faded from memory. After the French and American revolutions, the British were ready to boast of their attempt to introduce democracy through William's 'bloodless' takeover. On the 200th anniversary of William's landing in Devon, a statue of him was erected in Brixham. The white marble statue depicts him, minus his horse, with an air of intent. Like most statues, it has been vandalised and made the subject of pranks many times over the years, notably in 2018 when it was dressed up as a Dutch football supporter in readiness for a World Cup match.

Two statues of William III can be found outside royal palaces in London. In addition to the one previously mentioned at Kensington Palace, there is an equestrian statue outside St James's Palace. This was modelled on Rysbrack's statue in Bristol. Although planned at roughly the same date as the other, it was not completed until 1807.

The numerous portraits of William give us a better idea of his appearance. He is often recognisable by his long luxuriant curly wigs, which by all accounts distinguished him in real life also. Godfrey Kneller, Lely's successor as court painter, who had portrayed William's predecessor on the throne, James II, produced official portraits of William and Mary after their coronation in 1690, something of a new departure, although Kneller borrowed heavily from Van Dyck in terms of the style of the portraits. They were designed to be hung as a pair, with the man on the left and the woman on the right. Yet Kneller does not flatter William as much as Lely had, and clearly shows the determined mouth and large nose. His portraits of the king were much copied and used as the basis for many engravings. Kneller was also commissioned to produce a portrait of William that could be sent across the Atlantic to the colonial government of Maryland and put on display in their new state house.

One of these, by the engraver Bernard Baron, was published at the time of the second Jacobite rebellion in order to muster support for the Protestant monarchy. It shows William on horseback, surrounded by emblems of his military successes, and is titled *William the Third, King of England, of Glorious and Immortal Memory*. He may not have been handsome, but he must have looked impressive by comparison with King George II, whose overweight backside by then sat on the throne. Admittedly George had led out his troops at the Battle of Dettingen in Germany a few years earlier, but he had played little part in the actual battle.

During her time in Holland, William's wife Mary was painted by several Dutch artists, including Jan Verkolje (who died shortly before his subject) and Jan van der Vaart. Their portraits of Mary as a mature woman show her in conventional pose, with as much attention given to her hairstyle and costume as to her character. Willem Wissing's portrait of 1686, like several others, show her in loosened clothing, in accordance with a current fashion for 'luxurious negligence in attire'[4]. The purpose of this was to ensure that the mode of dress in such portraits did not appear out-of-date. However, Jan Van der Vaart also depicted her wearing the headdress known as a 'fontange', which has somehow become part of her image. Ironically, this was a French style that was generally disapproved of and whose popularity was short-lived. As with her husband, Mary became a popular subject for engravings, with the portrait by Lely being much reproduced. However, reflecting her much shorter lifespan, the National Portrait Gallery can boast only 97 portraits of her in its possession, as opposed to William's 140 plus.

In the BBC's 1969 blockbuster serial, *The First Churchills*, Mary was played by Anglo-French actress Lisa Daniely and William by New Zealand-born Alan Rowe. An early colour production, it was the first of many British programmes to be shown under the PBS *Masterpiece* banner in the United States, but the roles of the royal couple took second place to those of the main characters, John and Sarah Churchill, and the members of their circle, notably Sidney Godolphin, with Margaret Tyzack as Mary's sister Anne having a much larger role. Tyzack and Susan Hampshire (who played Sarah) had both recently starred in the last of the BBC's great black-and-white drama productions, *The Forsyte Saga*.

The 1986 serial, *Peter the Great*, produced for American television, was a star-studded pseudo-historical drama in which William was played by none other than the archetypal English actor, Laurence Olivier, then in

---

4. Royal Collection Website: https://www.rct.uk/collection.

his late seventies (readers will recall that William died at the age of 51). It includes a depiction of Peter the Great's Grand Embassy to England in 1697–8. Respecting historical accuracy, Mary does not appear since she had died by this time.

In a 1995 Channel 4 film, *England, My England*, in which Henry Purcell is a central character, Mary is played by Rebecca Front (an actress more usually associated with comedy) and Corin Redgrave, a scion of the famous British acting dynasty, is William. The film's script was written by English playwright John Osborne. A Guardian reviewer referred to Mary as 'arguably the most adored female royal personage before Princess Diana'. If that were so, she experienced the same ups and downs as Diana in relation to her public image.

In the 2003 BBC series *Charles II: the Power and the Passion*, Mary does not appear and the role of William was played by a Dutch actor, Jochum ten Haaf. The only other Dutch actor to have played him in an English-language production was Thom Hoffman in the 1992 film *Orlando*, based on Virginia Woolf's fantasy novel (in which the British actress Sarah Crowden played Mary).

The French/British 2015 series, *Versailles*, included William as a recurring and somewhat rascally character, played by George Webster. Mary appears in only one episode, in which Charles II offers his young niece to the adult William as a potential bride, as a diplomatic gesture. The child actress is uncredited, and the marriage of William and Mary is never followed up within the bounds of the series.

There are of course a number of films that include fictionalised, mostly historically inaccurate, versions of William and Mary in their cast list. One such is *Against All Flags* (1952), a pirate story starring Errol Flynn. King William makes a brief appearance, played by Scottish actor Olaf Hytten. In 1945's *Captain Kidd*, William is played by Henry Daniell, an actor who normally specialised in villains.

In addition, there are several Dutch films that deal with the period, the most notable being *Michiel de Ruyter*, a 2015 biopic of the admiral, in which William is played by Egbert-Jan Weber and Ella-June Henrard takes the minor role of Mary. However, most Dutch films that have

'William of Orange' listed among the dramatis personae are about William the Silent, great-grandfather of William III.

Laurence Sterne (1713–1768), an Irish clergyman and novelist, included in his masterpiece *Tristram Shandy* a character called Captain Toby, a military veteran who has served under William, along with his servant Corporal Trim. Sterne's own family were no doubt his inspiration for the inclusion of Toby, since his own father had served as an ensign in a British regiment, and had later married the widow of an army captain, who became Sterne's mother. The Sternes moved around a lot, including brief postings to Carrickfergus and Derry. There was another family connection with the period, since Sterne's great-grandfather was Richard Sterne, the Archbishop of York who had opposed James II's attempt to bring back Catholicism.

Alexandre Dumas included William of Orange and the de Witt brothers as characters in his 1850 novel *The Black Tulip* (not to be confused with a number of more modern stories of the same name). In the 1937 British film based on the book, William was played by Bernard Lee, later to become known as 'M' in the early James Bond films. There have been at least two television adaptations of the book. In the BBC's 1956 serialisation, William was played by the little-known Henry Davies, and in the 1970 serialisation by another New Zealander, Eric Woofe, best known for his subsequent leading role in *The Strauss Family*.

There is no shortage of lesser novels set in the period, such as Marjorie Bowen's 'William and Mary' trilogy, published in 1910–11. However, many such novels focus on fictional minor characters and do not include the king and queen among their characters. Victor Hugo's frequently-adapted 1869 novel, *L'homme qui rit*, (normally translated into English as *The Man who Laughs*), is partly set in the 1690s, but does not include William and Mary as characters, even though it does feature both James II and Queen Anne. Likewise, R D Blackmore's famous historical romance, *Lorna Doone*, possibly the most famous English novel set in the period, has James II as a major character, but does not mention William and Mary. Many other novels concern themselves with the events of Monmouth's Rebellion, but concentrate on its more sensational aspects rather than what came afterwards.

Jean Plaidy, the generally underrated author of popular historical novels, included William and Mary's reign in her multitude of well-researched titles. Whereas *The Three Crowns* (1965) was part of her 'Stuart saga', her later book, *The Queen's Devotion*, alternatively titled *William's Wife* (1992), deals mainly with Mary's personal struggle, and is written in the form of a fictionalised autobiography. Plaidy's portrait of William is almost entirely negative, possibly influenced by reading the work of the Strickland sisters, and she portrays the marriage, at least in the early days, as entirely loveless, which primary sources confirm was not the case. *The Haunted Sisters* (1966) is about the relationship between Mary and her sister Anne. William also makes an appearance in Plaidy's novel about Anne, *The Queen's Favourites*.

Philippa Gregory, one of the early twenty-first century's leading historical novelists and something of a revisionist, portrays a Royalist family in her 'Fairmile' sequence of novels. In *Dawnlands* (2022), set in 1685, some of her characters are drawn into the circle of Mary of Modena and are involved in a plot to replace the queen's dead baby with a changeling. It ends as William and Mary take the throne, but neither of them appears as a character in this particular book, though they may turn up in sequels.

In the 2005 black comedy film *The League of Gentlemen's Apocalypse*, William is portrayed by Bernard Hill and Mary also appears as a character; the fact that she is played by Victoria Wood marks the film out as something not to be taken seriously. The characters enter the plot as part of a 'play-within-a-play', in which the writers, playing fictional versions of themselves, toy with the idea of a historical production called *The King's Evil*.

In recent years, Mary's younger sister Anne has become a popular subject for playwrights and screenwriters. *Queen Anne*, a 2015 play by Helen Edmundson, is set in the years immediately before Anne's accession to the throne and therefore includes William, but not Mary, among the dramatis personae. In the Royal Shakespeare Company's production, William was played on the London stage by Dave Fishley and at Stratford-upon-Avon by Carl Prekopp.

Acknowledgements

I am not a professional historian. My highest academic qualification in the subject is a Grade 1 O-level. Almost everything I have learned about history has come from reading about the past, and for that I have to thank my father, Gerald Dickinson (born 1925); he and my late mother instilled in me a love of history that has never faded. Some people believe that there is nothing more to be learned about the past, yet every day brings new discoveries.

This book, like my work in the same series about King Henry V, was designed to comply with the original series title, *Following in the Footsteps of...* In other words, it is intended to encourage lovers of history, especially those for whom it is a recent interest, to visit places associated with William and Mary, as well as finding out more about the period without needing to tackle more traditional, perhaps less accessible, works about history. I chose William and Mary partly because no other women had yet appeared in the series, and I was repaid by finding out gradually that the real-life Mary was by no means the colourless character she is made to appear in fictional representations of the period and was well deserving of more coverage. As for William, his military record is noteworthy, in keeping with the name of my publisher, but the purpose of the book is not to go into the detail of his many campaigns. Having travelled to the Netherlands several times for work purposes, I have met (and liked) many Dutch people and picked up a smattering of the language, additional reasons for being attracted to this topic.

It is almost impossible to write a book about any period of history without finding that one's research has overlapped with that of other people, but I can assure the reader that I have tried to put my own interpretation on the information I have gleaned from the sources listed in the Bibliography (as I always do). At the time I began writing, I was unaware of the work of Professor Simon Thurley of Gresham College, an expert on the architecture of the Stuart period (and many others). I have drawn extensively on his writings and particularly on his filmed lectures available on YouTube, which I highly recommend to anyone interested in the topic.

Supporting me throughout my research were my sister, Rebecca Dickinson, a voracious reader with an encyclopedic knowledge of British history, and my husband David Fisher, whose extensive command of European military history was invaluable. Family members have been a source of support and inspiration to me in all my writing, most notably At the time of writing, I cannot predict whether I will ever be fortunate enough to have another book published, so I feel I must take this opportunity to thank the rest of my immediate family – my sister Ruth and my daughters, Roxane and Alex – as well as the many other friends and family members I cannot list for lack of space in this section.

Appendix

Artists and Architects Associated with William and Mary

Bakhuizen, Ludolf (1630–1708) was a German-born artist working in the Netherlands, where he became one of the leading painters of maritime subjects.

Baron, Bernard (died 1762) was a French engraver who came to work in England a decade after the death of William III.

Brandon, Jan Hendrik (1660–1714) was a French-born Dutch painter, who was director of the academy at The Hague and completed a portrait of William.

Canaletto (Giovanni Antonio Canal; 1697–1768) was an important Venetian painter, who lived in London from 1746 to 1755.

Chéron, Louis (1660–1725) was a French Huguenot painter who relocated to London after 1685. He worked on several great houses and submitted designs for St Paul's Cathedral.

da Maiano, Giovanni (died c.1542) was an Italian sculptor, who carried out work at both Hampton Court Palace and Greenwich Palace.

Danckerts, Hendrik (died 1680) was a Dutch Golden Age painter who spent periods working in Italy and England. He specialised in depicting great houses and royal residences, such as Whitehall Palace.

de Baen, Jan (1633–1702) was a Dutch portrait painter who worked for Charles II of England during his exile in the Netherlands. He relocated to The Hague following the Restoration.

de Formentrou, Jacob (died c.1670) was a Flemish painter from Antwerp, about whose life little is known.

de Hooghe, Romeyn (1645–1708) was a Dutch sculptor and painter who produced artworks of political propaganda for William III from the 1670s onwards.

de Keyser, Hendrik (1565–1621) was a Dutch sculptor and architect who designed the tomb of William the Silent, assisted by his brother, **Pieter de Keyser (died 1676)**. He visited London and it was probably there that he met Nicholas Stone, who became his son-in-law.

de Lairesse, Gérard (1641–1711) was a Dutch polymath, an associate and follower of Rembrandt. He lost his eyesight in 1690, but continued to draw.

Desgots, Claude (c.1658–1732) was a French landscape architect who learned his craft under André Le Nôtre, whose biography he wrote. He later worked in England and the Netherlands, and was heavily involved in the design of the gardens at Het Loo.

d'Hondecoeter, Melchior (died 1695) was a Dutch painter who specialised in animal portraits.

Dou, Gerrit (1613–1675) was a Dutch Golden Age painter based in Leiden. He worked under Rembrandt and built a high reputation that lasted until the 1860s. Interest in him revived during the 1970s.

Duval, Robbert (1639–1732) was born and died in The Hague, but also worked in Berlin and in Italy. He became court painter to William in 1682 and was instrumental in setting up the Royal Academy of Art at The Hague.

Eggers, Bartholomeus (died c.1692) was a versatile Flemish sculptor who worked in several media. He collaborated on the interior decoration of public buildings in Antwerp, Amsterdam and The Hague.

Elers, David (dates unknown) and John Philip (1664–1738) were Dutch silversmiths and potters from Utrecht. They eventually set up in Staffordshire, where they worked from 1690 to 1698.

Elsheimer, Adam (1578–1610) was a German artist who worked mainly in Rome but became popular after his death with collectors in England, including King Charles II.

Fabritius, Carel (1622–1654) was a Dutch landscape painter, a pupil of Rembrandt in Amsterdam and later a member of the 'Delft School'. He was killed in an explosion which also destroyed most of his paintings.

Grinling Gibbons (1648–1721) was a Dutch-born sculptor of doubtful parentage, best known for his work in England as a wood-carver. His work can be seen at Hampton Court Palace, St Paul's Cathedral and numerous other locations.

Gibson, Richard (1615–90) was a court dwarf whose height has been estimated at three feet six inches. Gibson's origins are unknown, but he worked for both King Charles I and Oliver Cromwell, and was a collaborator of Peter Lely before joining Mary's household as a drawing-master. He travelled with her to the Netherlands in 1677 and returned with her in 1689.

Hanneman, Adriaen (1604–71) was a Dutch painter based in The Hague, who briefly worked in England around the 1660s.

Hawksmoor, Nicholas (died 1736) was an English architect who worked under Christopher Wren and was Clerk of the Works at Kensington Palace from 1689. Under the Hanoverians, he worked on Blenheim Palace, Castle Howard and other major projects.

Johnson, Cornelius (Cornelius Janssen van Ceulen; 1593–1661) was born in London to Dutch parents. He relocated to the Netherlands during the English Civil War, and remained there. He signed some of his works with the English version of his name, others with the Dutch version.

Francis Johnston (1760–1829) was an Irish architect in Georgian Dublin, who was involved in the creation of the Chapel Royal within Dublin Castle. He also worked on the restoration of Slane Castle, overlooking the River Boyne.

Jones, Inigo (1573–1652) was a highly influential English architect, one of the earliest whose name is remembered. He made his name designing stage sets and costumes during the reign of King James I. As Surveyor-General of the King's Works, he served the monarchy until the downfall of Charles I, and his name has been associated with over 1000 buildings in England and Wales.

Kneller, Sir Godfrey (1646–1723) was a German-born painter, best known for his portraits of eminent people and British monarchs. He lived and worked in the Netherlands before coming to England in 1676.

Laguerre, Louis (1663–1721) was a French decorative painter, who relocated to Britain in 1683 and worked for William III on Hampton Court Palace.

Lujken, Jan (1649–1712) was a Dutch poet, painter and engraver from Amsterdam.

Maas, Dirk (1659–1717) was a Dutch landscape painter who accompanied William to Ireland in 1690, subsequently returning to the Netherlands.

Marot, Daniel (1661–1752) was a Huguenot refugee from France, who introduced artistic ideas from the court of Louis XIV into the Netherlands and later worked for William and Mary in England. He was prominent as an architect, interior designer, garden designer and engraver.

Neefs, Pieter (the Younger; died c.1675) was a Flemish painter, mainly known for his church interiors.

Netscher, Caspar (1639–84) was a Dutch portrait painter based in The Hague. He was a member of the Confrerie Pictura and William was among his patrons.

Post, Maurits (1645–77) was the talented son of Pieter Post, and succeeded his father as official architect to the House of Orange, but died in his prime. He worked for William at Soestdijk and other locations.

Post, Pieter (1608–69) was a Dutch architect and painter of the Golden Age, who was official architect to the House of Orange from 1645 onwards. He worked on Huis ten Bosch and the Mauritshuis in The Hague and the Noordeinde Palace, and also worked for William in Delft and Maastricht. He was succeeded as official architect on his death by his son, Maurits Post.

Quare, Daniel (died 1724) was a maker of clocks and scientific instruments. His origins are obscure, but he worked in London from around 1670. A Quaker, he was fined by King James II but William III soon became his patron.

Quellin, Arnold (Artus Quellinus III; 1653–86) was a Flemish sculptor from an eminent family of artists. He was an associate of Grinling Gibbons, with whom he collaborated on the altarpiece for James II's Roman Catholic chapel at Whitehall palace.

Ragueneau Abraham (1623–81) was a French artist who worked as curator of William's 'cabinet' of paintings.

Rembrandt (more correctly Rembrandt van Rijn; 1606–69) is one of the most important and influential of the Dutch Golden Age artists. Rembrandt worked in Leiden and Amsterdam. He is best known for his self-portraits and his painting *Militia Company of Captain Frans Banning Cocq* (popularly known as *The Night Watch*).

Rijsbrack/Rysbrack, Jan Michiel (1694–1770) was a Flemish sculptor who relocated to England with his brother in about 1720. By the time of his death he was one of the country's leading sculptors, responsible for many monuments and an equestrian statue of William III.

Roman, Jacob or Jacobus (1640–1716) was William's official architect in the Netherlands in succession to Maurits Post. He worked extensively on Het Loo.

Rousseau, Jacques (1630–93) was a French Huguenot painter, mostly of landscapes, employed by Louis XIV at Versailles. Religious persecution obliged him to leave France in 1685, and he lived and worked in England from 1690 until his death.

Rubens, Peter Paul (1577–1640) was a Flemish artist, best known as a painter. His workshop was in Antwerp, but he worked for the French and Spanish royal families as well as spending time in Italy and England. He also became a diplomat in later life.

Rysbrack, John Michael (1694–1770) was a Flemish sculptor, who worked in England and executed many of the most notable memorials in Westminster Abbey, including that of Godfrey Kneller, as well as the equestrian statue of William III in Bristol.

Saenredam, Pieter Jansz (1597–1665) was a Dutch Golden Age painter known for his depictions of church interiors.

Samwell, William (1628–1676) was an English 'gentleman architect', whose main interest was in the design of mansions and country houses.

Scheemakers the Younger, Peter (1691–1781) was a Flemish sculptor, who spent most of his working life in London, where many of his works survive

Schellinks, Willem (1623–78) was a widely-travelled Dutch landscape painter and poet, who visited England after the Restoration and left a journal and a collection of drawings from his travels.

Stickells, Robert (died 1620) was an English architect who worked on some country houses and on the Banqueting House in Whitehall.

Stone, Nicholas (died 1647) was an English sculptor and architect who was a master mason under both James I and Charles I.

Talman, William (1650–1719) was an English architect and landscape architect who became Comptroller of the Royal Works in 1689. He worked for Wren on Hampton Court. Many contemporaries are said to have found him difficult to get on with.

Tijou, Jean (died after 1712) was a French Huguenot wrought ironworker, who came to Britain with William III and stayed till around 1712. He was the father-in-law of Louis Laguerre.

Vanbrugh, Sir John (1664–1726) was an English architect of Flemish descent, and a successful dramatist.

Van Campen, Jacob (1596–1657) was a Dutch architect of the Golden Age. He collaborated with Pieter Post on the Mauritshuis in The Hague and was the main architect of the Noordeinde Palace.

Vanderbank, John (died 1717) was a Paris-born Huguenot tapestry weaver. He became the proprietor of the Soho Tapestry Manufactory and also supplied the royal family with wall-hangings.

Van der Haagen, Joris (died 1669) was a Dutch landscape painter and a co-founder of the 'Confrerie Pictura' at The Hague in 1656.

Van der Meulen, Laurens (1643–1719) was a Flemish sculptor who worked in England between 1675 and 1687, sometimes in partnership with Peter Van Dievoet.

Van der Poel, Egbert (1621–64) was a Dutch landscape painter of the Golden Age. He was based in Delft.

Van der Schuer, Theodoor (1634–1707) was a Dutch painter from The Hague and one of the founders of the city's exclusive 'Confrerie Pictura' in 1656. He had led a colourful life in Italy and Sweden prior to becoming a court painter.

Van der Vaart, Jan (died 1720) was a versatile Dutch painter who worked in London from 1674 onwards.

Van De Velde (the Elder), Willem (died 1693) was a Dutch marine painter who moved to England in the early 1670s, and set up a studio in Greenwich with his son.

Van De Velde (the Younger), Willem (1633–1707) was a Dutch marine painter. He worked with his father for both Charles II and James II before the arrival of William and Mary, and spent the rest of his life in England.

Van Dievoet, Peter (1661–1729) was a Flemish sculptor and wood-carver who worked mainly in Brussels and London.

Van Goyen, Jan (1596–1656) was a Dutch landscape painter of the Golden Age who moved from Leiden to The Hague, where most of his work was executed.

Van Honthorst, Gerrit or Gerard (1592–1656) was a Dutch painter of the Golden Age who worked in Italy and later in Utrecht and The Hague. He was drawing-master to the children of Elizabeth of Bohemia, and painted portraits of members of the House of Orange and other eminent individuals.

Van Scorel, Jan (died 1562) was a Dutch Renaissance artist based in Utrecht from 1530 onwards.

Van Swieten, Johan (dates unknown) was a Dutch land surveyor who was appointed William's court architect in the Netherlands from 1677, succeeding Maurits Post. He was dismissed in 1689 and replaced by Jacob Roman.

Verkolje, Jan (1650–93) was a prolific and versatile Dutch painter and engraver, best remembered for his portraits. He painted both William and Mary in the Netherlands.

Vermeer, Johannes (1632–75) was a Dutch painter known mainly for his interiors and views of his home town of Delft. His works are nowadays highly prized.

Verrio, Antonio (died 1707) was an Italian painter, a specialist in murals, who was largely responsible for the introduction of the Baroque style into Britain, where he worked for the monarchy from 1672 until his death. His work can still be seen in prominent buildings throughout England and Wales, including Hampton Court Palace and Windsor Castle.

Vincidor, Tomasso (died 1536) was an artist and architect. A pupil of Raphael, he was born in Italy but ended his life in Breda.

Webb, John (1611–1672) was an English architect and sometime collaborator of Inigo Jones. Webb is mainly remembered for his work on Greenwich Palace.

White, Robert (1645–1703) was a London engraver, known mainly for his portraits, which were frequently copied for wider circulation.

Wise, Henry (1653–1738) was an English gardener and garden designer, known for his work at Kensington Gardens and Hampton Court Palace.

Wissing, Willem (1656–87) was a Dutch portrait painter who worked in England as an assistant to Peter Lely. James II sent Wissing to the Netherlands in 1685 to paint William and Mary. He completed several other royal portraits, as well as those of nobles including the Earl of Rochester and the Duke of Ormonde, before his early death.

Wren, Sir Christopher (1632–1723) was an English architect, now best remembered for his role in rebuilding London following the Great Fire of 1666.

Wyck, Jan (1645–1702) was a Dutch artist who specialised in military subjects. His father, also a painter, took him to England after the Restoration, but returned during the 1670s, leaving Jan to settle in London. He later accompanied Dirk Maas to Ireland to record the military achievements of William III.

Bibliography

Primary sources
Abel Boyer, *The History of King William the Third*, 1702/3 (3 volumes)
Gilbert Burnet, *An essay on the memory of the late Queen*. 1695.
Gilbert Burnet, *History of my own time*. 1724 and 1734 (2 volumes)
Celia Fiennes, *Through England on a Side Saddle in the Time of William and Mary*. 1702
Narcissus Luttrell, *A Brief Historical Relation of State Affairs 1678–1714*. Oxford University Press, 1857.
Charlotte Sophie, Countess Bentinck (ed) *Lettres et mémoires de Marie, reine d'Angleterre, épouse de Guillaume III*. G. Fishbacher, 1880.
Christopher Wren (1675–1747), *Parentalia: Or, Memoirs Of The Family of the Wrens*. 1750

Books
C.C. Barfoot & Paul Hoftijzer (editors), *Fabrics and Fabrications: the myth and making of William and Mary*. Editions Rodopi B.V., 1990. ISBN 978-9-05183-182-5
Brian Best, *William of Orange and the fight for the Crown of England*. Frontline Books, 2021. ISBN 978-1-52679-522-9
Kerry Downs, *Christopher Wren*. Oxford University Press, 2007. ISBN 978-0-19164-752-9
Ferguson, Julie, *Visualising Protestant Monarchy: Ceremony, Art and Politics After the Glorious Revolution (1689–1714)*. Boydell Press, 2021. ISBN 978-178327-544-1
John Kiste, *William and Mary: Heroes of the Glorious Revolution*. History Press, 2011. ISBN 978-0-75247-097-9
John Miller, *James II: a Study in Kingship*. Methuen, 1991. ISBN 0-413-65290-4
David Onnekink, Esther Mijers (editors) *Redefining William III: The Impact of the King-Stadholder in International Context*. Taylor & Francis, 2016. ISBN 978-1-31706-987-4
Agnes & Elizabeth Strickland, *Lives of the Queens of England: Volume 10*. Blanchard, 1850.
Simon Thurley, *Whitehall Palace: an architectural history of the royal apartments 1240–1690*. Yale University Press, 1999. ISBN 0-300-07639-8
Arthur Trevor, *The Life and Times of William III, King of England, and Stadtholder of Holland*. Longman, 1836.

Olaf van Nimwegen, *The Dutch Army and the Military Revolutions, 1588–1688.* Boydell, 2010. ISBN 978-1-843-83575-2

David Onnekink & Esther Mijers *Redefining William III: The Impact of the King-stadholder in International Context.* Ashgate ISBN 978-0-754-65028-7

Stefan van Raaij and Paul Spies, *The Royal Progress of William and Mary.* D'Arts/De Bataafsche Leeuw, 1988. ISBN 90-6707-191-9

Lois G. Schwoerer (ed.), *The Revolution of 1688–89: changing perspectives.* Cambridge University Press, 1992. ISBN 978-0-5215-2614-2

Maureen Waller, *Sovereign ladies: the six reigning queens of England.* John Murray, 2007. ISBN 978-0-7195-6714-8

Articles

Hugh Aldersey-Williams, "Between Galileo and Newton". *History Today* Vol 70 (11), November 2020, pages 60–67

Ruth Battersby Tooke, Benjamin Redding, Francesca Vanke & Claire Jowitt, "The wreck that rocked the monarchy". *BBC History*, March 2023, pages 46–52

Rex Cathcart, "Ireland and 'King Billy': Usage and Abusage." *History Today* Vol 38 (7), July 1988

Chris Catling, " 'Not so much a residence as a tradition': the evolution of St James's Palace from leper hospital to royal court." *Current Archaeology*, Issue 394 (January 2023), pages 36–45

Alexander Dencher, "Daniel Marot and the painted staircase in the United Provinces." In *Deckenmalerei um 1700 in Europa* (Hirmer, 2020), ISBN 978-3777436388, pages 211–225.

K H D Haley, "William III as builder of Het Loo", and Florence Hopper, "Daniel Marot: a French garden designer in Holland". In *The Dutch Garden in the Seventeenth Century.* United States: Dumbarton Oaks Research Library and Collection, 1990.

Thomas E. Jordan, "Quality of Life in Seventeenth Century Dublin." *Dublin Historical Record* vol 61, no. 2 (2008) pages 136–54. http://www.jstor.org/stable/27806788.

Charles-Edouard Levillain, "William III's Military and Political Career in Neo-Roman Context, 1672–1702". *The Historical Journal* vol. 48, no. 2 (June 2005), pages 321–350

Rolf Loeber, "The Rebuilding of Dublin Castle: Thirty Critical Years, 1661–1690." *Studies: An Irish Quarterly Review*, vol. 69, No. 273 (Spring, 1980), pages 45–69

Thomas J. McSweeney, Katharine Ello, and Elsbeth O'Brien, "A University in 1693: New Light on William & Mary's claim to the title 'Oldest university in the United States'." *William & Mary Law Review*, 15 October 2020.

Richard Price, "An Incomparable Lady: Queen Mary II's Share in the Government of England, 1689–94." *Huntington Library Quarterly* vol. 75, No. 3 (Autumn 2012), pages 307–326

Brita Rang, "An unidentified source of John Locke's *Some thoughts concerning education.*" *Pedagogy, Culture and Society,* vol. 9, No. 2 (2001), pages 249–278

Bibliography

Hanneke Ronnes & Bob van Toor, "Restored and regretted: a history of staging authenticity at the Dutch palace Het Loo." In *Collections: A Journal for Museum and Archives Professionals* Vol. 16(2) 2020, pages 162–176

W A Speck, "William – and Mary?" In *The Revolution of 1688–89: Changing Perspectives* (ed. Lois G. Schwoerer; Cambridge University Press, 1992, pages 131–146

Mark Walker, "From William and Mary to William III: Transitioning the Monarchy at the Funeral Rituals of Mary II 1695." In *Royal Studies Journal* Vol 8(2), pages 146–160

Websites
Aronson Delftware: https://www.aronson.com/the-queens-passion-for-flowers/
The Irish Story: https://www.theirishstory.com/
https://www.metmuseum.org/art/collection/search/698848 but where?

YouTube videos
Simon Thurley: *William And Mary: The Court Divided.*
https://www.youtube.com/watch?v=7o0_iZuE3Lo

Simon Thurley: *The Last Stuarts and the Death of the Royal Powerhouse*
https://www.youtube.com/watch?v=aQ-dgXRnTHM

Simon Thurley: *English Architecture, 1650 to 1760: The Rise of Consensus*
https://www.youtube.com/watch?v=tBhx98WIM5w&t=874s

Simon Thurley: *Progresses: Royal Courts on the Move in Tudor and Stuart England*
https://www.youtube.com/watch?v=sdb8h4vqVis&list=PLU3TaPgchJtS tg9i2KFQ0DvrQbxN8P3P6

Note that web addresses may change over time. Some web content may become unavailable or a new search may be required to find it.

General reading:
Tristram Hunt, *The Radical Potter: Josiah Wedgwood and the Transformation of Britain.* Allen Lane, 2021. ISBN 978-0241287897

Places of interest

IRELAND
Aughrim Interpretative Centre
Ballinasloe, Co Galway
Admission charge
Website: https://heritage.galwaycommunityheritage.org/content/category/places/battle-of-aughrim-visitor-centre

Battle of the Boyne Visitor Centre
Oldbridge, Drogheda, Co. Meath A92 CY68
Website: https://www.battleoftheboyne.ie/
Admission charge

Christ Church Cathedral
Christchurch Place, Dublin D08 TF98
Website: https://christchurchcathedral.ie/

Dublin Castle
Website: https://www.dublincastle.ie/

St Patrick's Cathedral
St Patrick's Close, Dublin D08 H6X3
Admission charge
Website: https://www.stpatrickscathedral.ie/

LONDON
Banqueting House, Whitehall
London, SW1A 2ER
Website: https://www.hrp.org.uk/banqueting-house/#gs.fmbgbi
Open only on specific dates (guided tours) and open days

Greenwich Royal Museums
National Maritime Museum and Queen's House
Park Row, London SE10 9NF
Website: https://www.rmg.co.uk/queens-house

Hampton Court Palace
East Molesey, Surrey KT8 9AU
Website: https://www.hrp.org.uk/hampton-court-palace/visit/#gs.jubiqg

Kensington Palace
Kensington Gardens, London W8 4PX
Website: https://www.hrp.org.uk/kensington-palace/
Admission charge

National Portrait Gallery
St Martin's Place, London, WC2H 0HE
Website: https://www.npg.org.uk/

Richmond Museum
Old Town Hall, Whittaker Ave, Richmond-upon-Thames TW9 1TP
Admission charge
Website: https://www.museumofrichmond.com/

Westminster Abbey
Dean's Yard, London SW1P 3PA
Website: https://www.westminster-abbey.org/
Admission fee; free when attending a service

York House, Richmond Road, Twickenham TW1 3AA
Website of York House Society: https://theyorkhousesociety.org.uk/

YORK
Clifford's Tower
Tower Street, York YO1 9SA
Website: https://www.english-heritage.org.uk/visit/places/cliffords-tower-york
Admission charge (English Heritage)

King's Manor
York YO1 7EP
Telephone: 1904 32 0000

The Treasurer's House
Minster Yard, York YO1 7JL
E-mail: treasurershouse@nationaltrust.org.uk
Website: https://www.nationaltrust.org.uk/visit/yorkshire/treasurers-house-york
Admission charge (NT)
Open all year; visit by guided tour only during the summer

York Castle Museum
Eye of York, York YO1 9RY
Website: https://www.yorkcastlemuseum.org.uk/visitor-information/
Admission charge

York Minster
Website: https://yorkminster.org/
Admission charge; free when attending a service

REST OF ENGLAND
Althorp House
Northampton NN7 4HQ
Website: https://althorpestate.com/
E-mail: info@althorp.com
Admission charge

Belton House
Grantham, Lincolnshire NG32 2LS
Website: https://www.nationaltrust.org.uk/visit/nottinghamshire-lincolnshire/belton-house
Admission charge (NT)

Boughton House
Kettering,
Northamptonshire NN14 1BJ
Website: https://www.boughtonhouse.co.uk/
House is open to the public on bank holidays in summer: Admission charge

Bradgate House (ruins)
Bradgate Park, Newtown Linford, Leicester LE6 0HE
Website: https://www.bradgatepark.org/walks-talks-and-group-visits
Limited opening times; donations requested

Burghley House
Stamford, Lincolnshire PE9 3JY
Website: https://burghley.co.uk/
Admission charge

Castle Ashby (gardens only)
Castle Ashby, Northampton, NN7 1LF
Website: https://www.castleashbygardens.co.uk/visitor-information/
Admission charge; pre-booking advisable

National Horse Racing Museum
Palace House, Palace Street, Newmarket CB8 8EP
Website: www.nhrm.co.uk
Admission charge

Sheldonian Theatre
Broad Street, Oxford OX1 3AZ
Website: https://www.sheldonian.ox.ac.uk/visit
Admission charge

Warwick Castle
Warwick CV34 4QU
Website: https://www.warwick-castle.com/
Admission charge

Welbeck Abbey (estate)
Worksop, Nottinghamshire S80 3LL
Website: https://www.welbeck.co.uk/
State room tours:
https://harleyfoundation.org.uk/whats-on/event/welbeck-abbey-state-room-tours/
Also: The Portland Collection
Website: https://harleyfoundation.org.uk/

Bibliography

CONTINENTAL EUROPE

Both Belgium and the Netherlands have relatively flat landscapes, making walking and cycling easier for the visitor. Visitors can fly to Brussels or Amsterdam from several regional airports in the UK. KLM Royal Dutch Airlines also runs flights to Antwerp, and at the time of writing, direct flights are available from the UK to Maastricht and The Hague/Rotterdam.

Brussels is the nearest European capital city to London in terms of distance, and is easily reached by Eurostar in less than three hours. Eurostar to Amsterdam takes around four hours. Both countries are smaller than the UK and public transport is generally good. English is widely spoken in the areas most popular with visitors, and most of the websites listed are available in an English version. Many websites offer further advice on travel to the various towns and cities listed, and it is not possible to make specific recommendations as to which are best for your purposes.

Whilst cycling in the UK is not always an option for the tourist, the Netherlands (where 27% of all journeys are made by cycle) provides well for those on cycle tours, with specialist campsites and other facilities.

BELGIUM – ANTWERP

Cathedral of Our Lady
Groenplaats 21, 2000 Antwerpen
Website: https://www.dekathedraal.be/en

Fort Lillo
Scheldelaan, 2040 Antwerpen
Website (unofficial): https://www.livetheworld.com/activities/belgium/fort-lillo
Admission free; charge for guided tours

Museum Vleeshuis
Vleeshouwersstraat 38, 2000 Antwerpen
Website: https://museumvleeshuis.be/en
Admission charge

St James's Church
Sint-Jacobstraat 9, 2000 Antwerpen
Website: https://www.sintjacobantwerpen.be/

NETHERLANDS

AMSTERDAM
Rijksmuseum
Museumstraat 1, Amsterdam
Website: https://www.rijksmuseum.nl/nl
Admission charge (free to visitors under 19)

BREDA
Stedelijk Museum Breda
Boschstraat 22
4811 GH Breda
Website: https://www.stedelijkmuseumbreda.nl/en/

Waalse Kerk Breda (Walloon Church)
Catharinastraat 83
4811 XG Breda
Website: http://www.waalsekerkbreda.nl/

DELFT
Nieuwe Kerk
Markt 80
2611 GW Delft
Website: https://oudeennieuwekerkdelft.nl/
Admission charge

Oude Kerk
Heilige Geestkerkhof 25
2611 HP Delft
Website: (as for the Niewuwe Kerk)

Prinsenhof Museum
Sint Agathaplein
2611 HR Delft
Website: https://prinsenhof-delft.nl/en
Admission charge

GRAVE
Sint Elisabethskerk
Hoofdwagt 1
5361 EW Grave
Website: https://www.st-elisabethparochie.nl/

Stadsmuseum Grave
Hampoort
Sint Elisabethstraat 10A
5361 EW Grave
Website: https://www.stadsmuseumgrave.nl/

Bibliography

THE HAGUE AND AREA
Binnenhof
2513 AA The Hague
Website: https://www.rijksoverheid.nl/ministeries/ministerie-van-algemene-zaken/organisatie/gebouwen/binnenhof

Historical Museum
Korte Vijverberg 7
2513 AB The Hague
Website: https://www.haagshistorischmuseum.nl/nl/plan-your-visit

Mauritshuis
Plein 29
2511 CS Den Haag
Admission charge
Website: https://www.mauritshuis.nl/en/visit/

Paleis Het Loo
Koninklijk Park 16, Apeldoorn
Admission Charge
Website: https://paleishetloo.nl/en/about/location-events

LEIDEN
Academic Historical Museum
Rapenburg 73
2311 GJ Leiden
Website: https://www.library.universiteitleiden.nl/about-us/library-locations/academic-historical-museum

Bibliotheca Thysiana
Rapenburg 25
2311 GG Leiden
Website: https://www.library.universiteitleiden.nl/about-us/library-locations/bibliotheca-thysiana

Gravensteen
Pieterskerkhof 6
2311 SR Leiden
Website: https://www.universiteitleiden.nl/en/locations/gravensteen

Hooglandse Kerk
Nieuwstraat 20
2312 KC Leiden
Website: https://hooglandsekerk.com/

Meermansburg Almshouse
Oude Vest 159
2312 XW Leiden
Website: https://openmonumentendagenleiden.nl/en/informatie-monumenten/meermansburg-fmr-almshouse

Old Observatory
Sterrewachtlaan 11
2311 GW Leiden
Website: https://www.universiteitleiden.nl/old-observatory

Rijksmuseum Boerhaave
10, Lange St. Agnietenstraat
2312 WC Leiden
Website: https://rijksmuseumboerhaave.nl/english

St Peter's Church
Kloksteeg 16
2311 SL Leiden
Website: https://pieterskerk.com/en/museum/

MAASTRICHT
Fort Sint Pieter
Luikerweg 80
6212 NH Maastricht (LB)
Website: https://www.natuurmonumenten.nl/natuurgebieden/sint-pietersberg/monument/fort-sint-pieter
Admission charge

Helpoort
St. Bernardusstraat 24 b
6211 HH Maastricht
Website: https://www-vestingmuseummaastricht-nl
Limited opening hours
Admission charge

NAARDEN
Vestingmuseum
Westwalstraat 6
1411 PB Naarden Vesting
Website: https://www.vestingmuseum.nl/museum/
Admission charge

Index

Addison, Joseph, 129
Against All Flags, 168
Amalia, Princess of Orange, 9–11, 48, 59
Anglo-Dutch Wars, 14, 31, 143
Anne, Queen, viii, 14, 30–31, 33, 37–40, 43, 45–6, 58–61, 65, 72, 79, 82, 86–8, 93, 105, 109, 112–3, 118–9, 128–131, 133, 136, 138–9, 142, 151, 154–7, 159, 167, 169–70
Anne Boleyn, queen consort of England, 31, 82, 135
Anne of Cleves, queen consort of England, 32
Antwerp, 4, 8, 22, 50–3, 59, 124, 126, 162, 185
Apeldoorn, vii, 67
Apsley, Allen, 43
Apsley, Frances, 42–3
Ashby, Sir John, 104
Aughrim, Battle of, 103, 161, 181

Balcarres, Lord, 3
Banks, vii, 123
Banqueting House, Whitehall, 83, 85–90, 114, 117, 130–1, 176, 182
Barfleur, 110
Bathurst, Benjamin, 43
Beachy Head, Battle of, 103–4
Beeldenstorm, 1
Begijnhof (Breda), 56–7
Bentinck, Mary, 139
Bentinck, William, Earl of Portland, 45–6, 49, 59, 69, 71, 109, 117–8, 130, 133, 139–40, 142, 147, 150, 156–7
Bernhard, Prince, 68
Betterton, Mary, 40
Bibliotheca Thysiana, 17–18, 187

Bill of Rights, 80, 90, 154
Binnenhof, 2, 5–10, 47, 84, 187
Black Tulip, The, 169
Blow, John, 152, 97
Blue Guards, 97
Bonaparte, Louis, 68
Bonn, 26
Bornius, Hendrik, 15, 19
Boyer, Abel, 106, 108
Boyle, Henry, 79
Boyle, Robert, 79
Boyne, Battle of the, vii, 97–9, 101, 103, 143, 161–2 182
Boyne, River, 97, 162, 174
Breda, 12, 21, 50, 53–8, 177, 186
    castle, 55–6
    Declaration of, 53–4
    Treaty of, 55
Brixham, 78, 166
Bristol, 23, 113, 165–6, 176
Buitenhof, 7, 23
Burlington, Earl of, 79
Burnet, Gilbert, 65, 82, 108, 129, 152, 159

Cambridge, vii, 145, 149
Cambridge, Duke of (title), 45, 119
Canal, 11, 21, 49, 55–6, 60, 135
Caroline of Ansbach, queen consort of Great Britain, 118–9
Carrickfergus, 96, 101, 169
Cassel, Battle of, 29
Catherine of Aragon, queen consort of England, 134
Catherine of Braganza, queen consort of England, 30, 33, 36, 41, 46, 83–4, 124, 136

Catherine Howard, queen consort of
   England, 135
Celle, 61
Chamilly, Marquis de, 27
Chaplin, Sir Francis, 44
Charleroi, 24
Charles I of England, King, 1, 10, 16,
   30, 34, 38–9, 82, 87–8, 114, 118, 135,
   138, 174–6
Charles II of England, King, 2–3, 12, 14,
   19, 27–33, 39–43, 47, 50, 52–5, 59–66,
   71–2, 75, 79, 82–3, 85, 87–9, 92, 98,
   100, 102, 112–4, 123–4, 135–6, 138–9,
   143–5, 150, 152, 155, 168, 173, 177
Charles II: the Power and the Passion, 168
Charles III of the United Kingdom,
   King, 91
Charles, Duke of Cambridge (died 1677),
   45, 60
Charles Stuart ('Bonnie Prince Charlie';
   'the Young Pretender'), 156
Charlotte Elizabeth, Princess (Liselotte),
   3, 29
Cheere, John, 165
Christ Church Cathedral, 101–2, 182
Churchill, Arabella, 36, 41
Churchill, John (Duke of Marlborough),
   24, 36, 62, 78–9, 97, 103, 108–9, 120,
   128, 130, 151–2, 154, 167
Churchill, Sarah (Duchess of
   Marlborough), 36, 43, 62, 65, 79, 82, 93,
   109, 112, 129–30, 167
Clausius, Carolus, 17–18
Clifford's Tower (York Castle), 34, 183
Coffee, coffee houses, vii, 123–6
College of William & Mary, 79, 163
Compton, Henry, 39–40, 45, 66, 75,
   92, 152
Condé, Prince de, 26
Coppin, Sir George, 115
Coronation Oath, 80–81
Council of Nine, 103–4, 107–8, 110, 133
Covel, John, 61, 145
Croft, William, 129
Cromwell, Oliver, 1, 20, 31, 54, 98, 100,
   102, 138
Crowne, John, 40

Darien scheme, 110, 153
d'Artagnan, Count, 25
De Witt, Cornelis, 7, 23–4, 27, 55,
   110, 169
De Witt, Johan, 7, 13, 23–4, 27, 55,
   110, 169
Delft, 8, 16, 21–3, 57, 61, 70, 143, 174–7,
   186
Delft ware, 22–3, 73, 140
Denmark House, 84
Diana, Princess of Wales, 120, 168
Dieren, 19, 49, 59, 73
Dolben, John, 36
Downing, Sir George, 85
Drogheda, 98, 102, 182
Dryden, John, 93, 112, 125
Duarte, Diego, 52
Duarte, Gaspar, 52
Dublin, vii, 94, 97–102, 125, 127, 174, 182
Dublin Castle, 100, 174, 182
Dumas, Alexandre, 25, 169
Dundalk, 96
Dunkerque, 29
Dutch Church (London), 20
Dutch East India Company, 17, 122, 124
Dutch Gift, 13–14, 72

Edgar, Duke of Cambridge, 30, 38
Edward I of England, King, 91
Edward VI of England, King, 34
Edward VI of England, King, 135
Edward VII of the United Kingdom,
   King, 119
Edinburgh, vi, 127
Edinburgh Castle, 91
Edmundson, Helen, 170
Eighty Years' War, 2
Elizabeth I of England, Queen, 37, 86, 101
Elizabeth of Bohemia, Queen, 4, 10, 16,
   31, 54, 86, 177
Emilia of Nassau, 27
England, My England, 168
Evelyn, John, 46, 84, 153
Exclusion Bill, 60, 62

Fabritius, Carel, 22, 174
Fagel, Gaspar, 23

Farnese, Alexander, 51
Fawkes, Guy, 35
Fenwick, Sir John, 133, 158
Fiennes, Celia, 130, 140
Finch, Daniel, Earl of Nottingham, 103, 108, 115, 132
Fitzharding(e), Lady (Barbara Villiers), 79
Fleetwood, William, 132
Fort Lillo, 52, 185
Fort Sint Pieter (Maastricht), 25, 188
Forty Martyrs, vi
Foyle, River, 95
Frederick Henry, Prince of Orange, 8–10, 15, 48, 55–6, 151
Frederick William, Elector of Brandenburg, 2

Gaunt, Elizabeth, 62–3
Georg Friedrich of Waldeck, Prince, 24
George I, King of Great Britain, 118, 155
George II, King of Great Britain, 37, 113, 118–9, 142, 155, 164, 166
George IV, King of the United Kingdom, 99
George, Prince of Denmark, 65, 79, 109
George William of Celle, Prince, 61
Gérard, Balthasar, 21
Gibson, Richard, 38, 49, 174
Glasgow, 127, 162, 165
Glencoe, 110
Glorious Revolution, vi
Golden Age (Netherlands), 2, 5, 122, 173–7
Goldsmith, Mrs, 157–8
Goldsmith, Oliver, 159
Goose-Pie House, 89
Grand Pensionary (title), 13, 23
Grave (De Graaf), 26–7, 186
Gravesend, 82, 121
Greenwich Hospital, viii, 110, 112–5, 182
Great Fire of London, vi, 20, 123–4, 178
Green, Frank, 35
Gregory, Philippa, 170
Grey, Lady Jane, 148
Grote Kerk (Breda), 56–7
Grote Kerk (The Hague), 9
Grote Markt (Antwerp), 51

Grote Markt (Breda), 58
Guelders, 1
Guild of St Luke, 4, 23
Guildhall (London), 40

Hadid, Zaha, 51
Hague, The, vii, 2–12, 15, 19, 47, 49, 53–4, 60–1, 65, 74–5, 84, 105–6, 120, 144, 151, 155, 173–8, 185, 187
Hampton Court Palace, viii, 70–3, 84–5, 91, 93, 115–7, 134–145, 154, 156, 173–8, 182
Hanover, 61, 151, 155, 159
Hanseatic League, 51
Hawksmoor, Nicholas, 89, 113–6, 119, 123, 174
Henrietta Maria, queen consort of England and Scotland, 13, 30–31, 33, 39, 114
Henry III of England, King, 32
Henry III of Nassau, 55
Henry VII of England, King, 37, 131, 157
Henry VIII of England, King, 31, 78, 82, 89, 134, 148
Henry, Duke of Gloucester, Prince, 2, 14
Het Loo, vi-vii, 6, 11, 28, 67–75, 106, 117, 119, 152, 154–5
Historic Royal Palaces, 116
Holbein, Hans, 32, 86, 89, 118, 135
Holbein Gate, 89, 135
Holland House, 115
Hoonselardijk, 19, 47–8, 58, 71, 78, 105, 136
Hooper, Dr, 49–50, 60
Howard, James, Earl of Suffolk, 39
Hull, 165
Huis ten Bosch, 10–11, 175
Huygens, Christiaan, 56, 142
Huygens, Constantijn (the elder), 56
Huygens, Constantijn (the younger), 56, 69, 72, 118, 150
Hyde, Anne, Duchess of York, 3, 13, 30, 33–4, 36, 38, 41–2, 46, 62, 79, 131, 139
Hyde, Edward, later Earl of Clarendon, 13, 30, 33, 39, 53–4, 99, 149
Hyde, Henrietta, 46

Hyde, Henry, Earl of Clarendon, 53, 107, 149

Immortal Seven, 76, 120, 150, 152
innocent XII, Pope, 105, 121
Ireland, vi-vii, 12, 41, 91, 94–103, 109, 116, 127, 130, 153–5, 157–162, 175, 178

Jacobites, 81, 90, 95, 97, 102–5, 107, 110, 132, 158, 165–6
James I of England (VI of Scotland), King, 34, 82, 86–8, 92, 135, 145, 151, 175–6
James II of England (VII of Scotland), King, vii, 2,12, 30, 33–6, 38–43, 54–5, 60–6, 75–84, 88, 91–102, 105, 107–8, 110, 121, 123, 128, 133, 139, 145–6, 148, 151, 154–5, 158, 161, 166, 169
James, Duke of Cambridge, 31, 45
James Francis Edward Stuart, Prince of Wales ('the Old Pretender'), 117, 151, 154, 156
Japan, 11, 122
Jefferson, Thomas, 163
Jeffreys, Judge (George) 65–6
Jennings, Frances, 36
Jermyn, Henry, 54, 103
Johan Maurits, Prince, 7
Johan Willem Friso, Prince of Orange, 157
Johnson, Cornelius, 3–4, 15, 147, 174
Jonathan's Coffee House, 12–5
Jonson, Ben, 86
Juliana, Queen of the Netherlands, 29, 68

Ken, Thomas, 50, 60–61
Kensington Palace, viii, 70, 84–6, 93, 106, 111, 115–21, 128, 130, 133–7, 139, 142, 144, 149, 156–7, 166, 174, 178, 182
Kéroualle, Louise de, 83, 85
Kidd, Captain, 153, 168
Kilkenny, 102
Killigrew, Mary, 15
Killiecrankie, Battle of, 95
King, William, 97, 100
King William's Toleration, 81
King William's War, 150
King's Manor (York), 35
Kingston, Earl of, 147

Kinsale, 94
Kirke, Percy, 95
Kit-Cat Club, 126
Kloosterkerk, 12
Kneller, Godfrey, 81, 138, 141, 147, 153, 166, 175–6

Laine, Peter de, 40
Lambeth Palace, 108
Lamplugh, Thomas, 36
Landen, Battle of, 120
Langford, Mrs, 49
Le Nôtre, André, 72, 173
League of Gentlemen's Apocalypse, The, 170
Leiden, 15–19, 45, 156, 174–7, 187–8
Lely, Peter, 29, 49, 139, 166–7, 174, 178
Leopold I, Holy Roman Emperor, 151, 155
Leuze, Battle of, 106
L'homme qui rit, 169
Liège, 25, 106
Line, Francis, 88
Lloyd, William, 100
Lloyd's, 123
Locke, John, 81
London, vii, 6, 13–14, 30–3, 36, 44, 63–6, 72, 79–80, 82, 84, 86, 92, 106, 110, 114–5, 120–9, 131–5, 152–3, 157, 166, 173–8, 182–3
London Gazette, 90, 127
Louis XIV of France, King, 3, 20, 24, 26–9, 32, 53, 59, 64, 66–7, 69, 71–2, 79, 83, 85, 94, 104, 112, 144, 150–1, 154–5, 175–6
Louis, Grand Dauphin of France, 42, 44
Louis of Baden, Prince, 121
Louise, Princess of Orange, 10
Lowestoft, 33
Lowther, Sir John, 103
Ludewig, Frank Adrianus, 27

Maastricht, 24–6, 175, 188
Mackenzie, Lady Anna, 3
Margate, 46, 121
Marie de Medici, queen consort and regent of France, 48
Marie-Anne de Bourbon, 28

Mary II, Queen of England, vi–viii, 5, 7, 76, 78, 133–4, 136–40, 143, 171
  birth, 30–32
  childhood, 33–42
  death, 123, 128–132, 140, 157
  legacy, 158–9, 162–170
  marriage, 29, 42–47, 124
  as Princess of Orange, vi–vii, 10–11, 18–19, 28, 47–55, 58–68
  as Queen, 12, 20, 65, 69–71, 73–5, 81–95, 100, 103–122, 125, 133, 145, 150, 157
Mary, Queen of Scots, 42, 159
Mary Henrietta, Princess of Orange, 1–3, 10, 13–14, 53–4, 157
Mary of Modena, queen consort of England and Scotland, 41, 45, 58, 60, 65–6, 76, 80, 83–4, 92, 117, 155, 159, 170
Masham, Abigail, 112
Maurice of Orange, Prince, 6
Mauritshuis, 7–9, 12, 175–6, 187
Maximilian Emanuel, the Elector of Bavaria, 105
Meermansburg Almshouse, 19
Mesdag, Hendrik Willem, 5
Michiel de Ruyter, 168
Millington, Thomas, 156
Molendriegang (windmills), 5
Monck, George, 47
Monmouth, Duke of, 24, 61, 63–4, 75, 78–9, 146
Mons, 58, 106
Montagu, Lady Mary Wortley, 147–8
Museum Boerhaave, 17, 188

Naarden, 26, 188
Nagasaki, 11
National Maritime Museum, 115, 182
New Amsterdam, 55
Newmarket, 62, 144, 184
Newspapers, vii, 125–7
Newton, Isaac, 56, 81, 143, 149
Noordeinde Palace, 9–10, 59, 175–6

Oldenburg, Henry, 143
Orange, France, 28

Orange (Orange-Nassau), House of, 12, 18, 20, 55–6, 58–9, 75–6, 122, 175, 177
Orange College, 55
Orange order, 24, 160–1
Orangist party, 20, 23
Order of the Garter, 42, 61, 108, 118
Osborne, John, 168
Osborne, Thomas, Marquess of Carmarthen, Duke of Leeds, 36, 103, 150
Overijssel, 1
Oxford, viii, 31, 125, 138, 145, 149, 184

Pack, Mrs, 93
Palace of Placentia, 112, 115
Pepys, Samuel, 39, 81–2
Perth Academy, 127
Peter the Great, Emperor of Russia, 150, 152–3, 167–8
Philippe (brother of Louis XIV), 3, 29
Plaidy, Jean, 170
Plantin, Christophe, 20
Popish Plot, 60–62, 98
Portadown, 160
Post, Pieter, 7, 10, 12, 18, 28, 175
Presbyterian Church, 54, 96
Price, Robert, 150
Prince of Orange (title), 1, 20, 157
Prinsenhof (Delft), 16, 21, 70, 186
Prinsenhof (Leiden), 16
Purcell, Henry, 121, 129, 161, 168

Quare, Daniel, 118, 175
Queen Anne (play), 170
Queen's House, 112–5, 182

Restoration (of Charles II), 7, 12–13, 31, 34, 47, 63, 82, 87, 92, 112, 123, 163
Reynst, Gerrit and Jan, 14
Richmond Palace, 30, 37, 41
Rijksmuseum, Amsterdam, 8, 28, 38, 185
Rijksmuseum Boerhave, Leiden, 17, 188
Rijksmuseum de Gevangenpoort, 6–7
Rivet, Frederick, 4
Roman, Jacob, 5, 8, 18, 69, 73, 116, 176–7
Ronjat, 156
Royal Exchange, 124

Rubens, Peter Paul, 48, 52, 87–8, 176
Rupert of the Rhine, Prince, 39
Russell, Edward, 110
Rye House Plot, 62–3

Saint-Denis, 58
Saint-Germain, 80, 132
Sancroft, William, 66, 92, 107–8, 120
Sarsfield, Patrick, 79, 96, 103
Scheldt, River, 51, 121
Schellinks, Willem, 31, 82, 176
Scheveningen, 5, 13
Scotland, vi, 1–3, 7, 13, 23, 31, 34, 41–4, 49, 62–5, 70–1, 75, 80, 82–3, 91, 94–5, 109–110, 122–3, 127, 130, 132, 135, 151, 155, 157–9
Scottish Enlightenment, vii
Scrofula, 87
Sedley, Catherine, 41, 93
Sellar & Yeatman, 159
Seneffe, Battle of, 26
Seven Bishops, 61, 66, 75
Shaftesbury, Earl of, 60
Sidney, Henry, Earl of Romney, 75, 120, 152
Sidney, Robert, 75
Smallpox, 1–3, 14, 36, 46, 128
Smith, James, 36
Snellius, Rudolph, 17
Soestdijk, 28, 175
Sophia of Hanover, 151, 155
Spanish Gate (Breda), 55–6
Sprat, Thomas, 120
St Andrew's Church, Burnham-on-Sea, 88
St Mary's Pro-cathedral, Dublin, 101
St James's Church, Antwerp (Sint-Jacobskerk), 52
St James's Church, Piccadilly, 83
St James's Palace, 30–33, 37, 46, 62, 80, 85–6, 121, 133, 166
St Patrick's Cathedral, Dublin, 97–8, 100–1, 182
St Paul's Cathedral, London, 123, 137, 152, 173–4
Stadtholder, 1–3, 7, 9, 20–1, 24, 49, 54–5, 70, 73, 157
Stair, Earl of, 109–110

Stamford, Earl of, 148
Stanhope, Katherine, 3
Sterne, Laurence, 169
Sterne, Richard, 35–6, 169
Strickland, Agnes & Elizabeth, 159–60, 170
Swift, Jonathan, 101, 125, 127
Syon House, 109

Tate, Nahum, 111, 121
Teignmouth, 104
Temple Bar, 123
Temple, William, 58–9, 101
Tenison, Thomas, 122, 131, 157
Ter Heijde, 47
The Hague - *see Hague, The*
Thysius, Johannes, 17
Tillotson, John, 198, 122, 163
Titian, 14
Torbay, 79
Torrington, Earl of, 103–4
Tower of London, 32–33, 92, 107, 109, 124
Trelawny, Anne, 40
Trelawny, Jonathan, 40
Trevor, Arthur, 159
Trigland, Cornelis, 4
Trinity College, Dublin, 102, 127
Tristram Shandy, 165
Tromp, Cornelis, 24
Tromp, Maarten, 22, 24
Tulip Mania, 70
Tulip Stairs, 115
Turenne, Vicomte de, 25
Tyrconnell, Earl of (Richard Talbot), 95–6, 98

UNESCO, 26, 114
Utrecht, 1, 28, 54, 66, 152, 174, 177

Valkenberg (Breda), 56
Vanbrugh, Sir John, 89, 126, 176
van Campen, Jacob, 7, 9, 10, 151, 176
van Dijkvelt, Everard van Weede, 66
van Keppel, Arnold, Earl of Albemarle, 38, 109, 117, 157
van Kerckhoven, Johan Polyander, 15
van Wassenaer, Jacob, 9

Vaudémont, Prince de, 69
Vermeer, Johannes, 8, 22, 177
Veronese, 14
Versailles (TV series), 168
Victor Amadeus, Duke of Savoy, 104
Victoria, Queen of the United Kingdom, 32, 87, 92, 119, 143
Victoria & Albert Museum, 23, 141
Villiers, Anne, 47, 130
Villiers, Barbara, 39, 83
Villiers, Edward, 39, 69
Villiers, Elizabeth, 47, 49, 64, 93, 129
Villiers, Frances, 38–9, 46, 79

Wake, William, 132
Waldeck - *see Georg Friedrich of Waldeck*
Wales, vi-vii, 30, 150–1
Walsh, William, 112
Walter, Lucy, 63
Water Gallery, 140
Waterson, Nellie, 159
Waterline, 25–6
White's Club, 125–6
Whitehall Palace, viii 14, 40, 80, 82–90, 93, 106, 111, 114–7, 121, 130, 135, 149–50, 173–6, 182
Wigtown Martyrs, 63
Wijchen Castle, 27
Wilhelmina, Queen of the Netherlands, 67–8, 73–4
Williamsburg, Virginia, 163–4
Wisselbank, 123
William the Silent (Prince William I of Orange), 10, 16, 21, 52, 55, 57, 70, 169
William II of Orange, Prince, 1–2, 20
William II of Scotland, King (William the Lion), 91

William III of England, King (Prince William III of Orange), vi-viii, 1–7
   birth, 1–3, 7
   childhood, 3–7
   death, 25, 35, 72–3, 91, 99, 101, 119, 124, 127, 137, 151, 154–8
   education, 4, 15–19
   legacy, 158–170
   portraits, 3, 6, 29, 90, 113, 141, 166–7
   statues, 78, 102, 113, 119, 164–6, 176
William V of Orange, Prince, 7, 10
William III of the Netherlands, King, 1
William, Duke of Gloucester, 93, 106, 112, 118, 151–2
William, Prince of Wales, 119–120
Williamsburg, 163–4
Windsor, 38, 89, 103, 119, 149, 177
Windsor Beauties, 139
Wise, Henry, 139, 178
Wren, Christopher, viii, 31, 83–5, 92, 112–7, 123–4, 131, 134, 138, 143, 163, 174, 176, 178
Wroth, Jane, 50

York Castle Museum, 35, 183
York, Duke of (title), 34
York House,
York Minster, 34, 36, 183
Young, Robert, 120
Young, Thomas, 35

Zeeland, 1, 20
Zuylestein, Frederick Nassau de, 15, 24
Zuylestein, Willem Hendrik de, 15, 50

Dear Reader,

We hope you have enjoyed this book, but why not share your views on social media? You can also follow our pages to see more about our other products: facebook.com/penandswordbooks or follow us on Twitter @penswordbooks

You can also view our products at www.pen-and-sword.co.uk (UK and ROW) or www.penandswordbooks.com (North America).

To keep up to date with our latest releases and online catalogues, please sign up to our newsletter at: www.pen-and-sword.co.uk/newsletter

If you would like a printed catalogue with our latest books, then please email: enquiries@pen-and-sword.co.uk or telephone: 01226 734555 (UK and ROW) or email: uspen-and-sword@casematepublishers.com or telephone: (610) 853-9131 (North America).

We respect your privacy and we will only use personal information to send you information about our products.

Thank you!